Freedom with Violence

PERVERSE   MODERNITIES

A series edited by Judith Halberstam & Lisa Lowe

CHANDAN REDDY

Freedom with Violence

Race, Sexuality, and the US State

DUKE UNIVERSITY PRESS
Durham & London 2011

© 2011 Duke University Press

All rights reserved

Printed in the United States of America on acid-free paper ∞

Designed by Jennifer Hill

Typeset in Arno Pro by Keystone Typesetting, Inc.

Library of Congress Cataloging-in-Publication Data
appear on the last printed page of this book.

For my friends, without whom nothing . . .

CONTENTS

ACKNOWLEDGMENTS *Freedom with Violence* is a work that explores the legitimate violences that subtend modern political modernity in the United States. It argues against the political and theoretical concession to these violences, suggesting the limits of violence to foreclose, obliterate, or fully encompass that upon which it manifests. And, it focuses on race and sexuality as two formations that, albeit differently, manifest both US political modernity's geo-historical violences as well as the limits of those violences to shape, control, or restrict social formations of difference. Indeed, it is the recalcitrant racialized and sexualized communities shaped by modernity's dependence upon legitimate violence—communities whose practices of association remain nearly unintelligible within the modern structure of knowledge—that focus my attention and critique of violence in this book.

Even as I write these words, the United States continues its assaults and use of unmatched rational technologies of violence in the Middle East, North Africa, and West and South Asia. With the grievous and unimaginable loss of life the new US strategy of permanent war and global police actions continues to wrought, it can at times seem like little more than an intellectual exercise to speak of the limits of violence. However, it is important I think to remember that the practices of permanent war and global police actions that now seem a cornerstone of US foreign policy are themselves a response to the contestations of US Cold War policy in the Global South. That is, the post–Cold War era reveals the failures of US Cold War policy to determine the polities it sought to address through primarily military force as well as the rise of important new coalitions across national polities, regional geographies, class divisions, and cultural formations. The history of these coalitions and their conditions of possibility and impossibility are yet to be written. And, it is a premise of this book that our current division of knowledge and dominant modes of knowing must be historicized, deconstructed, and crossed if we are to fully grasp the force and limits of US Cold War–era violence in the inspiring popular struggles taking place currently in Tunisia, Egypt, Yemen, Bahrain, Libya, Palestine, Wisconsin, and New Orleans. These struggles will reopen our understandings of the global formations of race and sexuality in American studies and I hope this work can contribute in some modest way toward keeping such inquires available and ongoing.

Formations of violence, at once geo-historical and bodily, constitute my own conditions of possibility and impossibility in ways that can never be fully accounted. Yet it is my conviction that friendship, that uniquely modern formation, reveals more richly than any narrative account the unexpected practices of survival, meaning, solidarity, and alternative collectivities that emerge from and through modern racial and sexual formations. I have been uniquely lucky to be surrounded by friendships so dear and committed that I have little doubt about what a better modernity to come might be. This book is dedicated to my friends without whom historical and social violences might otherwise have had the last word.

For offering community and friendship I thank Faraz Ahmed, David Blackmore, Trishala Deb, Richard D'Souza, Zain Hadi, Barbara Khan, Martin Manalansan, Sonali Perera, Saeed Rahman, Dennis Shah, Atif Toor, Vinay Varghese, and Zahid Zaman. I admire Joo-Hyun Kang more than I can express; I am fortunate to have made her friendship. Javid Syed and Mohan Sikka make me miss New York every day. And they have taught me each in their own way to cultivate happiness, pleasures, and experiences of the beautiful as we endeavor for a more equitable and less violent world. They are heart, happiness, and family to me. I am inspired by the courage with which Gayatri Gopinath thinks and writes. And I am lucky for the laughter she always brings into my life. Nayan Shah has been a caring and sagacious voice at just the right times. Jodi Melamed could always see sooner and better than me what I was struggling to do and say. Her intellectual generosity has been humbling. I respectfully thank my graduate school teachers: Marcellus Blount, Ann Douglas, Kimberlé Crenshaw, Kendal Thomas, and Gayatri Spivak.

I discovered both the pleasures of thinking and political commitment as an undergraduate at the University of California, San Diego. And I still chuckle in disbelief when I take stock of who and what are meaningful to me and discover how often San Diego figures as an epicenter. For their friendship and commitment to radical work in the domains of race and sexuality, I thank Helen Jun, Lisa Cacho, Curtis Marez, Amie Parry, Randall Williams, Elenor Jaluage, Shelley Streeby, and Ruby Tapia. For making student activism memorable, I thank Leticia Juarez, Danny Calvi, Alex Garner, and Jorge Pelayo. George Lipsitz widens my horizons. Lisa Yoneyama and Takashi Fujitani define for me the meaning of principled commitment. My friendship with Tony Valenzuela is the oldest, longest, and sweetest that I have and the good fortune of that is all mine. Grace Hong and Victor Bascara know me and have cared for me like no one else and I'm still trying to figure out after all these years how I might weasel my way back into their apartment. Roderick Ferguson's friendship is a gift like no other. He never ceases to amaze me. I love him dearly. But for Judith Halberstam, I would not be a scholar and not a day goes by that I don't marvel at my great fortune to have found her. She is one of the most generous and loyal friends one could have. Rosemary George has been there for me over and over again. Her humor and guileless love are unique. Her unsentimental intelligence has opened important intellectual doors. There are some whose imprint is so immense that they defeat from the start the task of acknowledgment. Such is the case as I try to express my debt to Lisa Lowe. As a mentor and intellectual, there is not a page in this book that doesn't bear the trace of what I've learned from her. I am so profoundly enabled by the critical space she has labored to create, both philosophically and institutionally, for so many of us that citation would never suffice. And as a friend, I learn from her compassion and example always.

Since arriving at the University of Washington, I have found a community that inspires and nourishes me. I couldn't have found a better writing community in Ileana Silva-Rodriquez, Francisco Benitez, Rick Bonus, Habiba Ibrahim, and Naomi Murakawa. They kept me afloat during the most turbulent periods of writing. Few have the wisdom of Caroline Simpson, and I am lucky that she shares it generously and graciously. I cherish her friendship. I am grateful for Alys Weinbaum's incisive mind and deep sense of responsibility. I know no one else whose critical vision of social justice is as broad and thoughtful as that of Gillian Harkins. And on a more personal note, without her friendship and efforts this book would never have existed. Gillian sat with me day in and day out for a month reading my work, listening to my arguments and showing me a book I didn't think I had. Her contribution to this work is indelible. I miss Nikhil Singh's presence in Seattle profoundly. He has made me a better intellectual. Moon-Ho Jung is as solid as they get; I am honored to be his colleague. Stephanie Smallwood's arrival to Seattle changed everything. I am grateful for her deep intelligence and care. Stephanie Camp's return has made 22nd Ave. a home, plain and simple. Eng Beng Lim, Paul Rogers, and Anil Vora make sure that I don't lose sight of joy, and always with wit to boot. Dean Space is the "Sonic" of social justice workers. His unbounded energy and limitless capacity for friendship are mesmerizing. Priti Ramamurthy, Kathleen Woodward, and Gary Handwerk have been the most ideal of senior colleagues. Annie Fischer, Martha Mestl, Carolyn Busch, and Susan Williams make going to Padelford Hall something I look forward to always with a smile. I would like to thank the graduate students at the University of Washington: Sooja Kelsey, Julie Kae, Sydney Lewis, Ram Prasanak, Marites Mendoza, Jed Murr, Su-Ching Wang, Christian Ravela, Adele Zhang, Simon Trujillo, Rahul Gairola, Ryan Burt, Joe Bernardo, Vince Schleitwiler, Ji-Young Um, Caroline Yang, Kellie Holzer, Todd Tietchen, Madhavi Murthy, Amy Bhatt, Dipika Nath, Seema Sohi, Andrea Opitz, Mathew Southern, Soh Kim, Pacharee Sudhinaraset, Sharleen Mondal, Jeff Chiu, Balbir Singh, Junead Sheikh, Niroshi Sadanandan, and Kim Trinh. Our work together keeps me focused and I am inspired by the seriousness and ambition of their projects.

Much of the introduction and conclusion of this book was written at TwoDog Farm, and I thank Bill Collins for his patience, unwavering care, and deep kindness when I needed it the most. Peter Thompson helped me find the words where I thought there weren't any. He is a gift in my life. Michael Culpepper, Nicki McGaw, and Kelly Forrest are fellow travelers and I thank them for their honesty, compassion, and laughter. I thank my father for his quiet example and my mother for her tireless work in making community and family here in the United States. "Family" for immigrants defies biological conventions and I am so lucky for it. I thank my "siblings": Iqbal Anwar, Haroon Anwar, Yasmin Anwar, Rohit and Pavan Reddy, Alexander Eswar, Christopher Eswar, Ramesh Reddy, and Danielle Eswar. Mohammed and Rose Anwar are the "other" parents, and Ramesh and Uttara are the ones up north. Sounder and Diane Eswar were the first to show me worlds I didn't know possible. Nithin and Divya Reddy love me unconditionally. They have been my ballast and refuge for so many years. Kathan and Sanjana Reddy are happiness and joy incarnate. They have changed all our lives.

Ken Wissoker expressed an unflagging commitment to this project even when I didn't think I had one. He is responsible for so much of the good that has befallen me these past two years. I thank him for the generosity with which he extends himself and for his kindness. In plain fact, without him this book would never have been. Also at Duke University Press, I thank Leigh Barnwell for her help and Rebecca Fowler for her excellent editorship. Rebecca has dealt with the worst of my difficulties following directions and deadlines and has been nothing but professional and dedicated throughout. Jeanne Ferris did a heroic job copyediting an overgrown manuscript. The entire book is better because of Rebecca's and Jeanne's careful and thoughtful work on the manuscript. Finally, I thank Pacharee Sudhinaraset and Julie Kae for their lightning-speed editorial labors during the final weeks of revision.

INTRODUCTION Freedom's Amendments

Race, Sexuality, and Disposability
under the State Form

It seems that violence, be it "private" or "public," "domestic" or "international,"
has been reaching a degree that the very *idea* of politics is destabilized, since this
idea was always associated with an overcoming (*Aufhebung*) of violence. So had
said Hobbes and Kant: "we must find a way out of it" (be it called Power, Law,
or Civilization). It seems that the ambivalency of violence (. . . the difficulty of
identifying victims and oppressors [and] the difficulty of separating the positive and
negative kinds of violence) has reached such a degree that the traditional *negations of violence* (what we may call the strategy of *non-violence* and the strategy
of *counter-violence*) have lost the references they need to be meaningful (some
would say: "rational") political strategies.—ETIENNE BALIBAR, "Some Questions on
Politics and Violence"

There is really nothing more to say—except why. But since *why* is difficult to
handle, one must take refuge in *how*.—TONI MORRISON, *The Bluest Eye*

There is a tradition that is catastrophe.—WALTER BENJAMIN, *The Arcades Project*

On October 28, 2009, not even a year into
his historic presidency, US President Barack Obama signed into law the National
Defense Authorization Act of 2010. It was
hailed as a decisive victory in the struggle
against violence directed at gays, lesbians,
bisexuals, and transgender and queer
people.[1] This was because Congress had
attached an amendment titled the Matthew Shepard and James Byrd, Jr. Hate

Crimes Prevention Act to the original bill. This amendment expands the 1969 federal hate-crime law to include crimes motivated by a victim's actual or perceived gender, sexual orientation, gender identity, or disability. The act offers significant federal resources, both institutional and financial, to local law enforcement officials in the investigation and prosecution of hate-motivated incidents. It also extends federal authority to investigate and prosecute bias-motivated crime beyond the original restrictive grounds to cover any hate crime committed in any US jurisdiction, superseding state and local criminal statutes. For the purpose of this book, we can call October 28, 2009, a significant moment in a contemporary political culture defined by its *freedom with violence*. This requires some explanation.

The National Defense Authorization Act (NDAA), which is passed yearly by Congress and signed by the president, establishes the annual operating budget for the Department of Defense, which controls the various branches of the US military. The 2010 act appropriates $680 billion to the Department of Defense—during the worst recession and job market in the United States since the end of the Great Depression and the Second World War. Because the act establishes guidelines for the military as it apportions this staggering amount of money, its passage was hailed as a victory for the Obama administration and liberals: the 2010 act directly takes on the entrenched lobbying power and corruption of what President Dwight D. Eisenhower termed the military-industrial complex, canceling a host of long-standing private-industry projects that had little to no strategic value. The guidelines also target for reduction and elimination the George W. Bush administration's use of no-bid private contracts for military services—typically with corporations whose payrolls and boards included senior government and military officials—that were producing cost overruns in the hundreds of billions of dollars, all charged to US taxpayers.[2]

In spite of these claims of a victory for the White House over the entrenched powers of the military-industrial complex, the 2010 NDAA sets aside the highest amount of money for the Department of Defense in history. The budgetary increase covers the projected expenses associated with President Obama's controversial decision later in 2009 for a troop surge of up to 100,000 US military personnel in Afghanistan.[3] This was a defining tactic in Obama's extension of his predecessor's so-called global war on terror, which—as Obama suggested in his 2009 Nobel Peace Prize acceptance speech, delivered only days after the announcement of the troop surge—was a morally just war against evil founded on principles of national sovereignty, self-defense, and international norms for global prosperity. He opined that it was akin to the Allied fight against Nazism in the twentieth century: "I face the world as it is, and cannot stand idle in the face of threats to the American people. For make no mistake: Evil does exist in the world. A non-violent movement could not have halted Hitler's armies. Negotiations cannot convince al-Qaeda's leaders to lay down their arms."[4]

Still, the historic impact and value of the 2010 NDAA was portrayed in the US popular media as issuing from a single amendment—the Matthew Shepard and James Byrd, Jr. Hate Crimes Prevention Act, which added sexual orientation and gender identity to the list of federally defined hate crimes. This act's name recalls two instances of spectacular cruelty: in 1998 Matthew Shepard was brutally tortured, tied to a fence, and left to die near Laramie, Wyoming, because he was perceived to be gay; and a few months later in June, James Byrd Jr., an African American, was tied to a truck and dragged along county roads by white supremacists until he was decapitated in Jasper, Texas. The act extends the definition of federal hate crimes from crimes motivated by a victim's actual or perceived race, religion, ethnicity, or nationality to include crimes targeting a victim's actual or perceived sexual orientation, gender identity, or disability. The decision to attach the Shepard-Byrd Act to the 2010 NDAA was an act of genius on the part of Democratic leaders in both houses of Congress, as that approach prevented social conservatives from opposing the Shepard-Byrd Act and also prevented leftists from trying to combine it with antiwar legislation. Republican opposition to the expansion of federal hate-crimes protection to include gays, lesbians, bisexuals, and transgender and queer people (GLBTQ) had blocked the passage of such legislation for over a decade. In 2009 Democratic leaders were able to tie Republicans' hands, using the majorities they had won in 2008 in both houses to force Congress to pass the legislation by attaching it to the next military appropriations bill. Federal GLBTQ hate-crimes legislation passed with a defense appropriations bill that grew the military budget to its highest level in US history. The 2010 NDAA passed while the United States was officially engaged in two wars abroad, in the Middle East and South Asia. The act appropriated funding for the continued use of unmanned US drone strikes and bombings in countries that the United States is not officially at war with, such as Pakistan, disrespecting their national sovereignty and inflicting civilian deaths. And, as mentioned above, this unprecedented budget was approved during an equally unprecedented period of national joblessness for the US economy since the Second World War. The act funded the nearly 1.5 million people in the US armed forces, which has been made up entirely of volunteers since 1972, when public outcry against the failed wars in Vietnam and elsewhere in Southeast Asia ended the draft. Yet these matters were barely mentioned in the national discussion of the NDAA's passage. Rather, the passage of the NDAA with its federal hate-crimes amendment was perceived by the Democratic Party, liberal and progressive groups and constituencies, and national gay and lesbian rights organizations as nothing less than a historic milestone in US GLBTQ rights and struggles against violence. For example, Joe Solmonese—the president of Human Rights Campaign, the nation's largest gay and lesbian organization—called the hate-crimes measure in the defense bill "our nation's first major piece of civil rights legislation for lesbian, gay, bisexual and transgender people."[5]

And in his remarks at the signing ceremony for the NDAA, President Obama closed by saying of the Shepard-Byrd Act: "There is one more long-awaited change contained within this legislation that I'll be talking about a little more later today. After more than a decade of opposition and delay, we've passed inclusive hate crimes legislation to help protect our citizens from violence based on what they look like, who they love, how they pray, or who they are."[6] For Obama, the Shepard-Byrd Act extended the antiviolence protections originally designed by the federal government to combat white supremacy and to promote race-neutral liberalism within the nation-state. The executive director of the National Gay and Lesbian Task Force summarized the moral fulcrum of the Shepard-Byrd Act when she said: It has taken over a decade of perseverance to get to this momentous day . . . Laws embody the values of our nation, and through the enactment of this hate crimes law, our country has—once and for all—sent a clear and unequivocal message that it rejects and condemns all forms of hate violence, including crimes motivated by hatred of lesbian, gay, bisexual and transgender people.[7] Similarly, in a joint statement thirty-one national gay and lesbian organizations—comprising the most prominent national GLBTQ civil rights organizations, antiviolence groups, and medical and health advocacy groups—interpreted the passage of the Shepard-Byrd Act as a symbol of progress but "only one of the building blocks to full equality and . . . equal treatment under federal law in all areas of our lives."[8] These comments, and numerous others like them, evade altogether the context of the act's passage, as part of a defense budget nearly as large as all other countries' defense budgets combined. More striking than the unanimous affirmations of the hate-crimes bill from these incredibly varied—and, at times, even mutually antagonist—organizations and institutions is the almost equally unanimous indifference of these same institutional actors toward the stunning size of the defense bill through which the hate-crime provisions became law. Abstracting the amendment from the unprecedented NDAA of 2010 with which this symbol of progress and apparent "building block" of equality became law, none of these progressive voices show any equivocation, let alone concern, about the strange coupling of civil rights and national security. Not long ago it would have been inconceivable to propose that a US military appropriations bill incorporate the protection of homosexuality, or that homosexual emancipation cast its lot with the sustenance and growth of the military. How did this conjunction become a nearly unremarkable event? How did the differing institutions and political projects become undisturbed witnesses to this once impossible conjunction? What were the epistemological means for conveying this transition to ordinariness and acceptance in our changed political circumstances? That is, what structures, practices, and formations of thought enabled the felicitous conjunction?

Answering these questions is crucial because it helps explain the disorientation many Americans feel when they see supposedly progressive and egalitarian groups willing to share their beds with violent types like the military or the imperial actor. There are, I think, two different epistemological perspectives that organize the meaning and the felt sense of this no longer startling conjunction. The first sees the relation of the two bills as simply a pragmatic one. Even if hate-crimes legislation must be passed with a military appropriations act, that contingent context is in the end irrelevant, given the universal moral and ethical principle enshrined in the hate-crimes amendment. From this perspective, the conjunction between the two bills is explainable as a matter of pure strategy. And since contingency characterizes any context that yields transcendent values, it does not matter that the strategy used to politically ratify the universal principle betrays the very spirit of that principle. Indeed, this perspective is bolstered by the "fact" that once the principle is operative, it can be used effectively to censor and reform precisely those illiberal institutions through which it arrived into political life.

In contrast, the second perspective understands the conjunction in more felicitous terms, seeing it as expressive of a determining historical, structural, or positivist necessity. Here, the conjunction is an expression of the imbrication of the two bills, and of their common determination by the same contextual elements. What the first perspective renders as pure strategy, the second sees as the effect and expression of a complex historical process, an irrepressible tradition, or the virtue that organizes the social bond. Just as easily, this perspective considers the conjunction to express a constitutive dynamic that while at times suppressed can never be destroyed or upended. For example, this perspective might read the conjunction as revealing once again the development of personal liberties that attends the obligations and sacrifice demanded by citizenship in a democracy at war, or as affirming the cultural belief and meaning of an American exceptionalism that exempts US military actions from the charge of Western domination or capitalist imperialism.

We can name these two modes of thought liberal-individualist and republican-nationalist, respectively. The first privileges the standpoint of individual and personal liberty. Perceiving the 2010 NDAA as merely contingent context, it rescues the egalitarian principle important to liberal nationalism and state practice by transforming material and discursive conditions into a delineable and fixed context, one that is finally contingent in its relation to social progress and development over time. Seen in this way, these conditions are ultimately insignificant to the rational development of a national egalitarian principle expressed in the Shepard-Byrd Act. As an ideal law, this act is understood as a progressive refinement of a principle of individual liberty, one that not only moves toward a logical noncontradiction, but that also exhibits in the process an increasingly developed ability to trace and excise illegitimate acts of social and private violence and to abolish the cruelties and crudities of the past. The continued expansion of the moral and ethical principle reconciles the irrefutable functional, empirical, and logical primacy of community—from which individuals gain language, material sustenance, and knowledge—with individual development.

The second perspective, associated with the so-called republican tradition, affirms the standpoint of the nation-state or other political community as a distinct totality or unified whole. It sees in the unprecedented 2010 NDAA (in monetary terms) as both a necessary and an inextricable context for addressing anti-GLBTQ violence. From this perspective, the NDAA expresses the terms of the nation-state's sovereignty in international relations, a key element of the state's claim to a monopoly on violence within its jurisdiction. The NDAA and the hate-crimes bill express a complex interdependence between the social forces and means necessary for protecting the nation-state's sovereignty in international relations and the hegemonic struggles for consent that characterize a pacified civil society, which is achieved and maintained by the state's possession of a monopoly on violence within its boundaries. In the republican tradition, the passage of GLBTQ antiviolence law with the NDAA only dramatizes the inextricability of civil, political, and social rights from the martial obligations of citizenship. In this perspective, the state's enforcement of norms and behaviors, such as tolerance in the case of hate-crimes law, is predicated on the achievement of homogeneity in political society—whether that is the homogeneities of blood, race, tradition, and culture, or simply a set of defining civil values, as in the case of US exceptionalism. This homogeneous or multicultural citizenry is the real basis of social diversity in US civil and political society, its American character, whose way of life is the basis of its sovereignty. Like the enlistment in the US armed forces of Japanese American internees during the Second World War, or the Double V—victory at home and abroad—campaign promoted by republican-nationalist black intellectuals such as Ralph Ellison during the same war, the advancement of GLBTQ rights is necessarily and inextricably connected to the context of a republic at war. Here the performance of virtuous citizenship by second-class citizens, the construction of a foreign enemy against which to define the "American way of life," and the production of ideological contradictions between the state's demand for mortal sacrifice and internal juridical inequities of citizenship all produce the context in which national defense as the supreme expression of republican sovereignty expands democratic values.[9]

Though this second perspective appears to be a critique of liberal individualism and the idealist formalism on which that individualism is based, it is in fact a supplement and closely aligned to what it critiques. Both perspectives in their different ways reaffirm the nation-state as either the unsignified or exclusive frame within which the relation between the hate-crimes act and its context is decided. By the time of the Shepard-Byrd Act's passage in 2009, these two perspectives together constituted epistemological foundations for what I call the liberal egalitarian national state. At first the rise of liberalism in the early twentieth century was positioned as the effect of the urbanization and modernization of the US economy and society, integrating it with the historical course of the British and European nation-states. However, the integration or syncretism of liberalism and US nationalism in the early decades of the twentieth century into a distinct form of individualism quickly assimilated even liberal political thought into the traditions of exceptionalism and, to a lesser degree, national egalitarianism. Hence, both perspectives reproduce the form of the US nation as an exceptionalist topos within and among the national empires of Western modernity. The liberal state embodies a set of values that are ultimately the necessary foundation for the egalitarian attitude found among the peoples to whom movements for equality make their claims. These epistemologies promote an egalitarian principle that figures the liberal state as the ultimate embodiment of the values that enable and guarantee equality. Therefore, the liberal national state is also positioned in these accounts as the final outcome of struggles for equality. Even if this standpoint identifies the state as the source of a grievance, injury, or horrific exposure to arbitrary violence, its epistemological assumptions ultimately affirm the value of that very state formation.

Thus even when these political standpoints are critical of the state, they remain fundamentally reformist, since the liberal state embodies and figures the ethical fulcrum without which the movements and claims for equality would be both ineffective and dead.[10] To that end, these perspectives view the state as an apparatus that, on the one hand, conveys and establishes a legal order—itself designed to promote and protect egalitarianism—and, on the other hand, enforces through the threat and finally the use of violence the universality of the legal order for all within the nation-state. In these accounts, egalitarianism is the fulcrum of the liberal national state's existence, expressed most dramatically in the use of the state as a substantial threat against or counterviolence opposed to hate violence among the private citizenry, which curbs individualism's anomic tendencies. Additionally, egalitarianism is finally the basis for making the liberal state coincident with the very national people that it represents. If egalitarianism did not already exist as a virtue of the national people, neither the liberal state nor movements for equality would have any basis for existence, or conditions under which to speak or to be heard.[11] In this sense the nation—as the name for founding egalitarian conditions, figured variously as a constitutional or contractual community, a historical ethos or spirit, or a shared cultural tradition and ethnicity—is the source for the development of the state as a modern apparatus of liberal progress and social equality.

We can take the values of equality and tolerance that articulate hate-crimes legislation as one expression of this liberal egalitarianism, one that easily converts, as we will see, into an alibi for US globalism. Hence, despite the tethering of liberal egalitarianism to a budget that extends US interests globally, denying the principle of national sovereignty or alternative forms of regional development and international amity to the postcolonial states of the Global South, these perspectives both figure the United States as a bounded nation-state, the ultimate meaning of the processes and practices that sustain political modernity.

In their separate ways, both the liberal-individualist and republican-nationalist perspectives see the hate-crimes bill as a victory not only in the struggle to eliminate anti-GLBTQ violence, but also in the one to reaffirm and internalize the very state that was and remains in significant ways a primary cause of the now-outlawed violence. Both views abstract and idealize the acts passed by Congress, rather than seeing them as mediations of specific social and historical conditions. If seen as media-tions, the acts can be read to reveal the contradictions of racial forma-tion, the liberal national state, and the logic of disposability that struc-tures liberal and martial citizenship.

Yet even antiracist organizations like the National Association for the Advancement of Colored People (NAACP) lauded the passage of the Shepard-Byrd Act. Explaining the innovations the act makes in federal hate-crimes law, the NAACP noted that in addition to expanding the definition of hate crimes beyond its original meaning, enacted as part of civil rights legislation in 1969, the new act also expands the zones of the federal law's applicability to the national territory. Whereas previously, national hate-crimes law limited federal intervention in cases of bias-motivated crimes to those crimes committed on federal property or in re-lation to a federally protected activity, such as voting, the Shepard-Byrd Act expands the federal government's jurisdiction to any instance within the juridical territory of the nation-state of a bias-motivated crime, as defined by federal law. The act also includes specific penalties that target youthful perpetrators of hate violence. With the disproportionate arrests, convictions, and incarcerations of blacks and Latinos, it is fair to assume that these new penalties alongside the expansion of the federal govern-ment's policing power for the purposes of eradicating hate violence and enforcing civil rights laws will have a disproportionate impact on youth of color, or at least will deepen the ideologies that advance the policing practices of the racialized liberal security state as an answer to the per-sistent contradictions, conflicts, and struggles of the radically uneven accumulation of wealth by race that characterizes US capitalism.

Ironically, NAACP President Benjamin Todd Jealous believes that the new legislation, by expanding the categories of protection and extending the zone of application to all of the United States and its overseas territories and jurisdictions, makes antiracism identical with the US liberal state. Jealous argues that the new bill will enable the country to finally "begin to put an end to the vicious cycle of hate crimes that have plagued our communities for far too long." He continues: "This legisla-tion begins a new era in hate crimes protection and prevention. It sends a clear message to all that we will not tolerate hate crimes against any American."[12]

Jealous's comment, that the United States will not accept hate crimes "against any American" casts an unexpected racial and global shadow over his remarks about civil rights when we situate the hate-crimes act within the unprecedented NDAA of which it is a part. Breaking with the past, when the nation was mired in a vicious cycle of violence, Jealous views the hate-crimes bill as ushering in "a new era," one in which the state's apparatuses of violence finally coincide with true morality. In this present, the state has the ethical role of enforcing truly legitimate violence, of becoming the representative and material expression of that violence. State violence is legitimate only when there is a true equality among the "national people." It is a unique violence that brands all other expressions of violence in the United States as anti-American, and it can bring to bear the counterviolent force of the whole state if "any American" is victim to arbitrary violence. Only in this case can the nation break with its endemically racist past and emerge in the new era of a truly national history. For Jealous, a national "we" is assembled to send a "clear message to all," that violence against Americans will be met with the full force of the state. And anti-American violence—defined as that falling outside the core value of the national people and the US state (namely, tolerance)—has the unique character of being the defining limits of what can be tolerated.

Jealous's language cites and appropriates for his fight against hate violence the US governmental discourse after 9/11 and during the invasion of Afghanistan, events particularly evoked by the 2010 NDAA with which hate-crimes legislation passed. In doing so, his remarks trouble and ultimately blur the boundaries between reforming racial capitalism through the completion of the Civil Rights Act of 1969 and strategically advancing a racially organized US globalism as provided for in the NDAA. Indeed, the deeply buried borders between domestic legislation and foreign policy, between federal policing and military power, and between the racialization of the national population and the racial logics that organize US foreign policy all suddenly resurface. This citation of the logic of national defense and martial citizenship to performatively institute a national "we," this time united against hate violence, produces an isomorphism between the "hate" that defines America's enemies abroad and the "hate" of the domestic perpetrator—transforming geopolitical competitors and belligerent states into moral enemies. Within this iso-morphism, any violence not sanctioned by the state is characterized either as nonpolitical or antipolitical "hate," both conditions best ad-dressed by medicine, psychology, or the military (all institutions that, unlike the police, have the capacity and authority for the eradication or annihilation of the offending hate). That is, both conditions are figures of the limit of the human who exists within political society and con-ducts himself or herself freely within its domain. Practices of hate, then, are the kinds of violence that the state has an obligation to eradicate, so that political society can remain free—in this way, the state delivers not a political violence against a political enemy, but a nonpolitical violence against the enemies of modern political society.

Jealous's statement, set against a background of military appropria-tions, forces to the foreground the ideological dependence of the US lib-eral national state since the beginning of the twentieth century and the rise of Wilsonian foreign policy on its identity as the guarantor of individ-ual freedom from arbitrary violence and national self-determination. Thus his remarks remind us that in the twentieth century, it was the US state's guarantee to protect individual freedoms that reconciled or, more properly, integrated US colonialism, racial wars, and global violence with the state's persistent discourse of US exceptionalism. If understood as a caption to the image of President Obama signing a hate-crime rider to the NDAA, Jealous's comments force us to observe the unmistakable bond between the racial policies and practices of the liberal national state, which has sought to organize and manage the contradictions of racial capitalism within the nation-state, and the racialized modes by which—in its pursuit of dominance, hegemony, and control of global social relations—the United States addresses its global challengers and foils as anachronistic regimes of hate that are out of step with modernity. That is, like the "hate" that fuels the perpetrator of individual violence, these global challengers and foils, like Asian states susceptible to commu-nism and "Islamic fundamentalism" that commit a form of violence on a national or international scale, are the very limit of political society and modern publics.

Read in the light and shadows cast by Jealous's remarks, the hate-crimes act troubles its status as an amendment. Is it an amendment that depends on the body of the military appropriations bill to which it is attached, or is it an amendment that paradoxically authorizes, frames, and shapes the body of the defense bill of which it is a part? In one respect, the amendment does authorize the military bill to which it is attached. At a time when the United States is still involved in a brutal and illegal war that it instigated and when the military continues to use what it euphemistically calls "enhanced interrogation" as well as unmanned drone attacks in civilian areas, it is only the amendment—and not the appropriations bill—that reminds us that the secular state (and national sovereignty) is founded on the universality of human rights to which it is bound. To read state practice through the amendment is to obscure the mode of US power globally. Through the inclusion of the amendment, the appropriations bill writes that power not as the story of a persistent search for the possession of "assets" and "strategic" territories around the globe. Rather, that narrative is surreptitiously "amended" or rewritten for the citizenry, through the extension of US liberal values to formerly unprotected areas and zones, such as homosexuality.

Quite powerfully, if we follow the formal relation proposed by an amendment to the body of a text, it would appear in this instance that liberal values, in the form of hate-crimes jurisprudence, amends the sanctioned violence of the nation-state and its interests. Whereas for liberalism, normatively speaking, it is the authority of the nation-state that legitimizes its military force, in this instance, the bill's passage forces a reappraisal between a state organized through liberal political values (such as tolerance and negative freedoms) and the violence it uses. The amendment is a belated addition to the ratification of the military in-stitutions of violence. Allegorically, the material terms and conditions of US violence and globalism in the NDAA precede liberal political values. These values (in the form of the Shepard-Byrd Act) emerge like a growth on the institutional interests and material conditions and relations orga-nizing US racial and global relations, even as this growth seeks to reframe the violence from which it emerges. That is, there is a necessary gap and lack of identity between the violence figured in the body of text and the liberal political values that frame it. The violence out of which these liberal values emerge is both prior and heterogeneous to the amend-ment, and to the liberal epistemology that would interpret, taxonomize, and decide its meaning. As ideology, the amendment retrospectively authorizes and establishes limits on those apparatuses of the state that maintain US dominance globally, even as it depends on the agreements for the perpetuation of US illegitimate force globally for its very legislative existence.

This bill and the reformist publics that it elicits allegorize a different account of Western liberalism and the racial and global violence to which it was connected than is commonly understood. To further follow the formal logic of "body" and "amendment" in the 2010 NDAA, we notice, through an act of metalepsis, that the liberal values of the state that emerge belatedly nonetheless promote their applicability throughout the nation. As an example, we need only think here of what is empirically proven and well known of all US wars abroad: they are one of America's most successful tactics for recruiting so-called immigrants. While the migration of so-called immigrants and refugees to the metropole from US wars abroad was actually the result of these wars, their violent deterritorializations are figured prominently in US public culture as a racialized humanitarian crisis to which the US nation-state must respond. The granting of admission of these racialized war migrations to the United States is cited as evidence of a unique US exceptionalist sovereignty, in particular the bounded nation-state's openness to racial, national, and linguistic difference. In other words, rather than viewing these racialized migrations as the consequence of US wars in Asia, Latin America, Africa, Eastern Europe, and the Middle East, the granting of admission to racialized migrants figure, through a metalepsis, as evidence of the exercise of the democratic norms that are the supposed fulcrum of the state. In this manner, US wars are figured either as protecting exceptionalist sovereignty globally or as a declension of that sovereignty. The US wars abroad and state violence that makes possible the transformation of war migrations into racialized immigration are rendered as heterogeneous to the liberal and exceptionalist identity of the nation-state. In like fashion, the NDAA precedes and makes possible the liberal amendment, and more important, US political practice, even if the amendment and those political practices make their ongoing conditions of possibility difficult to remember or know. In relation to the NDAA—its excluded and heterogeneous conditions of possibility—the amendment seeks (as does US immigration policy after US wars abroad) to incorporate through its universal terms (of freedom from racist, sexist, sectarian, and homophobic violence) the heterogeneous histories and practices at its origin. What is constitutive of the amendment (or postwar immigration policy) slips surreptitiously into the status of being the amendment's subject and object of concern—another way in which amending liberal moral and political forms or clauses continues to frame and inflict unified meaning on the material body of the historical text.

If amendments belatedly modify and authorize the prior textual body, it is because only through their frames can the body continue to figure as meaningful—indeed, to persist. This suggests that amendments as frames conserve and reactivate the force of their textual bodies, even while displacing the origins of that force and restructuring its appearance, through the bestowal of meaning upon the original body. In like fashion, we might say that the Shepard-Byrd Act, far from being an unrelated and belated addition to the 2010 NDAA, in fact conserves the force of the military institutions funded by the main body of the legislation. It restructures those force relations by giving a frame or meaning, just as it displaces the original geographies, relations, histories, and peoples that have been the objects and means for the colonial and military institutions that give that body its force. And in this way the national "we" evoked by Benjamin Jealous and constituted by the hate-crimes law cannot escape the racial shadows that it casts itself.

There is one final way that the hate-crimes law's status as an amendment is noteworthy, one that is central to the argument and purpose of this book. The Shepard-Byrd Act is an amendment to the 1969 Civil Rights Act as well. As such, it triangulates race, sexuality, and US globalism in the twentieth century. Each of these terms on its own tells important stories of the struggle against the view that life is disposable, which has grown simultaneously with the rise of US globalism. Rendered as "intersections," we have been able to generate important critiques of the violence that inhered in the forms that gave those struggles their world-historical meanings, such as nationalism, self-determination, and identity-based rights. Yet when we set them in terms of amendments, I believe we can retrieve different histories and accounts of power, ones that could prove to be crucial alternatives to the current dead end that political modernity and the liberal nation-state have led us. To think of race, sexuality, and US globalism through and with "amendments," rather than through the metaphor of "intersections" is to suggest the importance of the historical, political, and epistemological structures that organize how these formations are linked or intersected, and what kinds of logic fasten their coincidence. It is not just that sexuality intersects with race or racial globality. It is, rather, that sexuality is in the specific position of an amendment within and for the production of these intersections. Just as liberal values amend the military violence on which they depend and which they now constitutively mediate, so too sexuality amends race and US globalism. As I argue throughout this book, we must read our current moment in the United States as one in which sexuality amends the racial and global formations of which it is a part. This includes using interpretative methods that approach sexuality as a site in which we can read these global and racial processes; we can understand this as a materialist account of sexuality. But it also suggests that we must take seriously the fact that in our historical moment, sexuality produces constitutive constraints on how the violence that in the twentieth century sustained asymmetrical racializations and modes of accumulation can be conserved, transformed, and reproduced. As I show in chapter three, the constitution of sexuality in the 1990s as a human right disorganizes Western sovereignty even as it conserves the divisions between the West and the non-West that organized the era of colonial capitalism. When sexuality is understood as an amendment to these historical force relations—that is, when we theorize how the intersections and conjunctions of lived epistemic objects are structured at a particular historical moment, of what their relation to one another is, and what this means for our inquiries—we gain a very different and crucial understanding of both the perils and the possibilities of conducting a contemporary politics and epistemology of sexuality. Thinking of these co-constitutive formations through the metaphor of amendments, then, stresses the fact that every effort to imagine, theorize, and practice alternative politics, to emerge from the intersectional or voided spaces of political modernity, to claim something other than autonomous life as the opposite to disposability will need to consider the histories of violence and alternatives that are conserved and still active within the new forms that seek to define our social relations. That is, we must pay

attention to the historically specific and amended contingent foundations that seek to finalize the meaning of our inherited social relations.

In this sense, seeing the passage of law against anti-GLBTQ hate crimes
as an amendment of both US racial globalism (the NDAA) and US racial
capitalism (the 1969 Civil Rights Act) suggests the critical importance of
sexuality in our contemporary moment as that which frames, redivides,
or seeks to offer synthetic "meaning," simultaneously conserving and
revising the relations and histories of force of both US globalism and
racial capitalism. It is sexual freedom—as the evidence of civilization and
progress—that at this moment most powerfully disallows a reckoning
with its own conditions of possibility, redeeming through its status as an
amendment the very state that these global and racial violences have
built. Yet if this is true, it is also the case that the amendment can never
fully manage the excess materiality and the allegorical meanings it produces. The discursive and historical formations or bodies that the amendment reanimates and keeps alive continually exceed its framing. If sexuality is an amendment of US freedoms at the close of twentieth-century
political modernity, then twentieth-century racialized social relations
(and their asymmetrical bonds and differences) inhere now within and as
sexuality. As I show in chapter four, as an amendment to the Civil Rights
Act, sexual equality cannot lose its own shadows of racial struggles
against the systemic disposability that defined the limits of the Civil
Rights Act. In other words, the legislative amendment allegorizes, in its
literalness, the fact that in our contemporary moment, sexuality is an
iteration of—an amendment to and of—race. It is for this reason that I
argue for modes of critique from the perspective of queers of color,
modes consciously and formatively tied to critical ethnic studies. We
might say that race is the political unconscious of sexuality, in its current
mode as an amendment to twentieth-century orders of legitimate violence. Therefore, forms of queer critique that refuse to engage their racial
conditions or that treat race as a discrete and intersectional variable do so
at great peril to any project concerned with expanding and proposing
modes of livability that do not accept racial, sexual, and gendered disposability as their dialectical consequence.

Throughout this book, I pursue the consequences of this historical
conjuncture, the idea that some of the richest and most pointed antiracisms opposed to disposability as well as ongoing impoverishment

emerge from current critical, social, and cultural practices of queers of color. Within current political and legal practices, sexuality has become a double amendment, mediating at once the history of the black freedom movement (the Civil Rights Act) and immigrant, diasporic, and de-colonizing struggles (the wartime migrations of the NDAA). For this reason, queer of color formations can be one site from which some of the most fragmented but crucial sediments, legacies, and formations of vio-lence of US globalism and US racial capitalism as an articulated whole can be excavated.

As a contribution to critical ethnic studies, this book argues that sexuality names the normative frames that organize our disciplinary and interdisciplinary inquiries into our past and into contemporary racial capitalism. It is the locus of important and vital contradictions between sexuality's institutional role as the promissory that will settle the past, cap-turing finally its meaning—even that of race—and the complex, overlap-ping, and imbricated racialized histories, migrations, wars, and social relations that sexuality now not only amends and regulatively frames but allegorizes as well. As a form of immanent critique, I position queer of color critique as the dialectical politicization of these contradictions. In this sense, queer of color critiques and practices share in the reimaging of ethnic studies and the study of race within American studies, in the context of changed modes and methods of racialization and more globally complex racial logics of uneven accumulation of wealth. To do otherwise —to fail to theorize about and engage our sexual amendments—would be to turn ethnic studies into another disciplinary institution that only amends the values of racial capitalism, its practices of racialization, and its extraordinary commitment and reversion to social violence. In *Freedom with Violence*, sexuality is an unstable and dynamic site for continuing our excavations of race as alternative trajectories of modernity.

In order to pursue these alternative trajectories, we must abandon political practices and epistemological standpoints that affirm history as a linear and progressive *telos* striving for unity and self-identity.[13] As I hope my discussion of the passage of the law against anti-GLBTQ violence suggests, political practices and epistemological standpoints committed to any such *telos* affirm those practices and subjectivities only through regulative idealizations that camouflage their material and dis-cursive conditions. The effects of these idealizations ought to be of central concern because they have historically been the means by which egalitarian efforts and politics in metropolitan contexts become the vehicles for creating devastating, crushing, and broad social violence— violence that appears again and again to Western metropolitan publics as antecedent, transitory, epiphenomenal, or coincidental to the project of real egalitarianism and the juridical politics of equality.

To be clear, I write expressly in the interest of expanding current projects for social transformation, which daily confront an empowered national public sphere that remains primarily organized by an ideal image of a universal political apparatus—namely, the modern state, reduced now to little more than security functions—that can or ought to effectively represent social practices and the capitalist societies in which those practices are embedded. Hence, I am interested in specific institutional, social, and bodily violences that emerge alongside the epistemic culture of twentieth-century American modernity and that are promulgated by national egalitarian forms of social change constituted through varying material regimes of perception. And that interest is part of a specific effort to generate modes of thought and forms of practice that can find in the very disclosure of these legitimate and desired violences the resources for developing alternative practices of collective transformation. Toward that end, this book makes a strong case for a critical ethnic studies, one that builds on earlier models of the discipline but deepens its comparative and intersectional work in a contemporary capitalist context characterized by a gendered transnationalization of previously national capitalist economic, institutional, and social practices.[14] Going beyond the parameters of liberal and nationalist modes of framing both social formations and movements for social change, critical ethnic studies seeks to understand race in the context of the dynamic political relations of the national within the international, of the nation form in conditions of empire, and of the microphysics of power that attend a Western context defined by national sovereignty and advanced technological and institutional conditions of capitalist social production and so-called national defense.

Through critical ethnic studies, we gain access to a different account of political modernity, the politics of knowledge, and the persistent reemergence of state violence. In its recountings of slavery, empire, wars, land seizures, deportations, and racialized immigrations as crucial and ongoing resignifications of the racial nation's dependence upon fictive ethnicity, critical ethnic studies produces contradictory genealogies of juridical equality and state-based and state-enforced freedoms. The genealogies narrate state-based freedoms as conserving, even as they produce anew, the racial and gendered inequalities for which these freedoms have historically been an alibi. Indeed for much of US history, the state has enforced a form of bourgeois freedom that liberalism would dub freedom from violence. It is a freedom upon which racial, patriarchal, capitalist, and slave-holding rights of enjoyment are predicated.[15] Throughout the nineteenth and early twentieth centuries, race figured as the central violence to be negated and eliminated in the dialectic of modern freedom. Through genealogy, we notice the degree to which race continues to figure in liberal and national projects even in the late twentieth century, an era of formal juridical equality, in ways that surprisingly expand the state's identity as the guarantor of a modernity free from arbitrary, irrational, and racial violence.

Far from diminishing the modern figuration of race as something that calls into being the political state as a counterviolence, the inclusion of race in the juridical and institutional forms of egalitarian freedom creates the inverse: at the end of the twentieth century, racial inclusion in the form of the US state has in important ways expanded and made more complex racial and racialized gendered inequalities, while simultaneously expanding the apparatuses of legitimate violence to do the work of securing and reproducing those inequalities through the very institutional sites, occasions, and acts that ensure racial inclusion. Especially as legal and social equality mediates the grossly uneven distributions of history and meaning that constitute racial capitalism, practices of racial inclusiveness are indistinguishable from what Ruth Wilson Gilmore calls the racialized workfare/warfare state that promulgates the structured asymmetries and divisions of contemporary racial capitalism.[16]

ANTIVIOLENCE LAW AND THE UNIVERSITY

The passage of GLBTQ hate-crimes legislation with the 2010 NDAA suggests a relation more complex than one of pure contingency, backroom politicking, or something that can be narrated simply as the idiosyncratic process of working with this particular legislation. The Shepard-Byrd Act is an amendment to a federal hate-crimes law passed in 1969, at the end of the civil rights movement. Studying the juridical history of US civil rights litigation and court judgments from the 1940s to the 1970s, the legal historian Mary Dudziak argues that state reform incorporated and attempted to absorb African American social movements that targeted the symbolic and material racial disparities of US society at midcentury through a Cold War–era liberal framework of universal civil rights. In this account, civil rights legislation and court decisions were less the effects of the successful transformation of state meanings by the ethical, moral, and political worldviews organizing the black freedom movement, and more the outcomes of the US Cold War initiatives to be globally hegemonic after the implosion of the European empires on their own continent.[17] That is, in a manner that is only partially resonant with current GLBTQ civil rights, the reformist state advanced individual civil rights as a way to restore its claim to political universality against growing antiracist antagonisms, as it sought to become hegemonic across a globe afire with heterogeneous anticolonial struggles. The racial reformist state's civil rights decisions do not, then, represent an advance in the historical self-creation of political universality. Such a proposition makes US geopolitics once again a purely contingent context for discerning the meaning disclosed by the state's civil rights decisions and legislation. Rather, the liberal reformist state narrated its delegitimation of white supremacy as protections against arbitrary local violence. Arbitrary violence became the terrain upon which the state attempted to settle the meaning of US racial projects in the context of the competing and at times conflicting interests of US postwar geopolitics and policies. Indeed, as historians and political theorists of US state formation remind us, the transformation of the Bill of Rights, originally composed to protect the rights of states, into its current status as the protection of individual civil rights—in the late-modern advanced capitalist conception of those rights—and its retrospective projection as the philosophical foundation of the US Constitution and its founding generation occurred in the United States in this very period of the mid-twentieth century.[18]

If pure contingency fails to characterize the relation between forms of antiviolence law and the material conditions within which such forms are advanced, so too does an account of social context as determinate cause. Instead, we must theorize about the contradictions of hegemonic social and political forms and knowledges—that is, we must investigate the ways in which the state rules through advancing formal resolutions to material antagonisms and ruptures. As scholars like Brenda Gayle Plummer, Kimberlé Crenshaw, Jacquelyn Dowd Hall, George Lipsitz, and Nikhil Pal Singh argue, the pursuit of African American civil rights was just one instance in a longer and more complex movement for black freedom.[19] Rather than settling what Singh terms the "relentlessly negative dialectics" of race that the "long civil rights" movement persistently opened, statist reform tactics only intensified the dialectical force and locations of race while shaping a national public sphere.[20] Advancing the negative dialectics of race, black freedom movements in this period discovered—through black political and cultural antagonisms to liberal and statist forms—practices for building and imagining a future global democracy in a canny understanding of social history as persisting beyond and after its seizure by the nation form. When the state advanced civil rights with a Cold War geopolitics that sought to control the terms and outcome of global decolonization, it clearly did so to orchestrate (often through recourse to the means of state violence) the limits of viable political speech and forms of antiracism. This enabled an attempt to sever the emerging radical, antipatriotic, nationalist, and anticolonial voices within the long civil rights movement from its self-identity. Yet it also unwittingly advanced the subject—as figured especially by legal discourse—as a crucial form by which the overdetermination of US racial contradictions, domestic black political and social antagonisms, and US state violence abroad (most glaringly, in the case of the war in Vietnam) could be resolved. The larger history that these scholars from critical ethnic studies offer reveals that racial meanings were not only provisionally settled in the state's attempt to gain the consent of black citizens. Rather, these scholars remind us, after the 1960s the US state attempted to govern through extending itself into practices of subjectivity across racial divides.

Subjectivity became a crucial element in constituting and reproducing the means available to the US racial state after the Second World War for the practice of legitimate violence, especially during the decades of the Cold War. This has often been understood as the promotion of a Cold War ideology, where a liberal-individualist theory of society became a practical imperative for the state. According to this account, the state operates as the ballast for the private pursuit of personal liberty and economic freedom, the latter concepts being the fulcrum of its Cold War campaign against communism. The antidraft movement, the post-1964 phase of the civil rights movement and emerging black nationalism, the 1960s student revolts, and the poor people's marches—originally led by Martin Luther King Jr. and later organized by the Southern Christian Leadership Conference (SCLC)—in particular revealed the state's need to mobilize a racially heterogeneous population for its military apparatus as it suffered stunning losses of legitimacy, both nationally and globally, in the late 1960s.

The state form in this era sought to address and demobilize the complex and heterogeneous political world characterized by a preponderance of social antagonisms across localities and regions of the United States, which—in the context of the civil rights, feminist, and antiwar movements—threatened to undermine the concept of the political sphere as a rational index of US society. As a result, the state form expanded in a contradictory fashion into the material practices of subjectivity that broke down previous borders between races, regions, classes, and genders. In other words, by providing alternative contexts for the growing social antagonisms, the civil rights, feminist, and antiwar movements threatened the state's capacity to mediate those antagonisms. The state's attempt to produce universality through practices of subjectivity must be read, then, as its response to alternative and heterogeneous mediating contexts. Richard Ohmann makes this point well in his account of the rise after 1968 of the professional-managerial class, whose dominance within the institutions that composed the state (especially those institutions that develop the ideological forms for the reproduction of state-based rule) was a consequence of its ability to champion cultural forms that interiorized social antagonisms and the contradictory conditions organizing social practices, as well as promoting techniques for their management. Yet this strategy was only successful because of the welfare state that, since 1947, had neutralized and outlawed labor agitation and militancy in social life and in the domains of economic production, while enabling American businesses to augment organized labor's material well-being by tying the fortunes of US businesses to US foreign policy, including the US-led postwar reconstruction, which took place mostly in Western Europe. It was due to these conditions that the tactics of the professional-managerial class became also the defining tactics of the liberal state. The cultural forms promoted by the professional-managerial class enabled the social rediscovery of political universality within a splintering social formation, by figuring that universality in the domain of subjectivity. Examining the kind of literary works that this class raised to the status of canonical, Ohmann argues: "The needs and values of the professional-managerial class permeate the general forms of these novels, as well as their categories of understanding and their means of representation . . . A premise of th[e] fiction [that they championed]—nothing new to American literature but particularly salient in this period—is that individual consciousness, not the social or historical field, is the locus of significant happening." Moreover, they promoted an understanding of subjectivity as primarily a private interiority that registers in affective terms, such as anger, the ongoing social conditions of racial, class, and gender disharmony. Lastly, these forms of subjectivity also mediate the increasing incorporation of bodily formations into institutional rationalities and knowledges, particularly those that enable methods of vertical control and management.[21]

Integrated schools, labor markets, hospitals, and neighborhoods, along with the enforcement at the private and governmental level of nondiscriminatory contracts, are just some of the examples by which the state form became increasingly indistinguishable from the institutions through which modes of subjectivity within a social formation were produced and reproduced. By the 1970s in the United States, subjectivity (and not simply abstract citizenship) became the contradictory locus through which the post-1968 US racial state reasserted and expanded the scope of legitimate violence, both nationally and globally. These new constraints, through which the state form expanded, simultaneously produced the conditions for black cultural and social expressions that engaged, stretched, and politicized the borders of subjectivity, from the aesthetics of black power to the power of black arts—revealing as well as reveling in the ambiguous limits of legitimate violence. These movements exploited the sources of legitimate violence for fighting a range of struggles against racial, class, and state inequalities.

The transformation and refashioning of the liberal state form in the 1970s through practices of subjectivity extended the horizons of struggles against racial inequities to the dominant social institutions responsible for the reconciliation of social and cultural meanings with the sources of state practice. The public university became a crucial terrain for this process. Indeed, the movements for ethnic studies and the Third World student movements at public universities such as San Francisco State University and the University of California, Berkeley, reveal well the contradictory aspects of the renovated state form. The late 1960s and early 1970s were a complex social and historical moment, characterized globally by broad, variegated, and splintering social movements as well as robust anticolonial movements. In the midst of these antagonisms, the US state sought to secure and expand its monopoly on violence; yet this expansion also extended the sites of racial antagonisms to the cultural institutions organized by the promotion of universality that was crucial to the state. The reorganization of the US state form through practices of subjectivity set the stage for the black power movement and the Third World student movements to contest the logic of formal rights as a legitimate approximation of social equality. As Glenn Omatsu argued, speaking to the Asian American student movement:

> Those who took part in the mass struggles of the 1960s and early 1970s will know that the birth of the Asian American movement coincided not with the initial campaign for civil rights but with the later demand for black liberation; that the leading influence was not Martin Luther King, Jr., but Malcolm X; that the focus of a generation of Asian American activists was not on asserting racial pride but reclaiming a tradition of militant struggle by earlier generations; that the movement was not centered on the aura of racial identity but embraced fundamental questions of oppression and power; that the movement consisted of not only college students but large numbers of community forces, including the elderly, workers, and high school youth; and that the main thrust was not one of seeking legitimacy and representation within American society but the larger goal of liberation (81).[22]

The Third World student strikes at San Francisco State in 1968 were the longest student strikes in US history. Though they were ultimately disbanded by the local police, whose violence was sanctioned by the university administration, the strikers did force the administration to create a College of Ethnic Studies, to change admissions criteria, and to redistribute financial aid and other resources. In addition, the strikes created an effective coalition of students of color linked by their marginality within academic knowledge and university space that expanded to other public universities across California and the country. The very name of the Third World student movement reveals a contradictory state formation that was constrained by its ongoing material needs to use legitimate violence to mobilize its racially heterogeneous population for making war and to wage unequal and technologically sophisticated wars of aggression along the rim of Asia that were central to US foreign policy in this period. We can situate the original development of ethnic studies as part of the activism of students who, in the context of the US war in Vietnam and the state's buildup of its Cold War apparatus, ruptured the state's contradictory extension into the practices of subjectivity. Yet the institutional pressures that forced the formal creation of the discipline of ethnic studies by the late 1980s in many ways displaced this aspect of its founding, as Omatsu suggests, normalizing the heterogeneous and intersecting quality of the Third World students' movement.

The first institutionalization of ethnic studies yielded forms for grasping the force of race disclosed in antiracist struggles, which translated the meaning of "race" through the terms established by liberal national idioms of inclusion and social representation within the state. Race became the basis upon which Americans constructed or elaborated their social identity, capturing race within a liberal identitarian framework governed by the core values of authenticity, originality, and wholeness. Ethnic studies was able to successfully become institutionalized within the university only to the degree that it reconciled the study of race to the epistemic divisions, forms, and modes of perception central to the reproduction of liberal political modernity. Crucially, the heteronomy and heterogeneity of race, expressed in the historically specific emergence of the US Third World student movement, was exactly what institutionalization designated as disposable in its biased and selective transcription of the social relations that the movement revealed and constituted. The first wave of ethnic studies programs yielded diverse intellectual and cultural projects, to be sure, but—like the cultural nationalist counterviolence that operated at the edge of legitimate violence—it made its point of departure, the assertion of counteridentities, the regulative frame or point of arrival for the critical, historical, representational, epistemic, and transformative work it undertook. The restriction of race to the terms of social identity produced a metalepsis in which race was itself regulatively constituted in a manner that made the abstract forms of representation that organized institutional practices appear identical to the racialized and gendered social relations those forms sought to describe.

Ethnic studies produced epistemic frameworks for social and political representation that at one level interrupted the state's monopoly on violence. As the universality of the state was reestablished in this period through practices of subjectivity, ethnic studies revealed the dark underside of previous and residual forms of legitimate violence in its historical and sociological investigation of race. That is, ethnic studies, like the urban black power movement, richly exploited the post-1968 reconstitution of the state through the promise and practice of subjectivity to forge a critical space within the institutional structures of the state. Yet to the degree that the field's representational framework for race restricted the word's meanings to the very terms by which liberal political thought in this period organized an ontology of legitimate violence—namely, to the view that the integration of racialized cultural subjects with the social formation would reinforce the pluralist values of self-unified, autonomous, and authentic collectives for which abstract representation (within the state) exhausted the horizon of meaning within social relations—ethnic studies risked legitimizing institutional modes of both knowing and representing race, and also racialized social differences. The normalization of race that the epistemic forms organizing ethnic studies practices generated was coincident with cultural nationalist practices within the larger US public sphere. To stay with African American social movements in this period, cultural nationalist modes of practice attempted to reappropriate the unstable—but heterogeneous, in terms of class—urban black power movement that emerged at this time. Its epistemes formed a thesis on race as an essence of or a fulcrum for the unification of diversely racialized black communities, transforming incommensurate practices within the urban black power movement into a more stable and substantive counterforce. This stabilizing counterforce—iterated in cultural nationalist social, cultural, and political practices—became the basis on which cultural nationalism addressed the violent persistence of white supremacy as coincident with state neutrality in struggles between races.

Ethnic studies risked creating a problem similar to that of cultural nationalism in the institutional context. Like the nationalist attempt to stabilize antiracist practices in nationalism's bid to undo the historical hijacking of the state form by white supremacy, ethnic studies, even as it contested racial inequality within the educational apparatus, risked disappearing into unthinkable transparencies within the structures that organized the institutional practices through which meaning is disclosed, most especially through the promotion of a self-coherent racial standpoint. For example, the gendered and sexual contradictions that organized the Third World student movement and mediated social expressions of race were based both on the strong female and queer elements within the student leadership and on the aggressive gendered Orientalism that organized both US state and dominant public discourse. This Orientalism was the result of the government's intensification of its use of technological means of mass destruction in Southeast Asia to reduce its reliance on politically meaningful citizen soldiers, a reliance that also intensified the racial antagonisms of the period. These gendered and sexual contradictions were central to the development of both normative cultural nationalist forms of cross-racial alliances as well as to the development of alliances resulting from shared experiences of existing within the incoherencies between multiple forms of social determination. As Grace Kyungwon Hong and Roderick Ferguson have recently argued, we can consider nonhegemonic, multiracial alliances such as the Third World student movement of the 1970s, as well as the activism of women of color and lesbians of color in the 1980s, to be expressive of the social possibilities that were generated by the complex racial heterotopias that emerged within the increased regulation, policing, punitive disciplining and political abandonment that organized the production of postindustrial urban space in the United States.[23]

These latter forms of solidarity are indeed inexplicable from the standpoint of both liberal and cultural nationalist modes of apprehending race. Although both forms of alliance, racial coalition and gender and sexual difference, were probably responsible for cementing the unexpected and broad coalition of diverse and, structurally speaking, historically divided students of color who took part in these strikes, we know very little about these latter formations of solidarity or the social practices within which they were formed.

This absence of collective knowledge within ethnic studies is itself a historically generated void. Indeed, it is for this reason that it would be good to rethink what it would mean to address this void in our understanding of the conditions that made the development of ethnic studies possible. In our desire to address this absence in our collective understanding, we may commit ourselves to a historiographical practice that places these nonnational gendered and sexual solidarities, socialities, and forces within the same representational schemas used by cultural nationalist thinkers to attest to the equally full presence of those excluded from our knowledge. But if we do so, we risk failing to note and reflect on two related and politically consequential aspects of these commitments for representation. First, we might fail to think about the relationship between the way in which cultural nationalist productions of race were in fact largely forged by the very representational schemas that required turning race itself into a divided space, containing both politically recognized presences and socially and politically consequential absences. That is, we would fail to ask how the terms for the representation of race created the very void we now seek to fill. The second and related aspect is that we may forgo the opportunity to develop and elaborate on alternative representational domains and practices for addressing the voids in our historical consciousness (in other words, a consciousness riven with structurally produced voids). Indeed, we might want to turn to these other domains because of their historical importance in mediating our engagement with those occluded socialities that emerged in and through the very representational regimes that turn race into a differential of presence and absence—socialities that thus persist in spaces different from but alongside those organized by normative representational schemas. In other words, these voids in our collective knowledge can help reveal the gendered and sexual political unconscious that organizes and subtends the first institutionalization of ethnic studies and the various forms of disciplinary practice that the institutionalization entrenched.

CRITICAL ETHNIC STUDIES

The Third World student movement that forced the establishment of ethnic studies on university and college campuses in the 1970s is part of a materialist genealogy of persistent antiracist critiques of US racial capitalism. These critiques served as an arraignment of the ontology of legitimate violence and the exploration of the possibilities of counter-violence. Yet the progressive institutionalization and disciplinary normalization of ethnic studies became part of the very means by which the conditions for legitimate violence were refashioned and the state was reaffirmed as the possessor of a monopoly on violence. The institutionalization of the study of race can become dangerously aligned with the normalization of the repressive functions of the state. These functions have historically produced race as the limit of ideological and discursive struggle, the illegible matter that we can interpret only through the vigilant infliction of legitimate violence. This is even more true when the terms and structures through which institutionality is achieved become the basis for the meaning and appearance of racial equality. With historical hindsight, we can see the liberal institutionalization of race within which ethnic studies programs were often forcibly contextualized—or made into pure context—in their emergence on college and university campuses. This produced a gendered and sexual political unconscious, which has restricted our ability to discover the alternative solidarities that generated cross-racial alliances challenging liberal and cultural nationalist models of alliance and solidarity. Additionally, we see that liberal institutionalization has sought from ethnic studies not a genealogical critique of the modern university within racial capitalism, but the development of a representative cross-racial class within the educational institution whose appearance and restricted space of effort it promotes as exhausting the meaning of racial equality. The liberal institutional promotion of a representative cross-racial class is an idealized and inverted image, a symptom of the deepening of the racial and gendered division of labor since 1970.[24]

Crenshaw has argued that the separation of social practices into distinct ontologies that defined state liberalism as well as the institutionalized variants of feminism and antiracist critique in this period had, by the 1980s, yielded a liberal pluralist juridical context in which black women's critiques of contemporary racial capitalism—in particular, of the post-1970s racial and gendered reorganization of industrial methods of production—were a disorganizing force for the liberal national state. Within the juridical context, black women's acts of representation were either elided, silenced, neutralized, or contradicted through their assimilation into existing so-called race- and gender-specific *standpoints* within the law, or, in an anxious act of supplementation, figured as a distinct standpoint within the existing legal account of social relations, with sharply restricted meaning. In this way, black women—women of color more generally, in Crenshaw's later work on the remediation by institutions, including nonprofit organizations, of racialized social and sexual violence in Los Angeles—are the "other" of liberal standpoint theory, its constitutive blind spot. But, as Crenshaw argues, the apparent political incoherencies of women of color's political practices and their social claims might in fact be the means by which we discover the historically specific structures of legibility and disposability that have become central to the racial and gendered US capitalist social formation since the 1970s. It is important to remember that for Crenshaw, intersectionality is not a distinct standpoint, available through structuralist or positivist modes of inquiry, but rather a critique of the way that both modes of standpoint theory normalize race and gender as part of a liberal metaphysics of substance that promotes the legal search for intention as the causative structure of harm. This becomes the very means by which particular regimes of racial and gendered domination and exploitation become both available to and unrelieved by the legal pursuit of universal equality. Crenshaw writes: "Perhaps it appears to some that I have offered inconsistent criticisms of how Black women are treated in antidiscrimination law . . . It seems that I have to say that Black women are the same and harmed by being treated differently, or that they are different and harmed by being treated the same. But I cannot say both. This apparent contradiction is but another manifestation of conceptual limitations of single-issue analyses."[25]

The feminisms of black and other women of color emerged in this period, then, as a critique of both the liberal theory of universal equality as well as the positivist regimes of the visible and the factual that delimit the horizon of the knowable, and through which universality is advanced, realized, and reproduced. For Crenshaw, intersectionality names the constitutive blind spots that emerge in the pursuit of knowledge that affirms the methods, terms, and frames upholding liberal universality in this moment. These blind spots are not spaces in which social power is absent, but rather spaces in which social power's first and foremost defining quality is the reproduction of distinct social practices of domination and exploitation that profit from the shadow of disposability cast by the liberal edifice of universality. Its second defining quality is that it generates distinct practices of oppositionality that are conventionally illegible within the modes of perception and knowledge that organize the reproduction and extension of liberal political modernity. These are practices that interrogate the division of culture and politics, and the division of subject and practice, producing critiques of those divisions as precisely prohibiting our grasp of the new determinations and ongoing transformations of modernity. In sum, intersectionality is a rethinking and reworking of the meaning of "standpoint," in a historical milieu in which the universality of the state (with its monopoly on legitimate violence) is created on the terrain of subjectivity itself.[26]

From the viewpoint of our historical moment, we can see a constant dialectic between the state's attempt to preserve the meaning of social antagonisms and the racialized formations that continue to reveal the material constraints that organize the making of meaning. As Ferguson argues, a cultural politics of alternative racialized genders and practices of sexuality within communities of color in the United States in the 1970s were negations of the logic of subjectivity through which the state asserted itself after 1968.[27] As a part of the negative dialectics of race, black lesbian and feminist collectivities exposed the limits of the forms of knowledge by which the meaning of the state is preserved. These racial, gendered, and sexual collectivities that sought to decipher the conditions their political moment emerged out of are dialectically connected to the post-1968 state's extension into and dependence upon what Evelynn Hammonds provocatively calls "the structure of what is visible" as its new limit. It is in this historical, institutional, and epistemological milieu of post-1968 liberal and juridical US state formation that Hammonds argues black lesbian and black female sexualities become the "not-absent-though-not-present" bodily "subjects" within both cultural epistemes and more formalized knowledge.[28] As such, they contribute to the racialized accumulation of heterogeneous material and practical remainders that find no comfortable home within the increasingly dominant positivistic and conversely structural historical expositions of subjectivity and collective practice upon which US state formation became dependent as it sought to address the crisis of legitimacy that its own blood lust produced in the Vietnam War. But these negations were also the basis for generating new and unexpected cultural objects that mediated urban black lesbian and feminist collectivities.

Ethnic studies, then, emerged within a social field defined by what Michel Foucault calls biopolitics and a late-modern political state determined by what he names practices of governmentality. And, as Timothy Mitchell has argued, the state form emerges through the repetitive production of mundane institutional practices. For Foucault, late modernity is characterized by practices that erode the ideology of separate spheres, that expand economic rationality into the political domain, and that extend the regimes of social control into social relations and the practices of subjectivity through which those relations are sustained. The regulation of late modernity by a biopolitical govermentality has submitted the political sphere and the domain of citizenship to an even stronger determination by instrumental rationalities, in which institutionally formed social practices become the violent omission of heterogeneous historical and social meanings.[29] Yet, it is imperative, I believe, to situate US governmentalized biopolitics as an effect of the ongoing and increasingly complex dialectics of race. That is, for the US social formation, the dialectical and critical practices of race have a distinct transformative power in eroding and upending contemporary regimes of violence. This is why we should not be surprised that it is at precisely this point in time, when biopolitical violence could not be more obvious, that it has been especially difficult to advance the study of race beyond the liberal institutional or Marxist rational critique of racism. It is uncontestable that practices of race are always under the threat of being appropriated for racist purposes. Equally, however, those practices are the way in which the forms of historical difference generated by the conditions of political modernity exceed their determination by that modernity. The practices are the basis of alternative publics—but only ones that undermine the self-evidence of contemporary disciplinary practices.

Race cultivates other modes and forms of investigation that constitute an infelicitous violence always threatening the conditions through which political modernity negotiates its dependence on capitalist regimes of social production. This is not an exercise of something called "violence," put into a taxonomy of uses from legitimate to arbitrary. I am interested in thinking about a regime of force that we can term "legitimate violence," distinct from other formations of violence because of the specific constraints and opportunities that "legitimacy" produces. It is a violence that carries social meaning. In other words, it is a violence that arrives with its own frames of interpretation. Or, to use earlier terminology, it always arrives with "amendments." In this way, it is also a violence that yields something more than a universal extension of rational violence. It also yields the conditions for a supplemental violence: practices that strive for absolute domination, a vigilant counterviolence against race itself. And by pairing the first US hate-crimes bill with the rise of ethnic studies, I have tried to suggest that the two are linked by a common historical dialectic: the negative dialectics of race in the 1970s and early 1980s were extended to and reappeared as social practices of gender and sexuality within racialized communities.

A FREEDOM WITH VIOLENCE

The critical frames opened up by the inquiries pursued in the subsequent chapters enable a different account of the 2010 NDAA's passage with an amendment against anti-GLBTQ hate crimes, an account that seeks to make sense of precisely what is figured in a contradictory way as either a merely contingent context for the emergence of a universal principle or as a historically determinative structural or positivist unity in the ongoing progressive development and refinement of the nation-state's self-identity. I offer genealogies of the specific legal and institutional forms of mediation that emerge from the challenges posed by identity-based social movements to the modern US state. These mediating forms are essential to our understanding of the historical conditions that mediation simultaneously preserves, advances, and displaces. I hope to show that specific contemporary antiracist and queer of color social and cultural movements reveal the social, material, and historical constraints or conditions of possibility that organize these forms of mediation, and that in doing so they destabilize the production of the representative state form from its diverse sources. Both the potency and the legacy of these movements are to be found in the way in which they show that forms of mediation presume the exclusion of alternative modes of subjectivity as an a priori requirement if they are to be effective as the simple, weak, and neutral frames that postwar twentieth-century liberal and national legal forms claim to be. My thinking here about certain twentieth-century social movements—especially those after the 1960s—as critiques of political and philosophical formalisms coincides in many ways with Butler's engagements with theories of universality in the context of the contemporary antiradical liberalization of US gay and lesbian politics through the movement for marriage rights and the repeal of "don't ask, don't tell," which I take up in the second half of this book. And my thinking resonates with Lisa Lowe's discussions of disidentification as a material effect of the complex neocolonial and late capitalist historical conditions that create the conditions for dialectical critique in the way that post-1960s state forms attempt to narrate or assimilate new racial formations of Asian immigrants.[30]

Like these thinkers, I read the exclusion of alternative modes of subjectivity not as forms of preexisting particularity, excluded by the drive for universality, that at a later moment simply appropriate that universality for their own interests. Nor are these exclusions simply points from which to discover the dissimulation of a hegemonic particular that alternately claims and passes for universality, as in the case of the masculinist and white supremacist structuring and appropriation of the presumed universality of formal rights and abstract citizenship in the founding of the US nation-state. Rather, these exclusions that emerge paradoxically into social representation as the racially and sexually excluded and excludable, through the very mediations that are responsible for their displacement, are best grasped as the bordering activities through and against which hegemonic forms assemble their frames or borders. It is only through these bordering activities, reiterated in every instance of mediation, that formalist schemas—such as universality and particularity, whose effect is to limit the horizon of the political—are both engendered and endangered. In this way, differing formations of exclusion have specific material and historical bearing, a certain historicity, even as they force an immanent reappraisal of traditional historical materialism.[31] That is, their historicity is inextricably tied to the limits that historically specific conditions of possibility establish for the production of culturally intelligible and sanctioned subjectivity.

Ironically, such subjects exist through social relations and practices that already exceed the regulative and constitutive limits set forth by these instituted and constitutive conditions of possibility. Ferguson elegantly argues that for this reason, queer of color cultural critique emerges as a "disidentificatory" practice within both revolutionary nationalist and western Marxist modes of historical materialism. For Ferguson, queer of color critique must refuse the universalizing empiricist and transcendent subject that both revolutionary nationalism and western Marxism attempt to preserve, offering in their place an understanding of political subjects as *gesturing* toward the social formations of which they are displacements.[32] That is, social antagonisms that emerge as a consequence of specific political forms of mediation have a historical and dialectical force in opening up materially specific alternative contingencies repressed by idealist conditions of possibility. These alternative contingencies can serve as the basis for critical practices that contribute to the development of cultural and political formations that collectively have adequate means and force to diffuse the state's disproportionate and counterinsurrectionary use of legitimate violence to direct the multiple horizons of politics.

The recent passage of legislation against anti-GLBTQ hate crimes cannot be the means through which the contemporary politics of sexuality confirms yet again the democratic value of the principles of institutional liberalism, since clearly the contradictory institutional contexts and material conditions of the passage subvert the principle of non-contradiction that is central to liberal political philosophy and thought. Equally, we ought not to pursue certain modes of leftist argumentation that figure contemporary sexuality politics as merely the convenient handmaiden to a US or even supranational military war machine (figured now as the true meaning of the nation-state, which is seen as a global apparatus of security and perpetual war)—either in a search for ideological cover and tactics of legitimation or in a discursive production of methods for near-total social control, tempting as this mode of interpretation might be in the context of daily revelations of the state's recourse to cruelty and illegitimate violence, both domestically and internationally.[33] Both narratives may settle too quickly the robust contradictions, aporias, and ambiguities that our contemporary historical terrain produces. Rather, I think that what we have is a unique structure of state violence and social emancipation that I designate a freedom with violence.

My attempt to speak to a contemporary conjoining of state violence and social emancipation through the phrasing of a freedom with violence seeks to draw out three different understandings of the relationship between violence and emancipation. First, I mean to draw out the sense in which twentieth-century modernity produced the material social forces and relations out of which developed a specific US state form, one in which the state could ideally claim to possess a monopoly on violence—what Max Weber termed the nation-state's drive to monopolize the apparatuses of legitimate violence.[34] Even in our transnational and global conditions of social production and accumulation, the US nation-state continues to assert its form as the best possible totality for worldwide social relations. Those who champion this position make their case through promoting the image of the nation-state as the preeminent vehicle for the conquest of arbitrary and irrational violence by a legitimate violence that it promotes as nearly bloodless in the supposedly ordinary times of market societies.

There have been varying liberal and republican strands of this argument, the former positing the so-called liberal representative nation-state as the site of the ongoing development of liberal values and principles in contrast to authoritarian state-based violence, while the latter promotes a vision of the nation-state as the exclusive apparatus for striking an ethical balance within liberalism, achieving social equality and freedom from state-enforced violence (especially of the monopoly capitalist marketplace) that modern liberalism—when transformed into a governing apparatus—would otherwise produce and sanction among the citizenry. Both these positions presuppose a vision of the state as striving not only for a monopoly on legitimate violence within its territorial jurisdiction but also for a monopoly on the terms of social rationality, since each position uses an explicit appeal to a persistent irrational and antirational threat. This is a threat that undermines the drive for a universal and ultimately nonauthoritarian communicative or procedural process and context. Every exertion of proper state violence subtends a thesis on rational practices figured in terms of a freedom from this or that arbitrary, though all-too-regular, experience of mainly private and civil violence. Stock figures in this narrative have been not only the authoritarian ruler, but also—in the context of early-twentieth-century industrial capitalism —the liberal contract, targeted by the welfare state as requiring countervailing regulations, and perhaps most powerfully the emancipated black slave class in the US South, which Jim Crow jurisprudence made a threatening and amoral group of vagrants. I examine the relation between vagrancy and modern sociology in chapter 1.

In this sense, a freedom with violence connotes the way in which, by the twentieth century, US state violence was operating through and constrained by a drive for a monopoly on rationality, figured most often by attempts to concretize the meaning of rational freedom as a freedom from the threat of arbitrariness.[35] The modern state establishes itself in and through practices and their apparatuses that, in a particular historical instance, generate the conditions for the expression of legitimate violence, seeking to conserve those apparatuses for the state exclusively. The state form, then, is made possible through epistemologies, epistemes, and institutions that collectively forge the conditions for the universalization of a specific expression of reason or rationality.

As this institutionally based formation of reason or rationality effectively mediates a nationalized social formation, it reproduces the unevenness in knowledge that is a consequence of asymmetrical social relations as the ongoing sources of arbitrary threat. In this way, we can see the varying US statist expressions of universal political freedom during the twentieth century as the rhetorical and linguistic residues of the complex material pathways that correspond to the state's drive to monopolize the use of legitimate violence. Each public demand for a freedom protected by the state threatens to expose these historically forged and variable material relations between a specific set of institutions—what Louis Althusser terms the ideological and repressive state apparatuses—which ironically the public call for freedom mediates.[36] Every effective expression of universal freedom arrives with the materially produced network of repressive and ideological institutions whose provisional unity is the basis of the state's claim to a monopoly violence.

Second, building on this understanding of institution-based force relations, I mean to indicate by my use of the phrase "a freedom with violence" the way in which socially and institutionally produced forms of emancipation remain regulatively and constitutively tied to the nation-state form. A contemporary antiracist and antihomophobic counterpolitics to state-sanctioned and state-produced violence, then, demands that we revise our understanding of the relation between violence, institutions of knowledge, and the modern nation-state form. Historically racialized groups and nonnormative sexualities gained their meanings in the early-twentieth-century US nation-state as modern irrationalities, atavisms, and perversities from the professional disciplines and institutional bodies that collectively constituted the first fully developed expression of the US research university.[37] Institutions of knowledge were central, then, to the process by which the state could exert its monopoly on force because they produced racial and sexual differences to designate the horizon of irrationalities against and through which state violence became identical to legitimate force. Legitimate violence can thrive only when its enactment produces excludable groups, formations, practices, and meanings.[38] Again, in this sense, the state's claim to legitimate violence is predicated on its ability to achieve a monopoly on rationality as well, most powerfully through the extension of universal citizenship. Hence, movements for social emancipation that use claims of universal citizenship to seek full inclusion within the modern state form will do little to change the conditions by which legitimate violence continues to be naturalized as a supposedly substantive attack on socially eradicable irrational practices and cultural expressions. In our current moment, it seems that every movement to validate a claim of social freedom produces a disparate and adversarial claim by the state elsewhere against what it determines to be irrational cultures and practices; thus, it will no longer do to simply claim the strategic use of the US state or its discourse of freedom. Rather, we need to ask what other orchestration of the institutions of knowledge might be necessary if we are to sever the tie between claims of social freedom and the sanctioned use (even extra-territorially) of the state's monopoly on violence, which includes not only the police and the military—as well as teachers, doctors, psychologists, judges, and social workers—but also unmanned drones, so-called smart bombs, and bunker blasters.[39]

And third, I mean to designate how contemporary identity movements that seek to open up practices of subjectivity (signaled by freedom) can figure as important contradictory formations. These movements (including how we represent them and interpret their scope) have the potential to either solidify or disrupt the functioning of the state's ideological apparatuses. These apparatuses are the source for the preservation of the nation-state's modern identity, as a distinct social form that can ratify what it enacts (legitimate violence). Indeed, legitimate force might best be described as those state practices that are constitutively tautological and iterative: they enact a regulative force, in order to promote a framework that ratifies that force even as the framework constitutes the very expression and occasions of that force. In this context, the passage of hate-crimes legislation as an amendment to a defense appropriations bill is disturbing in many regards, not least of which is the sense that a promised freedom from private violence is tied to a repressive state apparatus that appropriates the promise in order to supposedly free the state from constraints on its use of disproportionate force. But the passage is also a moment that disorganizes previous iterations of the state form. This disorganization can be registered broadly, but it is most clearly visible in the way that a particular arrangement of the elements or disciplines of knowledge, which at one time attested to the veracity (and facticity) of the various objects of social life, can no longer repress those objects' fundamental ambiguity.

For example, our contemporary interpretative and disciplinary traditions have historically kept the study of practices of subjectivity (upon which hate-crimes laws depend for their operation and their moral and ethical clarity) separate from contemporary global politics. Not only is the 2010 NDAA a historical, social, and cultural object relevant to GLBTQ, feminist, and ethnic studies, but it is also an object of interest in military and diplomatic history, area studies, and social sciences such as psychology, sociology, and political science. In these fields' collision at one and the same textual object, the object gains plural meanings. More disturbingly, the object reveals an important interdependence between those disciplines central to producing legitimate and national sovereign violence—such as area studies, military and diplomatic history, and the social sciences, all of which are driven by a separation of the rational, whose universality is achieved differently and variously, from the contingently irrational—and those disciplines and interdisciplinary fields that now address the apparent unevenness in institutional knowledge about the supposedly universal elements upon which practices of subjectivity are transacted, such as sex or gender, race, culture, and sexuality. These latter disciplines and interdisciplinary areas become valued and legitimate not because they uphold distinctions between the rational and the variously irrational. Rather, these fields promulgate the liberal promise that political modernity procures the means by which the subject's desire to persist on its so-called own terms is addressed and safeguarded. That is, within these cultural disciplines and interdisciplines the subject gains racial, sexual, national, and linguistic diversity. Ensuring that the subject remains autonomous and free is what determines the validity of these latter fields' systems of knowledge and their role within the university. The 2010 NDAA is a shocking instance of the complicity between these otherwise conflicting areas of the modern university. It reveals that the border between the former set of disciplines and the latter is no longer clear (if it ever was). And in doing so, the NDAA reveals important points of crisis and contradiction that can point a way forward in the attempt to undo the binding of freedom to violence. In particular, varied tactics of desubjectivation originate from this blurred border. These tactics are the basis for critiques of normative subjectivity, idealized in modern citizenship. From such critiques we gain an assessment of normative subjectivity as one important locus of constitutive violence, whose historical meanings are fundamentally global, capitalist, and modern.

VIOLENCE AND THE RUINS OF KNOWLEDGE

Of all the national civil rights organizations that commented on the passage of the hate-crimes amendment to the 2010 NDAA, the National Urban League may have been the only one to note publicly the historical meaning of the Shepard-Byrd Act as also amending the original civil rights legislation that offered federal protection against bias-motivated crimes. Opening his press statement by quoting and remembering Bayard Rustin, the black pacifist and nonviolent activist who was arrested by police more than once and publicly exposed by the Federal Bureau of Investigation for having sexual relations with men, Marc Morial, the National Urban League's president and chief executive officer, notes that despite Rustin's central role in the civil rights leadership—especially in organizing the 1963 March on Washington—"there were attempts, both by advocates and opponents of the movement, to marginalize Rustin's influence because of his sexual orientation, and through the years, some in our community have objected to including gay rights as a civil right." Like other groups, then, the National Urban League applauded the passage of the legislation, believing that it "takes us one step closer to full civil rights protections for all Americans." For Morial, the new legislation was evidence that "fortunately, [the] divide [between gay rights and civil rights] is closing as more of us embrace Dr. King's wisdom: 'Injustice anywhere is a threat to justice everywhere.' "[40] It is perhaps the cruelest and most vicious of ironies that King's words would be cited in this celebration of the hate-crimes amendment to the national defense bill, not least because King's choice of the adverbs "anywhere" and "everywhere" to characterize the struggle for racial justice were specific grammatical placeholders in a global critique of mid-century Western imperialism and the use of British, European, and American state violence to suppress the anticolonial movements taking place in Africa and Asia. Indeed, King used this sentence in a speech delivered at Atlanta University on May 13, 1959, when he had been asked to welcome and introduce the visiting Kenyan nationalist Tom Mboya, who was completing a nearly five-week tour of the United States. In 1958 Mboya had been elected chairman of the All-African People's Conference in Ghana, becoming a key voice in Africa's nonalignment movement. He chided the United States for its enormous defense spending since the onset of the US-instigated Cold War. Traveling across the country with the aid of the African American Students Foundation, he sought support for his Airlift Africa Project. His goal was to charter planes to fly Kenyan students to the United States and enroll them in US universities and colleges. In announcing his support for the nonalignment movement and Airlift

Africa Project, King reminded his audiences that "what we are trying to do in the South and in the United States is part of this worldwide struggle for freedom and dignity,"[41] calling on his audience to understand and situate civil rights struggles in the US South as an amendment to non-Western decolonization globally. "So we are concerned about what is happening in Africa and what is happening in Asia because we are part of this whole movement," King continued. The postwar worldwide movement for decolonization and antiracism constituted what King elegantly called "an inescapable network of mutuality" between the struggles. He extolled his audience to offer their moral and financial support to Mboya and his Airlift Africa Project: "Certainly injustice anywhere is a threat to justice everywhere. And so long as problems exist in Africa, or in Asia, or in any section of the United States, we must be concerned about it."[42] Mboya would convince both private citizens and the US government to fund his project and between 1959 and 1963, hundreds of East Africans would participate in it. For the US government and businessmen who funded the program, Airlift Africa was a crucial tactic in their broader strategy to figure midcentury US pro-business national liberalism as a universal model for the decolonizing movements and their regions, even as the United States sought to control and determine the local processes of decolonization through active military and covert operations, especially against Marxist social movements. As a Cold War tactic, Airlift Africa also furthered the incorporation of the public university into an apparatus of the Cold War state, nurturing the technical education sectors of academe—such as agricultural sciences, engineering, and medicine, which mediated and restricted the meanings of the Airlift Africa Project to the universalization of technical and instrumentalist knowledge.

However, for the civil rights movement, anticolonial nationalists, and other antiracist elements such as the nonalignment movement, the program offered yet another link in the global efforts to construct substantive alternatives out of the institutional and material ruins of global white supremacy. An "old order is passing away," King claimed, replaced by the "worldwide struggle for freedom and human dignity." King prophetically stated that there was an "inescapable network of mutuality" between anticolonial Asians and Africans and the struggle by US blacks against racial despotism, arguing that "whatever affects one directly affects all indirectly."[43] King could not have been more prescient. In 1960, a friend of Mboya and a fellow member of the Luo tribe left Kenya for the United States, caught up in the educational chain migration begun by the Airlift Africa Project. Once settled in Hawaii, Mboya's friend received financial resources from the program. His name was Barack Obama, and his son became the first African American president of the United States and later signed into law in a single moment both the largest US defense bill in history and the most unprecedented expansion of federal hate-crimes law since passage of the original 1969 legislation.[44]

I have tried to present here what Avery Gordon has called a "ghost," created as we assemble and look into that empirical image of a modern fatherless black prince of state, President Barack Obama Jr.—who, in losing his "king" to premature death, can only unevenly mourn the violence of US globalism that his signature continues to cast as shadows over the promise of a universal multiculturalism, as he signs an act for two destinies: the continued growth of a global regime of US state terror and the further protection of legal enfranchisement.[45]

This is a racialized haunting, constituted by the very normalizing and derealizing legal formalisms of freedom and human dignity that ironically conveyed and constrained King as a voice of the black freedom movement. It is not only a haunting by foreclosed trajectories in the national past, but more important, it also marks an absence that disturbs the self-evidence of the present and our perception of it. This is a meaning-laden void that interrogates the linked dominance of positivism and political and cultural formalism, an intellectual conjunction embraced as much by the liberal state as by many of the major institutional movements of counterviolence that together violently conserve a meaning of politics and the political sphere as at once postracial and postcolonial, with gruesomely inhumane consequences. These are intellectual projects that, now more than ever, seek through practices of disavowal, idealization, or disposability to manage the persistence of race, constituted by King's "inescapable network of mutuality" as both historically and materially produced. Though ours is a modernity that continues to persist through race, that network remains a little known and unevenly mined source of alternatives.

As I hope to convey in the chapters that follow, race is more than its manifestation as a specter, a haunting, an unmourned past. From the perspectives that affirm legitimate violence, the image of Obama signing the 2010 NDAA into law will give rise to accounts that stress poetic wholeness. Those accounts may stress unacknowledged pasts finally mourned and put to rest by Obama's election to the US presidency. Or they may focus on the tragic aspects of the institutional affect that evicts all of the allegorical possibilities available in this moment, believing that domination is total and that ignorance, false consciousness, and a facile multicultural capitalist subject sit and act exactly where the world-historical subject used and ought to be. Yet from the standpoint of queer of color formations that interrogate and dialectically manifest the incoherency of legitimate and sovereign violence within late capitalism, currently expressed through the legal forms that organize state-based emancipation, the past is restored as an unresolved problem for power. It is race, mediated in this instance through queer of color formations that interrogate hate-crimes legislation, that forces us to move beyond a melancholic fixation on the tragic, on a loss already conserved for the subject—tempting as it might be to stay its captive audience—so that we can see what all documents and practices of the modern state really are: snapshots and experiences of late modernity as a topography of livable ruins.

Indeed, at the edges of the national GLBTQ, civil rights, and anti-violence movements and entirely shut out from representation in the national public sphere were a number of queer of color; queer immigrant and diasporic; and working-class, racially mixed, urban transgender groups that interrogated precisely the violence that these national egalitarian perspectives promulgated and entrenched, contesting the abstract logic and ideal structures that made egalitarianism coincident with the state form.[46] Organizations such as the Audre Lorde Project, Incite: Women of Color against Violence, the Community United against Violence, FIERCE, Queers for Economic Justice, the Sylvia Rivera Law Project, and Southerners on New Ground spoke against viewing the hate-crimes bill as a step toward full equality. They note in their critiques the conditions that allowed the hate-crimes law to be tied to national defense, arguing that the two acts collectively mediate sexuality in a manner that violently reinstitutes racial divisions and appropriations of the egalitarian human as defended by national sovereignty, now within the human itself. Inhabiting the contradictions of egalitarianism, these groups ask what kinds of emancipation are being generated in and through sexuality at this historical moment. The groups interrupt the reconciliation of publics to the state, understanding emancipation or juridically recognized queer sexualities as, in Jasbir Puar's evocative language, a "process of racialization [that] informs the very distinctions between life and death, wealth and poverty, health and illness, fertility and morbidity, security and insecurity, living and dying."[47]

Queer of color cultural expressions and movements are in this moment crucial forces that reveal the specifically racial limits of egalitarianism and state reform; they reveal that every inhabiting of legitimate violence for more egalitarian ends will, in the absence of thinking and living with race, continue the racial cruelty that is inextricable from the nation's material conditions of possibility and the set of institutions that reproduce the state form. For some, our moment is decidedly mournful. The failure of postcolonial states, the resurgence of empire in the so-called exceptional nation, the imperial violence of so-called human rights, and the hierarchical affirmations embedded in egalitarianism itself have all produced political modernity as constitutively ambiguous and paradoxical. For many people who feel this way, this ambiguity emerges from an inversion of the interests of living (the rational and calculative institutions) with the ethical practices of living (those institutions in which values are formed and that express the life world), in which the instrumental rationality of the former has entirely substituted for and obliterated the forms and practices of living that it was originally developed to support. For others, this ambiguity is narrated as a contemporary effect of the state's entering so thoroughly into national practices and social life that the borders that constitute the autonomy of modern living have become not only permeable but fundamentally obliterated, sealed by little more than mist and haze. Karl Marx and Frederick Engels remarked about the Western experience of modernity: "All that is solid melts into air, all that is holy is profaned, and man is at last compelled to face with sober senses, his real conditions of life, and his relations with his kind."[48]

Race restores to the linguistic, numeric, and visual representational forms appropriated by and for the state their material character. It is what reveals these forms as ossifications, reifications, brittle structures crumbling from the invisible pressure of their own voided contents of historical and social difference. Race reveals the legal language, and the forms through which the meaning of that language is settled, as at once a means of communication and a field of ever-protruding trace structures. These traces are the deconstructive conditions of possibility, and they interrupt the displacement of historical and social differences through the terrain of mimesis, equivalence, and abstract equality. When appraised through race, they are material forms or ruins left in the wake of political modernity's global conquests, repackaged as representation's capacity for universal belonging or membership. Thus, we can study representational and symbolical forms such as the law as apparatuses that inadvertently record our contemporary lived ruinations—the cultural and representational forms on which the state depends can be understood in other terms. Above all, to embrace race is to restore to intellectual endeavor and the public university what both have lost almost entirely in our current moment, their immanent ambiguity.

It is only through political and ethical engagements of and with race, I believe, that we can restore to the educational apparatus its own ambiguity, which is the origin of an alternative political curiosity that institutionality and its disciplines and departments actively undermine. Race remains a crucial basis for any genuine openness to rethinking the meaning of the university and its methods of knowing, to restoring the university as an importantly ambiguous space. We need not be frozen by ambiguity; it is, rather, an effect of being contaminated by the histories, social groups, and formations that have been addressed only through a certain vigilance that subtends the legitimate violence that I have been naming "cruelty." Indeed, in these ambiguous times at the university, we might see the need to renew our efforts to make it open once again to those who are structurally marginalized—this time by the so-called egalitarian state—so that we might all know our objects and tasks of inquiry differently. To seize the university from the liberal national state and emphasize its historically contradictory and ambiguous identity as a lever for emergent modernities that the state seeks to repress through its authority requires sustaining many different kinds of publics—such as racial, sexual, subaltern, documented and undocumented, national and nonnational—within the university's apparatuses of knowledge. Organizing the division of knowledges so that we think and engage these incommensurate publics in the same moment will advance the university as a real tool for our collective fashioning of our ongoing relations to the global past and future without the imminent threat of violence or abandonment shaping the inquiry that we pursue. If we are to embrace this university in ruins as still having something we can use in building less violent and more responsible collective conditions of dwelling, we will need to recommit to race as that which remains our conditions of possibility for cultivating alternative trajectories of modernity.

OUTLINE OF THE BOOK

In developing the claims made in this introduction, I divide my study of the politics of knowledge, race, and state formation in the twentieth century into two primary sections. Part 1 focuses on the onset of the twentieth century in the United States, a period characterized by urban industrialization, US empire, and the formal extension of citizenship to African Americans. Chapter 1, "Freedom and Violence in W. E. B. Du Bois's *Souls of Black Folk*: The Land of Racial Equality," argues for an understanding of Du Bois's *Souls of Black Folk* (1903) as a critique of twentieth-century disciplinary modes of knowledge. From his unique standpoint as a racialized denizen, Du Bois interprets the onset of the twentieth century in the United States through the twin emergences of black male citizenship in the state and new positivist forms of disciplinary knowing within the modern research university. Although the latter emergence is the means by which the histories of violence connected to the former are displaced and transmuted by national representation, Du Bois argues that the former emergence develops an unexamined contingency within modernity. And it is in pursuit of this contingency that Du Bois's text produces a materialist theory of black culture as a suppressed difference from national capitalist modernity. For Du Bois, the twentieth century augurs the recognition of race as something irreducible to its functionalist representation as an object of and means for violence. Rather, race is, as in the account of black male citizenship, the production of the bodily subject as an experience of both freedom and violence. Thus race offers, as much as it demands, a different epistemology of US modernity than that institutionalized by emergent positivism.

Chapter 2, "Legal Freedom as Violence in Nella Larsen's *Quicksand*: Black Literary Publics during the Interwar Years," takes as its point of departure Larsen's modernist novella of 1928. If, as I argue in chapter 1, Du Bois excavates race as a condition of subject formation within political society at the turn of the twentieth century, then the material and political conditions of black women's lives within the industrial modernity of the United States in the 1920s compels Larsen to imagine racialized gender as the limit to the coincidence of subject, experience, and social practice within political modernity. Though black women gained citizenship through the back doors of the Reconstruction-era amendments to the Constitution and modern suffrage earlier in the decade, Larsen aesthetically renders black womanhood as a genealogy of mass citizenship in this period. I situate Larsen's critique within the chaotic imperatives of the newly established capitalist industrial administrative state. On the one hand, mass citizenship expanded the means and identity of the state into a regional security apparatus, protecting both the Atlantic basin and colonial Pacific shipping routes. The territorial acquisitions of Puerto Rico, Guam, and the Philippines; the military occupations of Haiti and Veracruz, Mexico; gunboat diplomacy; and covert operations along the Panama Canal are all evidence of a newly assertive regional security apparatus that developed within the constraints of mass citizenship, especially in relation to tax collection and popular conscription. On the other hand, the intensification of mass citizenship's identity as a security apparatus—the mode by which it addressed the meaning of mass citizenship—generated new imperatives and constraints for the state to pacify US civil society. If the parade of black soldiers on New York City's Fifth Avenue—the 369th Regiment's famous march in February 1919—expressed the former contradictions of the developing liberal white supremacist state, the suppression of white mob violence in urban race riots and lynchings across the United States in the summer of the same year vividly revealed the contradictions of that same supremacist liberal state. Black politics—with substantial participation by the sizable number of black immigrants from the Caribbean, whose presence was an effect of the state's transformation into a regional security apparatus—was animated by these contradictions, creating unique modern black public spheres that mobilized heterogeneous technologies of representation, from the printing press to photography and the cinema. Larsen's novella is a formal composite of these technologies central to the emergent black public, yet the work identifies national belonging as the means by which norms central to the emerging administrative liberal state stipulate a singular subject in that public sphere. *Quicksand* reveals the deadly and violent ground that is produced when the norms of the liberal administrative state demand a politically originating subject in the historically unexpected emergence of the twentieth-century black public sphere.

The first half of the book focuses strategically on what Edward Said terms twentieth-century "beginnings," suggesting that what is heterogeneous at the start of the twentieth century remains crucial to its later development. Part 2 examines the close of the twentieth century, in which US experience is marked by racial immigration, globalization, and wars of national sovereignty.[49] Extending Larsen's critique of liberal state formation as promoting a coincidence of the racialized subject with regimes of representation, generating a modern violence whose origins are national and epistemic, chapter 3 examines late-twentieth-century US human rights legal practices as they seek to mediate late modern economic globalization for the nation-state. Titled "Rights-Based Freedom with Violence: Immigration, Sexuality, and the Subject of Human Rights," the chapter focuses on the legal recognition by US Board of Immigration Appeals judges of homosexuality as constituting membership in a social group. First, the chapter asks to what degree a gendered and racialized homophobia detailed in the testimonies of gay Pakistani immigrants seeking asylum is relieved by such recognition. And, as the US state responds to late-modern economic globalization by repurposing itself as a competitive, neoliberal apparatus of contracts and enforcement, legal rationality gains a new purview in constituting the social meanings of civil society. Second, then, the chapter builds on its analysis of the liberal epistemological failure to comprehend racialized and gendered sexual alterity and violence within the nation-state, as represented in the legal resolution of a rights-bearing homosexuality, by arguing that queer of color and queer immigrant cultural politics critically define the borders of US neoliberalism as mired in a political modernity that can only be described as yielding freedom with violence. And it is from these borders that queer of color immigrant organizing rearticulates race as generating alternative contingencies that might yield a transnational social and cultural politics. The final chapter, "Moving beyond a Freedom with Violence: The Politics of Gay Marriage in the Era of Racial Transformation," extends from the preceding chapters the conversation on race, modern violence, and the politics of knowledge, inquiring into what possible social and political meanings and modes of inquiry can be cultivated by addressing the legal, legislative, institutional, and cultural movement for so-called universal marriage at the close of the twentieth century. Following Du Bois's distinct observational style and critical standpoint, this chapter observes the twin developments at the close of the twentieth century of the extension of US constitutional subjectivity to variously queer social identities and cultural persons, and of the institutionalization of positivist multiculturalism across the disciplines and professional schools of the late modern university, the representative apparatus of legitimate knowledge. The imperatives of the latter have significantly advanced the politics of the former, even as the civil rights analogy consistently made by the institutional movement for gay marriage unleashes the specter of the twentieth-century black freedom movement, whose heterogeneous modes of comprehending race continue to trouble institutionalized and disciplinary multicultural positivism. Rather than claim a new subject of late modern US political modernity, the chapter argues for a critical ethnic studies that comprehends the positivist domination of race as the means by which a liberal, state-oriented political field rearticulates racial transformation with gendered, sexualized, and extra-territorial violence. This chapter observes the apparently contradictory election results in California in 2008. The state overwhelmingly voted in the first African American president of the United States while it also voted to repeal extant so-called marriage rights to gays and lesbians. In excess of a unified positivist explanation of voting practices that would narrate the national coherency of the social realm, the results point us toward a social theory that is transnational in its scope. In closing, this chapter therefore tries to sketch out how alternative epistemological accounts of race—or, better, differing relations to our extant means of knowing—could defeat the fatal coupling of late modern US racial transformation with the growth of state, legitimate, and disciplinary violence against the noncontractual and the deterritorialized.

The book concludes by returning to the Shepard-Byrd Act and the National Defense Authorization Act of 2010 discussed in this introduction, offering a rethinking of race as designating the material conditions of possibility for our modern ways of knowing and acting. Here the conjunction of military spending and hate-crimes legislation is revealed to depend upon the military modes of subjection articulated through "don't ask, don't tell." Reading these acts together with the epistemology of human perception offered by this rethinking is, I argue, crucial if we are to comprehend and change how political modernity has produced representative and democratic states that repeatedly take horrendous freedoms with destructive violence.

PART I

ONE

Freedom and Violence
in W. E. B. Du Bois's *Souls of
Black Folk*

The Land of Racial Equality

But black nationalists have recognized since the time of Delany in the mid-nine-
teenth century that the location of the land of the *black nation is highly problematic,
as is the establishment of a state when the territory for the black nation has been
identified*... The status of land and statehood is ambiguous among the theorists
who embrace the nation-within-a-nation thesis. "Revolution is always based on
land!" Malcolm X argued in his speech entitled "The Black Revolution." Yet the land
over which the black revolution is to be fought was never specified.
—MICHAEL C. DAWSON, *Black Visions*

It is a bitter fact that the research university's great leap forward came in the
decades, 1890–1910, during which Jim Crow segregation was being systematically
installed in American life.—CHRISTOPHER NEWFIELD, *Ivory and Industry: Business
and the Making of the American University, 1880–1980*[1]

This chapter positions W. E. B. Du Bois's
Souls of Black Folk (1903) as a critique of
the emergent disciplinary organization of
knowledge within the newly formed US
research university. Du Bois interprets
US modernity through two distinct currents at the start of the twentieth century.
First, and the most apparent current by
which the text is opened, is the emergence of black male citizenship in the

state and the persistence of racial despotism after the abbreviation of Reconstruction. The second current, less remarked upon though no less central to Du Bois, is the development of the modern research university in the United States and the rise of positivist modes of knowing, especially for the sciences of government and state. The currents are not merely a contiguous development, and *Souls* renders each as constituting a unified and complex dialectic of US twentieth-century modernity. What emerges, Du Bois argues, is a modernity with distinct and marginalized contingencies and the possibilities they engender. It is in pursuit of these contingencies that I argue that Du Bois's composite text produces a materialist theory of black culture as a suppressed difference of national capitalist state modernity.

For Du Bois, the twentieth century forces the recognition of race as irreducible to its functionalist representation as an object of and means for violence, an emergent liberal-juridical thesis of the time. Rather, the text offers an understanding of race, as in the case of black citizenship, as the production of the bodily subject as an experience of freedom *and* violence. As such, race offers as much as it demands a different epistemology of US modernity than that institutionalized by emergent positivism. Rather than seeking to engage or resolve the current debates concerning the numerous inconsistencies in W. E. B. Du Bois's racial thinking in *Souls of Black Folk*, my goal in this chapter is to focus on a set of narrative occurrences that operate across the different empirical, historical, literary, and autobiographical chapters and that, taken together, reveal a suppressed narrative structure—a structure that I believe discloses Du Bois's theorization of race as one of twentieth-century liberal-

ism's conditions of possibility. In this way, I read Du Bois's *Souls* as a form of countermemory to the official narratives of national citizenship and emancipation that were generated by the liberal positivist methods that organized the university and the state in this period. Comparing Du Bois's work to that of the liberal progressive historian Henry Jackson Turner, who sought to offer narrative meaning to the state (conceived of as a field of practice and information), I read the two authors as offering conflicting accounts of the narrative of emancipation through which the nation and the citizen are naturalized and accorded the status of truth. Considered against the background of Progressive Era state building, Du

Bois's text can be read as more than an example of the contradiction of emancipation for African Americans. Rather, his text offers a theory of race as a genealogy of what the narrative of emancipation both cannot admit and seeks to subjugate as the outmoded, anachronistic, or the archaic part of state-based political modernity.

LIBERAL POSITIVISM AND THE POLITICS OF PERCEPTION

The work of the early Du Bois, including *Souls*, has generally been read as thoroughly complicit with the liberal and racial progressivism that organized academic thinkers and political elites in the United States from the 1880s through the First World War. Scholars and critics cite Du Bois's reliance on liberal theories of political representation as a countervailing force to the chaotic and degenerate conditions of mass democracy, and his belief in Lamarckian evolution and the civilizational discourse that overtook a country thoroughly engaged in imperial geopolitics.[2] For Adolph Reed Jr., many of Du Bois's most famous formulations in *Souls*— many of which, like "double-consciousness," he would never return to— were part of a larger Progressive Era worldview: "The many different expressions of 'alienage,' fragmented consciousness, and anxieties about overcivilization were articulated within an outlook that hypostatized dichotomous, essentialist categories as fundamental determinants of human existence."[3] That the concepts expounded by the early Du Bois fit so well within these Progressive terms convinces Reed that we ought to read *Souls* as part of a larger corpus produced by a university-trained academic elite that was both progressive and positivist and that sought to engage the ongoing social conflicts of the time. Reed writes: "Knowing what we do about Du Bois's faith in science and the nature of social scientific discourse about race during the era in question, it should not be too surprising to see that he operated within the parameters of mainstream academic conventions."[4]

Seen from this perspective, social and political history can help us decipher the politics of Du Bois's thinking in *Souls*. By engaging his racialist discourse or his commitment to the thesis of an elitist "talented tenth," this mode of interpretation suggests that we can discern the true political meaning and value of this otherwise generically and politically polyglot text. In my reading of *Souls*, I would like to break from this reading practice. I do so not so much to argue against it as to identify other strains organizing Du Bois's thinking and the ideas conveyed in *Souls*. I seek only to bracket these other forms of interpretation, rather than entirely displacing them, because I think that they are part of the text we have inherited, and their contributions make it richer. For example, radical black feminist critiques of Du Bois's talented tenth thesis must remain a central interpretation of the text and of his political thinking in this period—still many years before his turn to Marxism, communism, and decolonization.[5] These critiques present rich discussions of how deeply gendered, sexual, and civilizational norms organized Du Bois's thinking of the political—registered, for example, in his continuous appeal to "manhood rights" in this period. These critiques are crucial because they reveal the degree to which reformist movements such as Du Bois's progressivist NAACP are less a sign of the promotion of democracy than of the extension of political society's tentacles downward, inflicting violence on those excluded from political society in the guise of extending universal norms and values. Indeed, some critics have taken this argument to its most profound and historically accurate end: social reform doesn't just use universal values and norms for its own violent ends. Rather, the violence of political society—of universal norm and values—finds its best conduit in social reformers.[6]

But I also want to argue that to interpret *Souls* as a text that vacillates between affirming the violence of reform and communal rights against racism, has the potential to prevent us from seeing another central preoccupation of Du Bois's text: the questions of what is race, and what might it mean to speak of a politics of race? These are the questions that preoccupy *Souls*, traveling across the different chapters and different genres of writing that make up the text.

To ask these questions, I think, is to reverse our orientation for a moment: we do not use the positivist social science that underlay state reform in this period or the talented tenth thesis—a thesis that organized so much of Du Bois's actual social politics, his academic efforts, and his ongoing contributions to build the progressive state in this period—to read his literary text. Rather, in this instance we use the text and the orientations and questions it creates for its readers, to remark upon the apparent clarity of the social actions it advocates. In this way, the text undoes some of the clarity of meaning of the talented tenth thesis (of the idea of uplift as a part of racial or national intra-group class control and politics). It reveals the interruption of that meaning by the very conditions of race for which uplift is figured as the social solution. Indeed, like the opening salvo in *Souls*, the whole text reveals that bringing the empirical and positivist discourse of solutions into the domain of race— so that the "Negro" becomes an embodied question—is a way to regulate and control race itself.

What is so powerful about *Souls* is that text undoes, as much as any text can, some of the meaning and clarity of concrete social actions such as reformist uplift projects, from which much of the US state was constructed in this period. In reversing the priority we usually give to practice over thinking and experience over representation, especially in our engagement with politics and the state, although not abolishing these distinctions, *Souls* asks us to rethink social actions, their meanings, and their very quality, as those actions become incorporated into the text. *Souls* argues that what is primary is not interpreting the meaning of the text through the determinative lens of the concrete social action of Du Bois as the political subject of American progressivism. Rather, it is to read and rethink social actions as they are constituted by the text, to accept the text's challenge to our sense of political society as composed of clear and precise discrete actions. In following *Souls* this way, we see that a politics of race is not so easy to pin down. Indeed, Du Bois's view is that a politics of race might be exactly what undermines the clarity of the political sphere, of definitions of what is and isn't politics, of imperial violence as extraneous from progressive state building, and so forth.

Although suspicious of the empiricism organizing much research on race in this period, Du Bois does not advocate abandoning the empirical core of the positivist project that organized the social sciences and the state in this period. This is true even in those chapters or moments in the text when he excoriates the racist smugness and laziness of empiricists— those "car-window" sociologists, as he calls them. Du Bois was particularly incensed by the sociologists who surveyed the southern "Black Belt" from their train while traveling on vacation, only to rely on such travels in their academic study of the so-called Negro problem: "To the car-window sociologist, to the man who seeks to understand and know the South by devoting the few leisure hours of a holiday trip to unraveling the snarl of centuries,—to such men very often the whole trouble with the black field hand may be summed up by Aunt Ophelia's word, 'Shiftless!'"[7]

For Du Bois, these pronouncements revealed a secret transcendental being, unheard and unseen, but at the core of the positivist project—the liberal egalitarian citizen, who allowed otherwise rigorous scholars to pass off their southern vacations as scientific research. And for Du Bois, this is not so much a ruse as it is a genuine belief among white social scientists in this period that the social scientist could actually do the empirical field research (and what we would now call the ethnography) necessary to solve the Negro problem in the same amount of time that important male scholars carve out for taking family vacations. Needless to say, Du Bois offers an image of the academic sociologist for whom the hard work of thinking with and through one's own empirical conditions happened elsewhere, in another time, among peers, paradoxically producing the sociological authority to establish the meaning of the postbellum agrarian Black Belt while on leisure. It is precisely this *authority*, Du Bois seems to suggest, that enables the sociologist to miss the comedy behind ignominious academic pronouncements on "shiftless" black life that happily cite the sociologist's leisure time as the basis of such pronouncements. That is, in the context of professionalizing knowledge, it is the structure of sociological authority, and the racialized valuing of geographies and bodies that this authority conserves, that makes these leisure sociologists something other than shiftless academics by their own professional system of knowing. Furthermore, it is the slow pace of the racialized body—"shiftless!"—that guarantees leisure for the professionalized body we call a sociologist.

But Du Bois is also making a deeper criticism, beyond pointing out the lax standard for what qualifies as research, when it comes to racial inequality and representing the poor, racialized class of former slaves in his time. What he marveled at was that the car-window sociologist doesn't even think to ask (so committed is he to the positivist empiricism of the universal citizen subject) what he could and could not know as a free subject traveling in a region—the Jim Crow South—in which travel highlighted the differential conditions of race. For Du Bois, the car-window sociologist could have no reflexive capacities by which to interrogate his inquiry, as long as the conditions that made that inquiry possible—his freedom to travel—never once occurred to him as the organizing limit of his inquiry. In the wake of the Supreme Court decision in *Plessy v. Ferguson* in 1896, which permitted "separate but equal" train cars, Du Bois saw clearly that the transparent and universal vision that car-window sociologists were so committed to was indistinguishable from the juridical recognition of freedom that those (white) sociologists sought so desperately to exercise.

For Du Bois, this revealed something of the impossibility of the positivist study of race: to be a subject of positive knowledge, such as the use of the social survey in conditions where freedom to travel is a racially differentiated right, is to affirm a social world constituted through a juridical freedom that institutes racial divisions and appropriations through that very freedom. In Du Bois's view, this demanded a historical inquiry into race since sociology took freedom as a given, producing knowledge that formally sanctioned the racial divisions and appropriations that juridical equality produced. In other words, sociology could say nothing beyond reformist critiques about state power, as long as it remained entirely dependent upon that power in its methods and modes of knowing. It is only through a historical inquiry into race, Du Bois suggests, that the thinking subject can discover the conditions by which knowledge conserves juridical freedom as its unthinkable necessity—even, and especially, in those instances when the constraints of that freedom are perceptually registered, as in the case of the vacationing sociologist. Yet, as I argue below, Du Bois had to revise historical thought too, for the degree to which it affirmed the racial state as the outcome of its own investigations.

FREDERICK JACKSON TURNER AND THE POLITICS OF THE FRONTIER

Frederick Jackson Turner initially presented what came to be known as his frontier thesis in a talk for professional historians gathered in Chicago for the 1893 World's Columbian Exposition, which marked the four hundredth anniversary of the European discovery of the Americas. Titled

"The Significance of the Frontier in American History," Turner's speech concentrated on the significance of recent empirical data, particularly the census of 1890, for his profession and historical methods. Finding that the census offered data that the long history of US expansion and demographic movement westward was coming to an end, along with the closing of the territorial frontier, Turner argued that these data provided irrefutable evidence that the US state was a historical formation, dependent for its temporal persistence less upon its so-called Teutonic germs than on central positive dynamics unique to US modernity that only his progressive generation was in a position to grasp.

For Turner, the 1890 census data and the positivist information they conveyed were not a matter of mere happenstance. A proponent of intellectual historicism, Turner argued instead that 1890 was the culmination of a historical process that could be fully grasped only by the generation that was, temporally speaking, at the end of the process's development and formation. A follower of Leopold von Ranke for whom history was fundamentally ironic, Turner argued that although constituting the end of the first stage of American history, the closing of the frontier offered the historian as rich an understanding of the basis of US state formation as the state itself did. Though Turner's historical thesis of state formation roiled the perspectives on that topic offered in his time by the recently professionalized disciplines of sociology, political science, and historical economics, it shared a more fundamental conceit with all these disciplines. As Dorothy Ross has demonstrated, the professional social sciences—although builders and supporters of the modern state— were nonetheless entirely convinced of the doctrine of US exceptionalism. "From the very beginning," Ross argues, "American nationalists attached to their history the values of individual liberty, political equality, social harmony, and, to some variable degree, social equality as well. The millennial underpinnings of American exceptionalism made it possible to see those values as both present and potential, both the reality of American society and the ideal toward which reality moved."[8]

I see three recurring themes in Turner's frontier thesis that organize his narratives of emancipation in political modernity: territory, culture, and identity. My investigation of Du Bois consequently seeks to theorize how race recasts these themes, giving them different meanings. Indeed, the themes themselves are not arbitrary. Rather, they constitute some of the central terms by which the nation form is sustained, a form crucial to the modern political state.[9]

By the twentieth century, territory, culture, and identity had been fastened together into a powerful regulative fiction.[10] This regulative fiction of place-bound cultural subjectivity extended beyond the West, gripping the social consciousness of representative elites around the globe who were under the spell of what Frantz Fanon called the "pitfalls of national consciousness." Indeed the irony of this regulative fiction and its force on modern subjects can be grasped if we keep in mind that among the processes we associate with the rise of capitalist territorial states are emphatically human social dislocation and deterritorialization, effects of a capitalist mode of production. I argue that Du Bois produces race as a dialectical critique of the regulative matrix of territory, culture, and identity, offering up in the *figure* of "land" a trope that exceeds that matrix. In this way, we can appreciate Du Bois's trope of the "land" as a textual, rhetorical, and ideational figure that breaks from what Ranajit Guha has eloquently termed the "government of colonialist knowledge."[11]

Turner's essay is a melancholic lament for the closing of the national frontier. In contrast to a model of abstract citizenship proposed by other thinkers in the late eighteenth and the nineteenth centuries, what Turner describes is fundamentally different. I name his model "mass citizenship." Formally different in its structure and logic from abstract citizenship, Turner's mass citizenship tries to address the new meaning and function of citizenship in his era of popular enfranchisement and mass industrialization. Turner delivered his speech at a time of unprecedented social strife, mass conflict, and rapacious state power. The US economy that year was in a depression that had brought the unemployment level to what was then the highest in the country's history. The countermovements to corporate capitalism, communism, socialism, and anarchism, appeared as widespread around the globe as capital itself. Registering the threat of anarchist populism in particular, the United States officially extended its sovereign authority to anarchist thought both symbolically, by closing its borders to anarchists, and materially, by publicly hanging four of the so-called Haymarket rioters. Yet even to its erstwhile liberal supporters, industrial capitalism appeared to be a dangerous wagon to which to hitch their advocacy of ethical and moral individualism. The granting of personhood to corporations, the entrenchment of laissez-faire rules in the economy, and the withdrawal of state regulation of the market all had had devastating effects in 1893. In that year, the stock market had crashed, more than six hundred banks had closed, commercial houses were in utter disrepair, and the nation's transportation system was in chaos, with more than seventy railroad corporations in receivership.[12] In this light, Turner's frontier thesis can be seen as an attempt to relocate the source of modern individualism away from the market system and the economic sphere advocated by the then-dominant Spencerian liberal positivists, while nonetheless maintaining a strictly positivist and evolutionary account of moral individualism.

For Turner, land is frontier space. Writing after the end of the Seminole Wars in 1848 and the Mexican-American War of 1850, Turner's thesis considered the frontier to be a space cleared by the government and settled by the citizen. Historically, the United States was steadily being transformed by processes of industrialization, urbanization, and territorial expansion, and the strengthening of the federal government. Rising immigration was an index of these transformations, and there were more immigrants in the 1880s than in the previous five decades combined. When Turner delivered his frontier thesis in 1893 to members of the American Historical Association, foremost on his mind was how to enumerate the characteristics of an American national identity that was both distinct from and competitive with European formations. He chose the solid foundation of land, this time figured as frontier space, as the terrain on which the American citizen was to be formed and legitimized.

Although the nation's future resided inevitably in its urban cores, the nation's history, Turner argued, was in its frontier. In his rugged engagement with the frontier, the immigrant from Europe is remade into an American citizen. Breaking with traditional accounts of the nation as the product of its center, Turner argued passionately for focusing on the nation's margins. In this way, the frontier for Turner is on the margin of both national space and time. At the edge of American territory, the frontier is also the beginning of the nation in history. Turner suggests that the frontier provides the context for the citizen to "develop . . . out of the primitive economic and political conditions of the frontier into the complexity of city life." The frontier as margin constituted both the beginning and end of the nation, engendering *"a recurrence of the process of evolution in each western area reached in the process of expansion."* And, unlike the historical development of European nations along a single line, "American development has exhibited . . . a return to primitive conditions on a continually advancing frontier line."[13]

America, in Turner's account, has agentic qualities that precede European migration and colonization. Turner writes:

> In the settlement of America we have to observe how European life entered the continent, and how America modified and developed that life, and reacted on Europe . . . Now the frontier is the line of most rapid and effective Americanization. The wilderness masters the colonist. It finds him a European in dress, industries, tools, modes of travel, and thought. It takes him from the railroad car and puts him in the birch canoe. It strips off the garments of civilization, and arrays him in the hunting shirt and moccasin. It puts him in the log cabin and plowing with a sharp stick; he shouts the war cry and takes the scalp in the orthodox Indian fashion. In short, at the frontier the environment is at first too strong for the man. He must accept the conditions which it furnishes, or perish, and so he fits himself into the Indian clearings and follows the Indian trails. Little by little he transforms the wilderness, but the outcome is not the old Europe, not simply the development of Germanic germs, any more than the first phenomenon was a case of reversion to the Germanic mark. The fact is, that here is a new product that is American.[14]

For Turner, the land is a "wilderness" that "masters the colonist." The European is distinguished by his aesthetic disposition, his technological savvy, and his rationality. Though anthropomorphized in Turner's thesis, America is feminized and figured as the mother, while the European is returned to an earlier stage of development and figured as a child. The frontier mother picks our European out of the cradle of civilization ("from the railroad car") and "puts" him backward into primitive time ("in the birch canoe"). When Mother America encounters her young charge, he is inappropriately "European in dress." She is quick to "strip off the garments of civilization" and re-clothe him in "hunting shirt and moccasin." The mother is "too strong for" the juvenile migrant, and he must rely on the aid of his youthful brothers, "fit[ting] himself into the Indian clearings and follow[ing] the Indian trails."

In Turner's racialized narrative, the European male immigrant raised within the custodial boundaries of America is, at first, dependent on indigenous people. Yet, as is the case with most narratives of American citizenship, whereas white boys grow up to become adult citizens, the Indian is left in the position of child. The permanent juvenilization of Native Americans was a consistent trope in historical, literary, juridical, and legislative narratives of the time. Indeed, until the passage of the Dawes Act of 1887, Native Americans were officially wards of the United States, nationals who could not become citizens.[15] Even after the passage of the Dawes Act, which granted citizenship to Native Americans on the condition that they give up many of the rights of full (read: white) propertied citizens, this practice of government wardship persisted. Indeed, Turner's conservative narrative bears the traces of the nation's dominant political ideology concerning racialized denizens. During the first half of the nineteenth century, Indians were figured as inassimilable others, whose savagery posed a serious threat to the corporeal integrity of the American people, understood both individually and collectively. The reform movements of the latter half of the nineteenth century, after most of the large wars with indigenous native groups had subsided, figured the Native American as an assailable racialized population in need of Christianity, industry, and temperance. The Dawes Act was the culmination of that reform movement. The principles of democratic equality and republican virtue that figured in the trope of brotherhood and white male fraternity contradicted new laws in the period after Reconstruction that extended citizenship to certain racialized men—namely, African Americans and Native Americans. Turner resolves this contradiction by placing cross-racial brotherhood within juvenile relations, all under the powerful governance of the mother country. Whatever forms of brotherhood and cross-racial fraternities might develop, they all begin and end at the frontier. That is, they end precisely with the emergence of full citizenship for white men.

Hence, in Turner's thesis on the significance of the frontier in the making of Americans, land figures again as the social precipitate for producing

American citizens. The successive waves of European migration to the United States were matched by successive waves of frontier space: first as the trader's frontier, then as the rancher's and farmer's frontier, and finally as the military frontier. Nowhere is this more evident than in Turner's section on land, an abstraction that includes all four types of frontier space: "Obviously the immigrant was attracted by the cheap lands of the frontier, and even the native farmer felt their influence strongly" (74–75). Turner continues: "In the crucible of the frontier the immigrants were Americanized, liberated and fused into a mixed race, English in neither nationality nor characteristics" (76). Out of the frontier grew a national identity, a national economy, and a national government.

Turner's frontier space is less a trope of national ideology than it is one of democratic government. His expressed goal in this essay is to understand the vital forces that lie "behind institutions, behind constitutional forms and modifications" and to discover the "peculiarity of American institutions" (59). The frontier as the nexus of military and administrative government constitutes the "vital forces" upon which civil and governmental institutions are built (59). It is, however, a paradoxical space: on the one hand, it generates the individualism upon which American democracy is built; on the other hand, it can simultaneously be an "anti-social" space, within which is created an overbearing individualism that in turn creates monadic and ungovernable subjects.[16]

It is precisely this paradoxical nature that allows Turner to suggest that the frontier is indeed both the cutting edge of the national empire and its atavistic origin. If Turner tried to turn the historian's or the citizen's eye toward the nation's margin, it was always in the interest of viewing a margin that existed simply to understand the center better. Only governmental, educational, and religious institutions could keep the vital forces of the frontier in check, curbing its "anti-social" tendencies. Rather than seeing the dissolution of the nation at the "borderlands," and the creation there of alternative spaces to the nation form, Turner interprets the line of frontier as suturing the margins to the center through a logic by which the periphery must imply the universality of the core.[17] The frontier's closing, however lamentable, is predestined by its very condition of being primitive space.

In sum, Turner's frontier operates as a space within which Old World cultural identities and a variety of nationalities are stripped off the body of the European migrant and a new national identity is formed. The American citizen thus produced on the frontier is a member of no particular collectivity and is, rather, dressed in the garb of American individualism. The frontier breaks existing local and social allegiances and constructs the new citizen as the subject of the national government. By the end of the nineteenth century, when Turner delivered his speech, citizenship had increasingly come under the regulatory eye of the federal government. It is worth remembering that possibly the most important and contested jurisprudential issue during the nineteenth century was the question of whether state governments or the federal government had the jurisdiction to determine the rights and meaning of territorial citizenship. Although in the first half of the century, the courts sided with the rights of the states, after the Mexican-American War, the Civil War, and the passage of the Thirteenth, Fourteenth, and Fifteenth Amendments, the general legal view favored the federal government. Turner's frontier thesis, then, is as much about the Americanizing of the European migrant as it is about nationalizing (or Americanizing) the state, an apparatus of social control and social life indispensable to capitalist civilizations.

To be sure, Turner used the concept and metaphor of land to exclude the longer history of urban wage labor as constitutive to the development of political institutions in the United States. Yet the metaphor was also crucial to the development of what David Noble calls an "aesthetic authority" that "encourages us to remove Native Americans, African Americans, Mexican Americans, as well as Anglo-American women from our picture of the national landscape."[18] And in turn, this authority sought to reconcile the competing interests of professionalism, on the one hand—which discovered scientific continuities between American and European civilizations, subject to the rational forces of industrial capitalism, and which validated the positivist state—and, on the other hand, of mass citizenship—which used American exceptionalist discourse to suppress radical differences of perspective in the public sphere by appealing to the national character of American civilization.

Turner does more than invent the cultural origins of the American citizen in the national landscape. He also surreptitiously sutures state territory to the nation. Although he sees the emergence of the state and the institutions of government as a modern invention, he observes that the nation is as old and far-reaching as the land itself.[19] The citizen as the subject of both the nation and the state is the linchpin in the process by which governmental institutions conform to and ultimately embody the national spirit. It is also through the citizen that the state claims exclusive territoriality. The liberal theorist Michael Walzer writes succinctly: "Nations look for countries [that is, territorial states] because in some deep sense they already have countries: the link between people and land is a crucial feature of national identity."[20] The erosion of local attachments and forms of living generated the need for territoriality as a defining principle of national identity. These nineteenth-century narratives of citizenship, which connected national subjectivity and land, had the concomitant effect of making territorial placement and state enfranchisement the prerequisites for claiming a socially intelligible and meaningful subjectivity.[21] Finally, land was the unique basis of American civilization; it was what turned American civilization into a distinct amalgam of positivism and exceptionalism. Indeed, for Turner, the state is precisely what maintains this amalgam. That maintenance of the state as a positivist exception conserved popular sovereignty even as it compelled the aporetic practices of US empire and colonization that Turner lamented.

DU BOIS, DEBT, AND THE NARRATIVE OF ALIENAGE

Du Bois's *The Souls of Black Folk*—a monumental study of race, class, and culture in the United States—was released ten years after Turner's frontier speech. In it, we can observe the consequences of this logic of territoriality that structures Euro-American narratives of citizenship and social identity for the newly admitted racialized citizen of the nation-state after the passage of the Fourteenth Amendment.

In the work's opening chapter, titled "Of Our Spiritual Strivings," the entry of black people into citizenship becomes the occasion for the author's meditation on the modern epistemological crisis precipitated by the non-nation's becoming the nation. Here Du Bois, who had studied at Harvard University and the University of Berlin, discovers the contradictions of the Hegelian topography of state cultures from the standpoint of black history.[22] Whereas modernist histories and epistemologies appropriated the past for the interests of the nation-state, projecting backward and onto the land the origins and embryos of modern social identities, Du Bois notes the invention of national identity through narratives stressing the subject's identification with the land and relying upon cartographic practices and human geographies, with each territory representing a single and distinct race. Du Bois writes: "After the Egyptian and Indian, the Greek and Roman, the Teuton and Mongolian, the Negro is a sort of seventh son, born with a veil and gifted with second-sight in the American world" (5). The organization of social history through the division of social geography into nationalities and other forms of regional groups functions to repress modern blackness, producing "black folk" as a sort of seventh child, a prime integer or remainder outside the arithmetic of human progress. Du Bois conceives the "Negro" to be neither American (a category that denoted enfranchised whiteness) nor African (a category that, for Du Bois, signified less present-day Africa and more a common black descent). In contrast, for Du Bois, the Negro begins "to have a dim feeling that to attain his place in the world, he must be himself, and not another. For the first time he sought to analyze the burden he bore upon his back, that dead-weight of social degradation partially masked behind a half-named Negro problem. He felt his poverty; without a cent, without a home, without land, tools, or savings, he had entered into competition with rich, landed, skilled neighbors" (9).

For Du Bois, the forced labor migration of over twelve million Africans and the reproduction of slave labor through a racialized social structure had produced the first truly and purely modern social identity, "the American Negro." Du Bois understood the racialization of African slaves and their descendants as "black" to be a historically new practice, whose truth was repressed by contemporary epistemology. What Du Bois called the "strange meaning of being black here in the dawning of the Twentieth Century" became the site for a critical interrogation of modern political epistemologies and their reliance on social cartography (1). Two centuries of black existence and toil in national space meant something more to Du Bois than the brutal displacement of Africans in the United States. It meant a new race, or what today we might term a new racial formation, which disturbed modern regimes of classification by relating the origins of classificatory knowledge to modern fields of social power.[23] As Du Bois famously deduced, it was precisely this exposure of and disturbance in the epistemic foundations of modern knowledge and nationalist historiography that compelled the national citizen to project that crisis back onto black subjects, constructing black folks as the problem to be figured out: "And yet, being a problem is a strange experience" (*Souls*, 4).

Du Bois demonstrated for his readers that posing the African American as a problem to be solved was an attempt to escape the deeper contradictions of the nation form and the egalitarian state: on the one hand, the nation-state proposed cultural (and racial) uniformity within political and cultural spheres. On the other hand, it remained dependent upon an internally complex social and political economy of racial stratification and colonial violence.[24] Hence racialized labor, social practices, and cultural representations consolidating the nation and the citizen subject were repressed in the social histories of official nationalism.[25] As Du Bois understood it, black experience, as the return of that repressed racialized matter, exposed the contradictory relationship between racial and national ideologies—a dialectic critical for the consolidation of the nation-state in spite and because of its contradictions.

In the now-famous account of his first awareness of racialized embodiment and difference while swept up in a youthful game, Du Bois describes an erosion of the self in *Souls* that is powerfully constructed as the simultaneous loss of physical and social emplacement:

It is in the early days of rollicking boyhood that the revelation first bursts upon one, all in a day as it were. I remember well when the shadow swept across me. I was a little thing, away up in the hills of New England, where the dark Housatonic winds between Hoosac and Taghkanic to the sea. In a wee wooden schoolhouse, something put it into the boys' and girls' heads to buy gorgeous visiting-cards— ten cents a package—and exchange. The exchange was merry, till one girl, a tall newcomer, refused my card,—refused it peremptorily, with a glance. Then it dawned upon me with a certain suddenness that I was different from the others; or like, mayhap, in heart and life and longing, but shut out from the world by a vast veil. I had no desire to tear down the veil, to creep through; I held all beyond it in common contempt, and lived above it in a region of blue sky and great wandering shadows. (4)

The passage begins by giving only minimal attention to time, saying nothing more than that something happens in the "early days of rollicking boyhood." By using the indefinite pronoun "one" to describe the interpolative encounter by which the child becomes the "black boy," as Richard Wright might put it, Du Bois foregrounds racialization as a collective experience. Or, more accurately, Du Bois suggests that racialization is exactly the movement from the personal and singular pronoun to an ascriptive and forced impersonal collective. This brief anecdote about becoming black is not recounted as a generic experience universally applicable to all black persons; instead, it is recounted to stress that generic applicability *is* the experience of racialization.[26] Although the anecdote conveys the story of a child ostracized from the group, for the community of racists, racialization—the ascription of Du Bois to a larger black collective—recodes the child's ostracism as the exclusion of the black race from individual, private actions.

When the shadow of collectivity swept across Du Bois, he was "a little thing, away up in the hills of New England, where the dark Housatonic winds between Hoosac and Taghkanic to the sea." At first it might seem unclear why Du Bois would go to such pains to mark the specific location of the events of his anecdote, but if we understand racialization as the loss of independent subjectivity and expulsion, we can appreciate the erosion of social space that Du Bois narrates as its worst consequence. Of course, on an explicit level, the spatial coordinates operate to locate for the reader the specific and exceptional nature of Du Bois's blackness, as an American Negro in northern New England, who grew up in a primarily white town (a condition that more deeply highlights the injustices of racist collectivization). At the same time, Du Bois also uses spatial figures and settings specifically to mark the tragedy of racist social practice—that it disconnects subjects from locality and scripts them within a collectivity for whom the very denial of space is only symptomatic of the deeper losses of social particularity. As we get closer to the racist encounter, the spatial forms and objects become increasingly generic (the perpetrator of the act is a newcomer, a girl), and spaces of nature are succeeded by spaces of culture. From the hills and river, Du Bois is now in the "wee wooden schoolhouse" where there is an exchange, but he is spurned by a girl, a newcomer. Du Bois cannily renders racism as a perversion and denial of the exchange relation. His allegory places racism squarely within that relation and economic space, but also within the affective registers of coupling and conjugality. Racism knows no limit between the public and private spaces of social life. Indeed, it perverts their very distinction for the racialized subject.[27] Du Bois consciously places race within spaces of culture as opposed to nature, and more specifically within the institutions of civil society and its social relations, suggesting that the expansion of generic forms of state culture such as the schoolhouse—what Turner optimistically saw as the expansion of democratic institutions across the line of the frontier—will only continue to erode from the social topography a growing number of forms of particularity.

The ultimate experience of loss for Du Bois is figured in the total erosion of territorial encasement. The forced awareness of his difference and the dropping of the veil at once forces Du Bois off national space: black racialization signifies the disinheritance of the national landscape: "I held all beyond [the veil] in common contempt, and lived above it in a region of blue sky and great wandering shadows" (*Souls*, 4). It is precisely this loss of national identity through black racialization, an uprooting from the national landscape, that dialectically opens up a new set of possibilities—perspectives on the nation form from the nonplace of the sky and drifting shadows. As this brief anecdote shows, Du Bois clearly recognized the regulative fiction that connected subjectivity to national identity and territoriality. And he critiqued this fiction for the way it left the educated black subject unmoored, uprooted, and dislocated. Yet, most powerfully, *Souls* is a rearticulation of black meanings, rescripting nationalist narratives that would otherwise dissipate black experience into illegibility and the invisible air.

Yet if blackness emerges out of the dispossession of national belonging, Du Bois quickly discerned the dual antipodes within a single chain of representation for figuring black racialization: either blackness was a hard fact of biology and science that required surveillance and regulation, or blackness was invented—nothing more than an illusion, a mongrelization of blood and genealogy. In moving from one pole of representation to the other, from representations of black blood as ancient, solid biological matter to portrayals of American blackness as contemporary ephemera and trivial social artifice, Du Bois perceptively observed that both figurative strategies aimed at black obliteration. Indeed, these poles of blackness were both signifiers in a system whose signified was the citizen subject and his or her placement in the nation-state. In Du Bois's allegory, these regions in the sky are imaginary sites opened up by the encounter of the black subject with the racist apparatuses of the state, specifically the cultural institution of schooling. As unreal spaces produced out of the pressures and violations of racist and supremacist violence, these imaginary spaces are not purely virtual or in any simple way solely symbolic. Instead, they are part of an emerging repertoire of a black imaginary, born of the black encounter between the nonnational subject and the nation-state. Du Bois continues: "Why did God make me an outcast and stranger in mine own house? The shades of the prison-house closed round about us all: walls strait and stubborn to the whitest, but relentlessly narrow, tall and unscalable to sons of night who must plod darkly on in resignation, or beat unavailing palms against the stone, or steadily, half hopelessly, watch the streak of blue sky above (5)." In this metaphorics of space, contingency and juxtaposition prevail in the description of the racial social structure. The contiguous placement of spatial types works rhetorically to enforce a Manichaean logic of both race and space. Du Bois contrasts the "sons of night" and "the whitest" and juxtaposes private dwelling ("mine own house") and public enclosure ("the prison-house"). The racialized subject's confrontation with the institutions of the nation-state is rendered in binary terms, within which imaginary spaces of racial transcendence for the individual and the group are contrasted to the burdens of embodiment and particularity on national terrain. Following Du Bois's spatialization of the racial social order and his metaphor of the sky, we might define these spaces of racial transcendence from the nation form as supranational formations that exist symbolically, in a vertical relationship above the nation-state.

Institutionally formed black subjects—what Du Bois called in this essay the "black artisan" and elsewhere the "talented tenth"—were for Du Bois supranational subjects located within virtual spaces above the nation-state.[28] As mediators and mediums for black consciousness,

Du Bois and his talented tenth were cosmopolitans whose task it was to bring black folk into the "kingdom of culture" (5). Black cosmopolitanism is a formation whose transcendence of blackness must be understood in the context of the racialized denial of black membership by the nation-state, and as the effect of physical and social displacement. In focusing on spaces above and beyond the nation-state, and on cultures of supranational space formations, black cosmopolitanism must be distinguished from its European variant, even if it maintains an ambivalent relationship to that variant.[29]

Binaries abound in the first chapter of *Souls of Black Folk*, exemplified by the spatialization of social relations either through contingency and juxtaposition or through hierarchy and synthesis. Although the binary construction of racial difference is an unresolved matter in the first chapter of *Souls*, later in the text, we can see that Du Bois suspects that it reproduces racism, even as it seems to equate black and white striving.

For Du Bois, the black subject's coming to knowledge was not simply the extension of contemporary modes of knowing to blackness, but rather the dialectical recognition of blackness as a form of knowing that worked to criticize dominant modes. It is through this sense of a dialectical critique of bourgeois nationalist modes of knowing and classifying humanity that Du Bois posits the idea of double consciousness. Double consciousness is more than the revelation of black otherness within public culture, the voicing of the suppressed segment of the white/black or "American/Negro" binary. Instead, double consciousness criticizes the binary organization of modern knowledge for the ways in which it manages and distorts the existence of the latter half of any binary construction.[30] Scholars of postcolonialism, feminism, queer studies, and poststructuralism in the last two decades have exposed the ways in which binary epistemes are monolithic constructions that privilege and reinforce the dominant component of the binary, especially when the latter term in the pair comes into self-representation. For this reason, we must pay equal attention to the mode by which representation and knowledge is organized, interpreted, and disseminated, if we are to displace reigning discursive formations. If we follow the narrative structure of *Souls*, we notice that Du Bois slowly builds to a discussion of the sorrow songs as sites of countermemory. This is also a movement in *Souls* from blackness as the racialization of the black male educated citizen, in his encounter with state apparatuses, to blackness as the sites of alternative culture behind "the veil." Although one of Du Bois's goals is certainly to register the collective consciousness of black slaves and their descendants in the United States, he first engages the binary discursive formation by which blackness is socially mediated.

Double consciousness, as the essence of blackness, is the displacement of the dominant schema of difference by which whiteness is equated with selfhood. For Du Bois, double consciousness requires a questioning of the mechanisms by which black existence is tied to whiteness, always in a necessarily derivative and devalued position. Du Bois's critique refuses the integration of blackness into a white/nonwhite binary, whose system of operation will always already position the black subject as simulacrum and copy. Or, as Du Bois puts it, the binary forces the black subject to "look at oneself through the eyes of others, of measuring one's soul by the tape of a world that looks on in amused contempt and pity" (*Souls*, 5).[31] By suggesting that the meaning of blackness inheres in the recognition and critique of binaries and spatial dualities that would demand the reduction of black existence to the position of the "other," Du Bois moved toward a nonbinary understanding of racial formations. For Du Bois, true self-consciousness existed outside the binary constructions of race. As evidenced by its location in *Souls*, double consciousness for Du Bois is the beginning of an epistemic fracture that is precipitated by the black subject's coming to consciousness, which is the studied realization of the significance of race to modern epistemology. As the reader moves through the text, alternative spaces and spatializations emerge in the fractures, crevices, and gaps—what Du Bois calls the "eloquent omissions and silences"—opened up by double consciousness (211).

In contrast to the landed spaces of national culture, Du Bois posited the supranational space formation of a kingdom of culture within which the tensions between racial difference and nationalist uniformity might be resolved. Yet, however much the imaginary spaces of sky and other supranational space formations attempted to convert the conditions of black nonidentity into a critical posture, they left uninterrogated the authenticity of territorially vested nationalist identities. We can argue that instead it is the move from pursuing blackness in the unreal and utopian regions of elevated space to seeking it in the materialist sites of the sunken and forgotten spaces of the Black Belt that constitutes the most important trajectory of Du Bois's narrative. Such a trajectory requires a second glance at the corrosive effects on the nation form of processes both beyond and below the scope and space of the nation-state and nationalist representation. It requires us to situate blackness not within the kingdom of culture but rather within the scarred lands of what Du Bois named in his narrative the "Cotton Kingdom." In the shift from kingdoms of culture to those of cotton, Du Bois situates race within social and economic processes that we might interpret as subnational. In the process, he provides us with a third definition of culture, an alternative to its aesthetic and anthropological versions.

As many critics have noted, *Souls* is a heterogeneous text, containing a multiplicity of narratives and pursuits that the author weaves together. Among them, for example, we find Du Bois's own selective autobiography, overlaid with and ensconced inside of the larger narrative sequence and chronology. This autobiography opens with Du Bois's childhood and concludes with his mature position as a member of the Fisk University faculty. The narrative sequencing, then, also corresponds to a spatial movement that is highly orchestrated and develops as a formal element of the narrative structure. Robert Stepto's narratological description of *Souls* elegantly captures this coordination of space and time: "Du Bois' journey in *Souls* from infancy in the Berkshires of western Massachusetts to adulthood amid the western hills of Atlanta, complete with symbolic disembarkings in Tennessee, Philadelphia, and that part of the Black Belt surrounding Albany, Georgia, is not simply the story line of the volume but also the narrative manifestation of Du Bois' cultural immersion ritual."[32] The connotation of descent that Stepto's use of "immersion" carries is matched by Du Bois's own sense that to enter the Black Belt is to descend into spaces organized by racialized social relations that could be considered subnational only in comparison with the projected ideals and legal forms of the industrial nation-state. The narrative turn toward what Stepto terms the "geo-cultural"[33] spaces of the black and red subaltern in the South grounds Du Bois's study of race within subnational space formations.

Stepto argues that Du Bois's narrative is tightly organized by a "symbolic geography,"[34] a notion that suggests "that a landscape becomes symbolic in literature when it is a region in time and space offering spatial expressions of social structures and ritual grounds on the one hand, and of *communitas* and *genius loci* on the other." Stepto pursues this argument, showing the reader the repetition of certain spatial motifs in Du Bois's narrative. For example, the spatialization of racialized social structures— like the dialectical combination and interrelation between the verdant spaces of the rollicking hills that represent for Du Bois genesis and death (that is, the spaces of utopian freedom) and the expanding and eroding red spaces of dust and dirt that represent violence, toil, and enclosed homelessness (that is, racialized peonage and indenture)—creates a "structural topography"[35] that can be found within both the northern and southern sections of Du Bois's narrative. Yet Stepto's most powerful and unsettling intervention into the study of *Souls* is his identification of important ritual spaces within Afro-American cultural production that function as *genius loci*, where the "local integrities or imagery of the tribe are given bounding outline" and "spirit of place."[36] The *genius loci* manifest themselves in the "lilt and imagery" of the sorrow songs: "Thus, when they occur in *Souls*, spatial expressions of *genius loci* bind spirit of song to spirit of place. The only 'problem' with this strategy is that it defines the Afro-American *genius loci* more by charting its circumference or 'bounding outline' than by attempting to gauge its interior; as a result, circumference is sometimes mistaken for interior."[37] Stepto argues that there are three constitutive places of black self-creation in Du Bois's narrative: the revival campgrounds, Jubilee Hall, and Du Bois's private dwelling place and study at Atlanta University. I suggest that however much these spaces provide a rich index of African American cultural *genius loci*, they are ultimately only partially successful as representative sites. *Souls* never achieves a complete symbolic geography of blackness, in part because "what is national about Afro-America is that it is without dominion."[38]

Du Bois's narrative as a socially symbolic act is cast within a form that privileges space and temporality equally. Yet his poetics of space expresses important ambivalences and contradictory impulses that emerge from his gradual awareness that neither space nor place is congruent with the territorial nation-state. Nowhere is this articulated more strongly in *Souls* than in Du Bois's descriptions of his travels to the edges of the Black

Belt: "We had come to the boundaries of Dougherty, and were about to turn west along the county-line, when all these sights were pointed out to us by a kindly old man, black, white-haired, and seventy. Forty-five years he had lived here, and now supports himself and his old wife by the help of the steer tethered yonder and the charity of his black neighbors. He shows us the farm of the Hills just across the county line in Baker, a widow and two strapping sons who raised ten bales (one need not add 'cotton' down here) last year" (98). Although outsiders to the social spaces of the Black Belt can see only the invisible lines of territory and state, it is the "old . . . black" man who points out what is beyond rationalized vision. In pointing out these spaces, he provides neither a simple catalog of distant objects on the horizon, nor a historical account of their emergence. Instead he points out spaces constituted below and beyond the dividing spatial practices of the state, attaching stories of habitation and modes of survival to each spatial referent. For the farmer, the Hills across the county line are less distant objects than they are figures of the social relations by which the spaces are reproduced and transformed. His own space is not a static possession but is maintained by "the steer tethered yonder and the charity of his black neighbors."

Du Bois and his weary travelers continue on their way: "We turn now to the west along the county line. Great dismantled trunks of pine tower above the green cotton-fields, cracking their naked gnarled fingers to-wards the border of living forest beyond" (98). In this instance, the logic of property and spatial domain inscribe themselves onto nature, dis-mantling and gnarling the bordering trees. These barren and grotesque bounded spaces provide for "little beauty in this region, only a sort of crude abandon that suggests power," making Du Bois's weary travel-ers increasingly desperate for reassuring markers: So when, as here at Rawdon's, one sees a vine clinging to a little porch, and home-like win-dows peeping over the fences, one takes a long breath. I think I never before quite realized the place of the Fence in civilization. This is the Land of the Unfenced, where crouch on either hand scores of ugly one-room cabins, cheerless and dirty. Here lies the Negro problem in its naked dirt and penury. And here are no fences. But now and then the criss-cross rails or straight palings break into view, and then we know a touch of culture is near (99)." Du Bois deftly enfolds the relation between culture as a mark of civility and the system of property relations by which civilization is established. The county lines of political jurisdiction are replaced by the palings and rails of the fence in civil and economic society. Du Bois is not only suggesting that culture is to be found within the boundaries of the fence, evoking a sigh a relief from the traveler who has been lost within crude abandon; he is saying that "culture" *is* the fence. Culture is not the bounding outline of a *genius loci*, it is boundary making. It is the set of inscriptions and practices by which boundaries are made and remade, centers are constructed, and truths are framed in "home-like" fashion. By relating the aesthetic conception of culture to modern apparatuses of security such as the fence, Du Bois disinters and reveals the discursive functions of culture to inscribe social relations in spatial terms. On the other side of fenced spaces are the ugly lives of "the Unfenced," cheerless and dirty. Against the figuration of culture as fencing that Du Bois connects to the modern practices of property, security, and borders exists culture as dirt. Dirt is that upon which the fence stands erect; it is the microscopic forms and particles that cross and pollute fenced divisions. Cultural formations strapped to the dirt do not exist for Du Bois as negations of civilized space or as utopian elements outside of boundaries and form. Instead they are cultural formations that survive in the context of their loss and disinheritance, left to make life in that "crude abandon that suggests power" and for which state and civil practices of division, boundary, and border both fragment and constellate the raw shapes of cultural difference. Against the invention of parceled spaces through the enframing practices of modern culture emerge the clustered formations of "scores of ugly one-room cabins" that exist in "naked dirt and penury."[39]

Breaking, then, with Stepto's attempt to assimilate Du Bois to nation thinking, one that would evaluate cultural forms based upon their ability to capture the national spirit through symbolization, and shifting our focus from cultural circumferences to culture on the color line, we can propose that Du Bois's conception of unfenced spaces (like his understanding of the sorrow songs) redefines in fundamental ways how we approach the study and situating of cultures in space. Du Bois's ideas did not conform to either the aesthetic nor the anthropological definition of culture—that is, to culture as *bildung* or *Kultur*. Rather, they propose a form of cultural study and meaning that emerges through grasping the social reality of racial alienage, a term that I define more fully in chapter two. Suffice it to say here that "racial alienage" signals the paradoxical status category produced by the conjunction of universal legal citizenship within the nation-state and the racial formations it produced. In this sense, black citizenship particularly after 1877 may be better rendered through the heuristic of racial alienage than through the other two definitions. Culture for Du Bois is not spirit, essence, or private transcendence—the defining elements of a national culture organized through liberal citizenship—nor is it locatable within space and place presented as objective elements. Instead, culture is that which is formed through the iterative practices of the fractured social body in labor, at work, and in motion.

I conclude this reading of *Souls* and the chapter by turning to one final representation of land in order to sketch the outlines of what I call in this book "narratives of racial alienage." It has been my intention to describe the changing modalities of state incorporation. I have examined the narrative of mass citizenship and have suggested that it proposes a set of imperatives and loci of meaning around the concept of national and state culture—imperatives and meanings that have been shaped by the changing demographic composite of citizenship. Yet the narrative of mass citizenship seeks to connect the modern subject to the nation-state by investing the citizen's intelligibility on its territorial emplacement. As I turn now to this final figuration of land in Du Bois, I will stress not citizenship but alienage, not topography but temporality, and not stasis but crisis and transformation.

After a long day's ride in a "Jim Crow car," surveying Georgia's Black Belt, Du Bois meditates on the significance of the land for capturing the racialized subject's relationship to the nationalist narrative:

> How curious a land is this—how full of untold story, of tragedy and laughter, and the rich legacy of human life; shadowed with a tragic past, and big with future promise! This is the Black Belt of Georgia ... It is full of historic interest. First there is the Swamp, to the west, where the Chickasawhatchee flows sullenly southward. The shadow of an old plantation lies at its edge, forlorn and dark. Then comes the pool ... In one place the wood is on fire, smoldering in dull red anger; but nobody

minds. Then the swamp grows beautiful; a raised road, built by chained Negro convicts, dips into it, and forms a way walled and almost covered in living green. Spreading trees spring from a prodigal luxuriance of undergrowth; great dark green shadows fade into the black background, until all is one mass of tangled semi-tropical foliage, marvellous in its weird savage splendor . . . And as I crossed, I seemed to see again that fierce tragedy of seventy years ago. Osceola, the Indian-Negro chieftain, had risen in the swamps of Florida, vowing vengeance. His war-cry reached the red Creeks of Dougherty, and their war-cry rang from the Chattahoochee to the sea. Men and women and children fled and fell before them as they swept into Dougherty . . . Then the false slime closing about them called the white men from the east. Waist-deep, they fought beneath the tall trees, until the war-cry was hushed and the Indians glided back into the west. Small wonder the wood is red.

Then came the black slaves. Day after day the clank of chained feet marching from Virginia and Carolina to Georgia was heard in these rich swamp lands. Day after day the songs of the callous, the wail of the motherless, and the muttered curses of the wretched echoed from the Flint to the Chickasawhatchee, until by 1860 there had risen in West Dougherty perhaps the richest slave kingdom the modern world ever knew . . . Twenty thousand bales of ginned cotton went yearly to England, New and Old; and men that came there bankrupt made money and grew rich. It was the heyday of the *nouveau riche*, and a life of careless extravagance reigned among the masters . . . Parks and groves were laid out, with rich flower and vine, and in the midst stood the low wide-halled "big house," with its porch and columns and great fire-places.

And yet with all this there was something sordid, something forced— a certain feverish unrest and recklessness; for was not all this show and tinsel built upon a groan? (*Souls*, 101–2)

For Du Bois, space is a socially produced and mediated form. Official designations of space, such as "Georgia" and "Dougherty County," are subordinated to the everyday meanings of the space at the west end of the Black Belt, once called the Egypt of the Confederacy. Both nature and human artifice clutter and give the space its bounding outlines and complex interior. Next to swamp and river, we discover the plantation of old, now forlorn, dark, and deteriorating. In fact the division between natural objects and those of artifice blurs, as the road built by chained Negro convict labor dips into the swamps and is covered in living green. In the abstract forms created by the grafting of nature onto artifice, Du Bois sees the past actions of "Osceola, the Indian-Negro chieftain." Spaces are collected sites of the historical past. But unlike Turner's rendering of the past as simply primitive space destined for modern progress, in Du Bois's narrative the past exists as a threatening presence in the present. History for Du Bois grows and expands wildly over the land, threatening to overtake the present by its layers and "savage splendor." Language and song—the war cries of the Creeks and the wails of the slaves—are like the material objects of nature and human artifice in their ability to inscribe and transform space, becoming part of its material sediment and geology. All conspire to produce "a land where a history can be read but a future can barely be expressed."[40] The social space of the Black Belt is created in the constant emergence of historicized racial struggle and conflict.

In Du Bois's time, space is produced by a series of networks and relations, none of which is reducible to or exclusively constitutive of the others. The transatlantic markets and economic networks of King Cotton in the 1850s that most surely constitute the Black Belt, connecting it to "England, New and Old," are contrasted with and contested by the disjunctive networks of indigenous uprisings that similarly shape the changing boundaries of the Black Belt as Osceola's "war-cry reached the red Creeks of Dougherty, and their war-cry rang from the Chattahoochee to the sea." To these intersecting networks and flows, Du Bois adds "the clank of chained feet marching from Virginia and Carolina to Georgia," a sound that transforms the "rich swamp lands": "Day after day the songs of the callous, the wail of the motherless, and the muttered curses of the wretched echoed from the Flint to the Chickasawhatchee." The land for Du Bois is neither the projection of a static totality nor the image of linear progress. It is instead a node within conflicting and overlapping networks, relations, processes, and flows. Du Bois's description of the land as a haunted and historicized space is most clearly grasped in his descriptions of subalterns, whose voices ring in the air as interrelated noise:

clanking, singing, wailing, crying, and cursing. Even apparently empty spaces are filled with the presence of an "otherness" that refuses to blend into retrievable language, remaining instead a haunting noise that transforms the sociality of space.

Unlike Turner's suppression of historical difference through his discursive construction of the land as frontier space, Du Bois posits the land in his Black Belt chapter as a form of social space. Both land and space in Du Bois's text disrupt chronology and narrative organization. In the long passage above, certain narrative markers seem to suggest chronology and development: "First there is the Swamp . . . Then comes the pool . . . Then the swamp grows beautiful . . . Then . . . the Indian glided back into the west . . . Then came the black slaves . . . until by 1860 there had risen in West Dougherty perhaps the richest slave kingdom the modern world ever knew . . . It was the heyday of the *nouveau riche*." Indeed, the passage seems to narrate the transformation of the natural landscape into the parks and groves of the slave regime. It figures historical progress as the development of bourgeois gentility and private space, "with its porch and columns and great fire-places," out of "savage splendor." The past seems to be organized into a set of determinative events whose meanings are prescribed by their placement within the narrative structure: the land is discovered; the Indians cleared out; the slaves transported; and the *nouveau riche* entrenched, and the Black Belt exists as the composite text of that history of transformation. Yet, on closer inspection, chronology and narrative progression are displaced and disorganized by the emergence of elements and spaces into the narrative before their proper time, like the "shadow of an old plantation" ensconced within the natural topography, a "raised road, built by chained Negro convicts" before the Indian wars, and "a war-cry . . . from the Chattahoochee to the sea" far beyond the Black Belt, all of which suggest an excess of meaning that cannot be related to any single historical frame. It is the eruption of these spaces and crumbling structures that cannot be assimilated to narrative chronology or to the retrospective organization of past events into linear form that enables Du Bois to construct the Black Belt as an allegory of racialized space, unhinged from the nation form. Organizing racialized experience within spatial forms such as the Black Belt enables Du Bois to recast the historical past in ways that saturate spatial frames more deeply with historical processes and networks than is allowed by the formalist and symbolizing representations of land that we find in the writings of Turner. Moreover, it is the eruption of sound and song in scenery—"for was not all this show and tinsel built upon a groan?"—and of discursive and expressive forms, by which the land is recast as unstable social space. For Du Bois, language, song, and cultural practices are technologies of space and place. Additionally, alternative spatial experiences and forms of living house themselves in the shapes and spaces of language and song.

Dougherty County, once the seat of the most rapacious slave economy in the world, is by the time of Du Bois's writing on the edge of postemancipation black life. At first it might seem odd to choose Du Bois's Black Belt chapters to introduce the concept of racial alienage. Yet for Du Bois, the period after emancipation and Reconstruction ironically inaugurates a new mode of racialization for black people. The emancipation of former slaves by government decree has the paradoxical effect of expanding the state's function as an apparatus of racialization. In the postemancipation context, not citizenship but its continual deferral and denial are characteristic of black political and social status.

The Black Belt encompasses "vast stretches of land beyond the telegraph and the newspaper [where] the spirit of the Thirteenth Amendment is sadly broken" (124). Outside the means of cultural and political representation, black folks along the belt were particularly vulnerable to supremacist violence and renewed enslavement. In the anecdote that closes his survey of the Black Belt, Du Bois relates a final conversation between himself and some local "folk." Du Bois asked if they owned land: " 'Own land?' said the wife; 'Well only this house.' Then she added quietly, 'We did buy seven hundred acres up yonder, and paid for it; but they cheated us out of it. Sells was the owner' " (110). This remark leads a local man to tell Du Bois and his fellow travelers that Sells, his former employer, cheated him out of more than a month's wages: "He paid me in cardboard checks which were to be cashed at the end of the month but he never cashed them—kept putting me off. Then the sheriff came and took my mule and corn and furniture." To which Du Bois responds, in astonishment: "Furniture? But furniture is exempt from seizure by law." " 'Well, he took it just the same,' said the hard-faced man" (110). In this final scene of his chapter "Of the Black Belt," Du Bois leaves little doubt of his assessment of black civil and political status after emancipation. The seizure of the furniture marks the transgression into personal space by the state and repressive authorities, marking racial alienage as more than denial of citizenship rights. Instead, state action actively invades black folks' lives to the point of rearranging their material conditions, by moving furniture.[41] It constitutes racialization as a process that negates the boundary between the legal and the extralegal, and between de jure and de facto practices. As Du Bois's anonymous interlocutor suggests, with his use of the masculine pronoun, the state is aligned with Mr. Sells. Sells and the state act in unison to disarrange black modes of living. As their actions transgress the limit of legal permissibility, we gain a perspective not only of the state as productive of racialization, but also of the state as itself produced through racialization.

The homes of the slave regime are mostly empty and left to deteriorate, while the agricultural belt carries on its work with former slaves and their descendants. Du Bois writes of a former plantation in the region: "The Big House stands in half-ruin, its great front door staring blankly at the street, and the back part grotesquely restored for its black tenant. A shabby, well-built Negro he is, unlucky and irresolute. He digs hard to pay rent to the white girl who owns the remnant of the place. She married a policeman, and lives in Savannah" (97). In account after account, Du Bois figures the shift from ante- to postbellum life in the Black Belt as the transference of power and modes of domination from the slave owner to multiple state instruments. The expansion of indenture, debt peonage, and convict labor among black residents of the belt followed, with the fall of radical Reconstruction in 1876. Forms of racial violence and terror are no longer exacted by the direct owning class, as was the case under slavery, but by the legal practices of the state. In his reconstruction of the structure of ownership of the plantation upon which the farmer toils (an absentee white female landowner living in Savannah), Du Bois argues that, in the 1890s, it is not the master/slave dialectic, but the contradiction between the national citizen and the racial alien—the black tenant farmer—that structures the relations of production in the Black Belt. In his vivid rendering of the social relations within which the belt is embedded, Du Bois expresses the ties and networks between the country and the city as a relation between the new visible middle classes and the projected "otherness" of the racialized poor. The national citizen who appropriates the surplus value of the racial alien through legal networks and financial markets is represented as white, urban, and heterosexual and is thoroughly subservient to the state as its civil servant (working in the police force); the black peasant, on the other hand, is represented as irresolute, shabby, desolate.[42]

I have chosen Du Bois's Black Belt to introduce the relationship between migration, alienage, and the formation of recalcitrant social spaces. Chief among the elements of Du Bois's formal and structural analysis of Dougherty County are statistics that report its denizens as overwhelmingly black, outnumbering the whites "four or five to one— and predominantly migrant labor with only ten percent of the adult population . . . born in the county" (126). Furthermore, the population of the Black Belt of Dougherty County is composed of migrants from elsewhere in the South—mostly black peasants who migrated to escape violence, imprisonment and renewed enslavement in other parts of the Belt, such as Mississippi, Louisiana, and Arkansas. The interstate migrations are not only the consequence of economic imperatives, and they become a structuring force in the reshaping of Dougherty County, constituting a specifically racialized labor market. If the county is only part of the Black Belt, the Black Belt is part of a cotton kingdom that extends transnationally into Mexico, wherever the "hum of the cotton-mills . . . [those] gaunt red buildings" can be heard (112). Du Bois embeds the Black Belt within a transnational economy and an international market for commodities and raw materials, suggesting that the dynamics of displacement, migration, and racialization found in the belt are more than local manifestations of a global economy. Rather, the "Negro forms to-day one of the chief figures in a great world-industry; and this, for its own sake, and in the light of historic interests, makes the field-hands of the cotton county worth studying" (112). That is, the local contradictions and antagonisms of black social life constitute a system of constraints by which the global is realized. Du Bois situates the conditions of black racialization within a global national economy for which race had become a constitutive social process.

Describing what we might term the "space of 1898," Du Bois places the belt in synchronized relation to other sites that are equally mediated by the racialization process, emphasizing racial alienage in respect to the American imperial state as the link between them: "The Negro farmer started behind,—started in debt. This was not his choosing, but the crime of this happy-go-lucky nation which goes blundering along with its Reconstruction tragedies, its Spanish war interludes and Philippine matinees, just as though God really were dead" (122). In the space of 1898, Du Bois connects legal Jim Crow racism in the South to American colonialism, articulating black, Caribbean, and Filipino racializations. He eschews black identification with the imperial state and instead suggests that black debt is sustained, not relieved, by American imperialism. In his synchronic spatialization of nonbinary racializations, he never eclipses difference by uniformity. Instead, he emphasizes the very different racialization of each group in relation to the American state. The different forms of racialization—from tragedy to interlude to matinee—also emphasize the unevenness of encounters, intensities, and historical engagements with the US nation-state for the differently racialized formations of US slavery, circum-Caribbean colonialism, and the recolonization of the Philippines. The epic-like duration of Reconstruction tragedies are contrasted to the interludes and matinees of young imperialism. Connecting each context through dramatic forms, Du Bois emphasizes the interconnecting discursive formations and practices by which nonequivalent yet linked racializations are mediated and gain public representation.

Just as the Black Belt is a social space that is linked to a multiplicity of sites and sets of relations, it is also not internally homogeneous. Instead its microspaces are eloquent testimonials to the modes of local survival. Houses of prostitution are located next to the county jail, suggesting that spaces of social crisis are also sites of emergence. Black accommodations are barely homes, operating as dwelling spaces for "widows, bachelors, and remnants of broken groups" (115). For Du Bois, the loss of proper dwelling places is both symptom and cause of "sexual looseness" (117) and "immorality," causing a "plague-spot" in sexual relations (116). In his nearly dystopic figuration of the Black Belt, Du Bois's racialized subject constituted through land is most certainly not the normative citizen promoted by Turner. Instead, the constitution of political and cultural subjectivity through racialized social space eschews the symbolization of the citizen formed by the landscape, promoting instead narrative spaces within which allegories of racial alienage emerge and proliferate.

If interest is the category that aligns aesthetic, political, and economic representation in liberal theories of citizenship, then debt is the category around which a cultural politics and poetics of alienage is organized. Du Bois writes: "The keynote of the Black Belt is debt; not commercial credit, but debt in the sense of the continued inability on the part of the mass of the population to make income cover expense" (113). The anti-migration laws and the peonage practices of Jim Crow tie the racialized denizen to the land, forcing an inheritance of the past that denies the racialized subject the ideological promises and resolutions of citizenship. But it is also the inheritance of the past as a debt that disorganizes and defers nationalist forms, creating strange inheritances that both weigh down and give weight to alternative social formations. Although the figure of land is a projected essence of objective space in Turner's narrative, the figure of land in Du Bois is social space constituted through and against the complex networks and webs of social relations that characterize the racialized industrial mode of production. Finally, if the national myth of territoriality suggests that the land exists to be inherited by the citizen, then, in the allegories of racial alienage, the land is already mortgaged and in debt. Where the citizen projects beginnings, alienage suggests a loss, a struggle, and a displacement. Debt is the precondition of the social field and an animating social force in the production of black migrancy.

TWO

Legal Freedom as Violence
in Nella Larsen's *Quicksand*

Black Literary Publics during
the Interwar Years

"But why?" Irene wanted to know, "Why?"
    "If I knew that, I'd know what race is" [replied her husband].
—NELLA LARSEN, *Passing*

You need not believe this if you do not want to. They do not care what you believe.
They have the POWER. They are settling the world's problems and you can believe
what you choose as long as they control the ARMIES and NAVIES, the world
supply of CAPITAL and the PRESS.—W. E. B. DU BOIS, "Returning Soldiers"

Nella Larsen's 1928 novella *Quicksand* has
been variously situated as a diasporic
novel, a product of the Harlem Renaissance, a modernist text, a black feminist
critique of patriarchal racialism and capitalist inequality, and a cosmopolitan work
about urban commercial modernity's
production of gender and sexual masquerade. Building on these interpretative
frames, I want to position *Quicksand* as a

text that both extends and intervenes in the black counterpublics of the interwar period, established shortly before Larsen wrote. However, rather than reading for particular historical and cultural themes contemporaneous with *Quicksand*'s writing that Larsen takes up, impacting her account of subjectivity in this period, I argue that we can read *Quicksand* as a materialist intervention into the use of subjectivity for the purposes of political governance over shifting populations, historical meanings, and social practices during the turbulent period of national capitalisms between the world wars. Indeed, I argue that *Quicksand* is a critique of the very logic of belonging that organized transatlantic economies, a logic that in our time has become the means by which literary critique engages the modern state.

The modern reader of *Quicksand* has the sense of being anticipated by the author. This is especially true for the literary critic. A defining labor within literary studies since the 1980s—when institutionally validated critics belatedly noticed the contradictions of postcolonial freedom and US civil rights—has been a critique of national literature. Since at least the publication of Benedict Anderson's *Imagined Communities*, literary critics of all methods—formalist, new historicist, Marxist, deconstructionist, psychoanalytic, and so on—have worked to denaturalize the idea of national literatures, studying the intricate modes by which national identity was produced by literature. Just as Western capitalism in its postcolonial phase found the very idea of nations to be an artifice that impeded and blocked its development, literary criticism shifted its definition within the modern categorization of academic knowledge from conveying the spirit and ethos of nationally produced literatures to revealing the modes by which language and literary practices were central to the invention of that spirit. It comes, then, as something of a surprise when entering into the text of *Quicksand* to find that Larsen has anticipated the critics of the late twentieth century.

At the end of the novel's opening chapter, Larsen writes in the voice of her protagonist, an approach that wouldn't be discovered, let alone used, in modern literary criticism for another sixty years, well after Larsen had died in obscurity. Staging the conflict that will drive the narrative plot, Helga Crane, Larsen's mulatta protagonist, discovers the reasons for her alienation: "If you couldn't prove your ancestry and connections, you were tolerated, but you didn't 'belong.' You could be queer, or even attractive, or bad, or brilliant or even love beauty and such nonsense if you were a Rankin, or a Leslie or a Scoville; in other words, if you had a family. But if you were just plain Helga Crane, of whom nobody had ever heard, it was presumptuous of you to be anything but inconspicuous and conformable."[1] The African American literary critic Jennifer Brody reminds us, in her ingenious book about punctuation, that "to 'see' the quotation marks is to question their straightforward, direct meaning—to highlight through a specific ironic staging a queer multiplicity or polymorphous perversity."[2] Scare quotes draw attention to the performativity of reading and the materiality of modern language. We might also say—marking a matter that will be significant to the reading of Quicksand—that they have the power to suddenly shift the registers of the aesthetic sense, from that of reading (meaning) to that of viewing (the sign). In other words, as Mieke Bal argues, quotation marks render the text as a mixed medium, bringing the practices of visual culture into literary culture. To put a word or phrase in quotation marks forces a shuttling between aesthetic registers, being both a form of intertextuality (citing previous meaning through signification) and an act of iconography (appropriating this or that motif without the meaning).[3] Helga Crane already suspects that to make belonging into an icon is a queer and perverse thing, presumptuous in its conspicuousness. Quoting here not only interrupts meaning but works like an archaeology to call attention to the material formation of a language community in a given time. Though it has been traditional to read Larsen's narrative as a female bildungsroman —that is, as a story of alienation and belonging—it would be more profitable to think of Quicksand as a historical metafiction, one that uses that story of a failed bildungsroman to map out the racial, gendered, and historical limits, aporias, and impossibilities produced as a consequence of the narrative of belonging that organizes our inquiries into cultural subjects and their practice. To follow Larsen's punctuation is to read the text as an archaeologist might, and to wonder, as Larsen did, what kind of society would make it possible for Helga Crane to desire belonging. Considering the opening chapter as a frame to the story that ensues, we might also suggest that Quicksand is an aesthetical history of belonging, in which the varied scenes of belonging and unbelonging are tableaux in mixed media, presented for the study of belonging.

I interpret belonging as a structure of feeling that connects persons and groups to the symbolic forms of liberal political life. Belonging emerges within the transatlantic system of Western modernity. It mediates between those collectivities that have political value within this system and other collective elements and practices that have come to be felt as alienation, expropriation, and something that is foreign to the self. Belonging constitutes the set of bodily, affective, and aesthetic norms and dispositions that regulate social participation and social presence within contexts organized by the transatlantic system of political modernity. This includes minimally formal civil equality, rights, territoriality, and the gendering of social practices.

Larsen's own experience of migration and immigration made her acutely aware of the emerging documentary or identification apparatuses that sorted US populations through the categories of citizenship, alienage, wards, and racially excluded groups. Many scholars have followed Paul Gilroy's generative metaphor of The Black Atlantic to interpret Quicksand, situating Larsen's own Atlantic crossing and European experiences within their accounts of the novel's critique of racial nationalism and essentialism, and its envisioning of black subjectivity—diasporic, transnational, and otherwise—as a break with, departure from, and dislocation of the regulative powers of the US nation-state to determine modern cultural identity. However, I find in Larsen's transnational cultural identity the contours of the transatlantic and the social formation controlled and administered by the Anglo-European system of states whose hegemony comes to an end during the interwar years, as well as an emergent transpacific increasingly dominated by the strategies of US racial capitalism.[4] Indeed I argue for a reading of Quicksand as part of an emergent structure of feeling, the consequence of a dialecticization of transpacific social forces at the height and end of the transaltantic system.

Gilroy's important definition and description of a black Atlantic space as a counterculture of modernity constituted by the diverse roots and routes of black diasporic identity has tended to stress the circuits of movement that defined black aesthetic and political modernisms, together with an understanding of diasporic cultural identity as the dialectal critique of the nation form and the spatial and temporal logics that naturalized its domination of black cultural memory.[5]

Yet what this critical project ignores, in favor of focusing on the nation, is the state formation and inter-state system that was controlling human movement and migration within the Atlantic system by the end of the first quarter of the twentieth century.[6] That is, without a concentration on the modern technologies of surveillance, control, regulation, policing, surveying, and governance that shaped and made transatlantic modernity a particular kind of experience, it fails to comment on the technologies that produce transatlantic bodies and subjects. These technologies are not manifested exclusively in the form of material objects and changing social forces—such as those that enabled the commercialization of travel, or new forms, spaces, and rules for sovereignty, national capitalism, and seafaring war machines.[7] Nor are these technologies exclusively the production of new perceptual and epistemological forms and the bureaucracies and institutions that sprang from them and that produce such items as passports and visas, customs and immigration records, medical reports, and immigrant detention centers. To focus on twentieth-century modernity's institutional production of the transatlantic world is also to study the political technologies that were produced by and that regulatively articulated new social forces. Larsen's transatlantic novel, I would argue, is less concerned with matters of national identity as ideological ruses or exclusionary and exclusive cultures than with trying to theorize modern belonging as an emerging political technology of the transatlantic system of globalization (a phrase I will clarify below) and the racial and gendered fulcrum that supported it. I read an emergent figure of a transpacific structure of feeling within the institutionally constituted transatlantic novel. A figure of "racial alienage," I argue, Larsen's central trope ironizes the mimetic tradition as central to the transatlantic novel as to the juridical system within which it took shape.

Larsen's novella is better grasped as a genealogy of belonging. For reasons that have to do with the geopolitical structure of the state in the political economy of US racial capitalism at the onset of the twentieth century, the novel as a genealogy of belonging returns us to the unstable figure of racial alienage that, as I argued in chapter 1, attempted to recast or de-subjugate the meanings and conditions of blackness *enclosed* by twentieth-century citizenship. In Du Bois, racial alienage emerges in the double address of, on the one hand, the phenomenon of post-slavery black subaltern migrancy internal to the South, the legacy of the violent suppression of radical Reconstruction, and, on the other, of the development of the modern institutions and disciplines of knowledge that not only produced the modern state but also became the institutional matrix for the racializations of modern populations and for the control of race itself—its integration into the sovereignty of the national state. Out of this double address Du Bois gestures at and calls up the strange affinities of blackness with the racial category of "Asia," producing a metonymic chain of US racial capitalism that moves from "Reconstruction tragedies, with its Spanish War (Caribbean) interludes," to its "Philippines matinees."[8] What Du Bois saw in 1903 as the alien specter that haunts and presages the permanent fracturing, fragmentation, and deferral of the embodied meanings of black citizenship (its alternative maps of ethical and political life) and that identifies the condition of post-Reconstruction black migration as suspended and not at home in the institutions of meaning of the recently established modern university becomes in the hands of Nella Larsen two decades later a phantasmagoric icon for the impossibilities of black women's citizenship in the interwar years.

Between Du Bois's *The Souls of Black Folk* and Larsen's *Quicksand*, the United States completed an unprecedented phase of consolidating power in the hands of the federal government, expanded its overseas territories and imperial footprint, and integrated its economy with those of European, creating the first period of globalization—which ended in the spectacular crash of 1929 that began the Great Depression, and the rise of militaristic states that led the Second World War.[9] Internationalism became a crucial node of black political thought, bringing the contradictions of colonial Asia and Africa into the subject of the recently established print-based public sphere. What Du Bois could only speculate about in 1903—the linked destinies of racial and colonial groups, of black and Asian histories, of Jim Crow democracy, and the supposedly benevolent occupation of the non-Western world—had become in Larsen's time the defining conditions of racial politics. Even in the heyday of a black Atlantic that asserted itself within the metropoles and modern liberal governments of European and American modernity in the first quarter of the twentieth century, a new cultural and social formation was making its presence felt: the beginnings of what some have called a black Pacific, which stretched from the Philippines and the islands of the

Pacific to Haiti and the Caribbean.[10] Though without a political public sphere like that of the black Atlantic—which developed in the transatlantic cities and command centers that managed the economic globalization of the Atlantic, particularly Paris, London, and New York—the black Pacific had a growing structure of feeling, one that developed in the shadow of belonging and in the national structures of feeling that consumed the Western empires. This Pacific was the theater of America's sovereignty, the site of its skirmishes and wars that settled its sovereign status among the crumbling European states of the Atlantic world. Thus the black Pacific within this US-dominated transpacific addressed the colored masses of the world, who—through European wars, the modernization of Europe's colonial economies, and Atlantic globalization—were becoming just that: racialized masses.[11] The black Pacific names the cultural life, pleasures, and imaginings that emerged alongside racialized and migratory masses for whom the Pacific registered not citizenship and the promise of European modernity, but the colonial and racial battles, wars, and migrations that remained the conditions of possibility of the Atlantic treaties that channeled the wealth of this first twentieth-century globalization to the modern citizens and urbanities of Europe and North America.

In conveying both dominant and alternative structures of feeling, Larsen's *Quicksand* is exemplary of the instability of racial belonging in the early twentieth century. In updating the mulatta trope, Larsen added her labors to a standing frame that was produced by and supported the counterrepresentational strategies and counterpublics of black women's critiques of American citizenship, racial capitalism, and the changing gendered, racial, and sexual violence on which they were predicated. As Cherene Sherrad-Johnson has argued in her excellent and original book, *Portraits of the New Negro Woman*, the iconographic mulatta is "a fraught, continuously reinvented figure in black literary and visual culture." Black women's counterpublics emerged in the interstices of numerous other counterpublics—the women's movement, the Harlem Renaissance (also called the new Negro movement), the Communist and labor movements, the Hull House reform movement, and so on—but they consistently exposed the gendered racial violence that particularly attended the dominant US print-based public sphere, as well as those counterpublics that strived for representation and identity in the state, such as the liberal feminist movement for suffrage. The mulatta was a defining trope of black women's fragmented counterpublics, "born from a complex melding of aesthetics and activism."[12] Larsen's appropriation of the trope of the mulatta brings to this alternative public sphere, in a way that only the blend of aesthetics and activism can, a powerfully new set of social relations.

Indeed, Larsen's text of black life powerfully draws out the Orientalist histories of the mulatta icon. As a figure that calls forth the dialectical relations between the empowered discourse of white liberal citizenship and the black social worlds that are its negation, the mulatta in my reading of Larsen's novel figures the lines of intersection and fragmentation of the alternative structures of feeling of the gendered black transpacific in contrast with the dominant structure of feeling of transatlantic national belonging.[13] I deviate from those accounts that read in this figure the travails of black-white mixedness, of the American Negro, and cosmopolitan European cultures and communities, for example.[14] Rather, we could say that Larsen's mulatta represents—or, more accurately, locates—an unstable blackness that abruptly shifts, like the affects of grandiosity and shame, between the registers of the black Pacific and the black Atlantic, between black alienage and black citizenship, between the foreclosed conditions of possibility of US Atlantic modernity and an emerging black transatlantic that is the leading edge and the border of European global modernity's national cultures. She is, finally, a trope for the imbricated conditions of being reduced to muteness and rising to autonomy, of being the gendered masses in the literary object and of claiming the literary subject for black counterpublics, of being speech or just being seen.

In the previous chapter, I examined the South-South black rural migrant as both a concept-metaphor and allegory in Du Bois's text for theorizing black racial formation as a form of persistent alienage even after formal emancipation. In this chapter, I seek to engage the black working class and Caribbean migrants as the "subjects" of contests within the recently established black public sphere over the meaning and "being" of blackness caught between citizenship and migrancy. My focus on Nella Larsen's *Quicksand* allows me to explore the relation between migration, race, and the instability and incoherence of the US nation-state within the international political and economic arena. In particular, my treatment of *Quicksand* and the broader workings of the interwar black public sphere focuses on three main points.

First, the interwar years are significant as the time when US society became increasingly structured by the liberal state, with its heavy reliance on classically liberal jurisprudence, isolationism, and an expansive disciplinary network—whose contradictions resulted in the hegemonic New Deal welfare state. However, this period is also significant for its continuation and expansion of forms of antiracist and anticapitalist internationalism (after the ending of the slave trade and slavery) that muddied the transparency of the nation-state, offering us evidence of forms of political critique that circumvented nationalism and were founded on the imbrication of race and class.[15] Second, the history of the failed state that I recount exposes the incoherence and instability of the US state and its social forms in terms of the management of the interwar racial order. It suggests that in the United States, the state has always been a racial state, and that one primary function of the racial state is to regulate and rationalize racialized meanings.

Third, I seek to expose the way in which citizenship, as an effect of disciplinary power, broke down as an abstract form in its extension to African American migrants in this period. That breakdown revealed that citizenship subtends a particular discursive and material order of gender, sexuality, morality, property, and so forth—one that was severely challenged by the material conditions and cultural practices of the migrants. And the breakdown produced language for an alternative figuration of social relations within the hegemonic order, or for a black subject position within those relations. This alternative figuration was produced through various media in the black public sphere. In particular, the literary representations of these racialized conditions of political modernity do not simply reflect new cultural subjectivities, nor are they acts of private transcendence achieved through aesthetics. Rather, the literature of the new Negro movement consists of modes of figuration that reveal the emergence of black alternative modernities, as yet only an uneven structure of feeling; this is its richness, in contrast to the ossified and dominating cultural form of political life, signified by belonging, as well as its limits as a form of activism.

BLACK LITERARY PUBLICS

The black counterpublics of the interwar years were mediated by news-print and enabled by the soaring rates of black literacy and black urban-ization. This was a public sphere that was heavily constituted by alterna-tive visions of internationalism, ones that sought to link the material and political conditions of racialized minorities (a term that emerged from the dominant internationalism of the transatlantic states) to those of African and Asian colonized peoples, engaging the contradictions of both Marxist and liberal theories of self-determination. As Brent Hayes Edwards has elegantly argued, there may not have been a single US black intellectual or producer of culture in the Harlem Renaissance who did not address the international dimensions of blackness and race in this period.[16] In this era of successive pan-African congresses including Afri-can Americans and colonial Caribbeans and Africans in 1919, 1921, 1923, and 1927 in Europe and New York City, blackness was seen as the basis for the formation of what we now call a transnational identity. By this term, Edwards and others mean that black identity was understood as both sub- and supranational with regard to the international system of the interwar years, crossing the borders of competing capitalist states in the development of antagonisms that went beyond national and class politics.

Black transnationalism in this period was multilingual, geographically dispersed, and composed of uneven and discrepant material histories of race. As a transnational identity, blackness in the interwar years was a signifier and mode of sociality that presumed immanent differences and heterogeneity; it was the basis for ongoing practices of translation that expressed both counterglobal solidarity and material incommensurabil-ity among differing black worlds in the United States, the Caribbean, Europe, and Africa. In many ways, the black internationalism that devel-oped during the interwar years—represented, for example, by the Pan-African Congress of 1919, where delegates from fifteen countries gath-ered for the purpose of petitioning the powers at the Versailles Peace Conference—was a rich exploitation of the contradictions of develop-ing a postwar global political economy through the ideology of self-determination and the nation-state system that was nonetheless con-trolled by the Western imperial nation-states, making it an economy that

depended on the Western ownership of vast colonial holdings and strategic non-Western territories.[17]

Blackness and race more generally were refigured during the interwar
years through an internationalism that stressed a worldwide color line,
and these transformations were registered in the literary forms that
developed during the era. Nearly every novel and narrative that stressed
a black coming-of-age tale relied on a plot that had at least one Atlantic
crossing, creating what Edward Said calls a "distinct structure of reference and attitude" within these stories of formation.[18] Others, including
W. E. B. Du Bois, returned to the genre of literary romance in the hope of
rendering an emerging alternative globality in the age of Western empires in terms of an affective and private life.[19]

Yet within the US scene, blackness and race were also transformed by
the rise of migration in general, and black migration in particular. The
state form that emerged in the interwar years was a consequence of the
largest population movements the United States had ever experienced.
Feeding the country's expanding industrial economy, nearly thirty million immigrants arrived from Europe from the 1880s to the 1920s. US
political elites responded to this massive transformation of society, which
deposited large numbers of noncitizen industrial workers in nearly every
major city, by building the administrative state and formalizing civil
society through a complex of institutions. Academic experts—especially
in the social sciences—became directly involved in state building, help-
ing to produce the state and its various institutions and bureaucracies, as
well as the logics that linked them together, that the experts' knowledge
sought to describe or reform. As Mae Ngai has argued, by the interwar
years, liberal political and social elites were addressing the social crises,
contradictions, and political antagonisms that had emerged in this period of industrial capitalism by seeking strategies for controlling the
population through an assertion of sovereign territoriality.[20] From modernizing the census to securing and controlling the US borders, the
modern social sciences were crucial to the development of a new system
of social rule that linked population, territoriality, and the state in a
manner that generated a new legal social body and a variety of dangerous
social subjects, including the illegal alien, the Asian who was ineligible
for citizenship, alien citizens, and racial alienage. Racial alienage is of

particular importance to this chapter, which focuses on black alienage as both a juridical status and dialectical figure of critique of the US immigration state. Racial aliens named those so-called non-white migrants whom the US state distinguished from so-called white European immigration. Indeed in the case of Caribbeans and some Asian migrants in the United States, racial aliens were formally and juridically considered subjects of the European states from which European immigration hailed and that claimed colonial power over their regions. The racial alien, and Caribbean migrants in particular, revealed the dual strategies of US racial capitalism at the century's opening, which included the recruitment of (European) labor for mass industry, mediated by the legal system of juridical alienage, and the development of colonies, territories, holdings, and other emergent forms of land and maritime ownership in the Caribbean and Pacific for the expansion of US industrial capital, of which race was a central formation. Though a juridical term, "racial alienage" is a dialectical figure in my account, revealing the transpacific as the emergent negation of the transatlantic economies of mass industrialization to which it was materially tied.

During the interwar years, the social sciences—particularly statistics, geography, and sociology—produced ways to organize the population by nationality, giving each group its own enumerated traits and racial status. Progressive and liberal thinkers in this era displaced national capitalist contradictions, political conflicts, and antagonisms, producing instead a crisis of social control, an antihistorical and scientistic thesis on social rule that argued for the development of institutions that could universalize the behavioral and social structures that the middle-class elites believed would ensure social cohesion through the proper development of individuality across social classes.[21] If social control operated at the level of individuals or the subject—though always racially defined—then population control, most significantly through the regulation and restriction of immigration, operated as a totalizing procedure. The population was understood by social scientists as a collection of nationalities and races that could be analyzed, managed, controlled, and optimized. Particularly in the form of immigration control and exclusion, the liberal democratic state could develop immense apparatuses of state violence such as Ellis and Angel Islands, the new US-Mexico border, and medical and eugenic bureaus without appearing either to be an authoritarian state or to wrest sovereignty from the people. By the interwar period, the state power had been organized into an immense juridico-administrative system, which used nationality and race as the primary principles by which social relations were submitted to the dual forces of institutionality and productive development on the one hand, and state power and violence on the other hand. Just as European immigration in this period tells us much about the tremendous institutionalization of US society and its new forms of administrative violence, which together forcibly gave shape and regulatory form to the population, and assigned race and nationality to everyone in it, Asian exclusion in this same period provided racially inassimilable populations and shows how the administrative state with its network of institutions could function as the vehicle for simultaneously gathering and expressing—through violence, if necessary—the state's sovereign authority.

By the interwar years, the modern regulation of population as the technique of ruling had made racial and national identity basic to the human person. Belonging to this or that community was now innate to the human subject. Even as modernity intensified the movement of peoples—and perhaps because of this intensification—the immigration state interpreted those movements through a lens that attributed belonging to all migrating bodies. All bodies had national origins, and the Immigration Act of 1924 (which included the National Origins Act of 1924) set numerical quotas by nationality as a way to regulate the arrival of impoverished immigrants from southern and eastern Europe. Using social scientific knowledge as its fulcrum, the newly formed juridico-administrative state restricted immigration, excluded some groups altogether, and carried out other illiberal practices, such as the sterilization of women, within US society, ironically through citing the forms of belonging that it claimed existed prior to political society: the various national, racial, regional, religious, or linguistic communities that the National Origins Act codified.

The state engaged the social relations on which it was dependent through the reified category of the population. The population was the aggregate of the scientific categories of belonging—including in the terms of the day, "Greek," "Negro," "Oriental," "Hindoo," and "Latin."

The juridico-administrative state of the interwar years addressed not so much the citizen or the alien, as the world of belonging. By this I mean that by the interwar years, US knowledge institutions had transformed the world into a cartography of human belonging, and this formalized knowledge enabled the state to cite a nonpolitical basis for its political violence. Indeed, to the degree that the state used social scientific knowledge to legitimate its political ruse, it enshrined the authority of the social sciences as a true discourse of social relations. It was through belonging that the state conducted its practices, discovering not only new techniques of rule but also new forms and sites of authority and legitimate action.

Black migrations in this period were unevenly addressed by the juridico-administrative state, in part because of a legacy of nineteenth-century knowledge that understood blackness within the national territory as a problem of belonging, a troubling of the claims of whiteness and a free republic as the origin of the national community and territory. The social scientific construction of nationality excluded black social groups, classifying them as belonging to race instead of nation. By the end of Reconstruction, however, and with the Supreme Court's *Plessy v. Ferguson* decision in 1896 enshrining the doctrine of "separate but equal," the state figured blackness (and all other racial formations) as a form of racial belonging, upholding the legality of Jim Crow segregation for the way in which it treated the races symmetrically. In other words, the liberty claims of black persons were now secondary to their membership in or belonging to a racial group. It was this belonging that the state had an obligation to respect in its laws, administration, and policing. Social science in this era blurs the distinction between white supremacy and liberalism in the manner in which racial and "national difference operates as a universal and neutral framework for classifying human populations. Hence, the famed white supremacist and nativist Lothrop Stoddard, author of *The Rising Tide of Color*, sounded much like the social scientists of his era when he declared that "when we discuss immigration we had better stop theorizing about superiors and inferiors and get down to the bedrock of *difference*."[22]

Racial alienage was pervasive within the black public sphere in this period. In New York, a site of particularly heavy black alienage, nearly one in four black persons was an immigrant.[23] Yet although there was significant black immigration in the interwar years, black immigrants were not enumerated according to their true national origins but according to their race, gaining for the purposes of immigration control and restriction the nationality of the Western powers—such as England, France, or Denmark—that ruled the regions they had migrated from. This meant that Caribbean colonized subjects belonged to the "Negro" race, while also being the "belongings" or possessions of European states. Additionally, upon gaining entrance into the United States and settling in de facto and de jure segregated societies, colonized West Indians were quickly marked as black. Larsen's own parents' immigration history suggests the multiplicity of statuses that racial immigration could create. Although Larsen's mother immigrated from Denmark, Larsen's father immigrated from the Danish West Indies. US immigration laws gave colonized populations the nationality of their colonial dominators, so Larsen's father, like her mother, was probably admitted as a Danish national rather than as a national of his native Caribbean society. The Fourteenth Amendment meant that he could eventually become a naturalized US citizen. Ironically, because of the gendered logic of nationality that persisted though the 1920s, though Larsen's mother was white and from the colonial metropole, she was dependent on her black colonized husband's naturalization to gain US citizenship. And because a woman's nationality and citizenship was always tied to that of her husband, when she remarried, even if she had been naturalized by the time of her second marriage, she could have lost her American citizenship, had her husband's nationality been other than American—a problem that was exclusive to women. As Nancy Cott argues, by the beginning of the 1900s, "nations in the Western political tradition translated modern respect for the elective quality of national allegiance to mean that, in the case of women, a choice in marriage expressed a decision about national belonging."[24]

Much black immigration in the early twentieth century came through the Panama Canal. The United States recruited Caribbean migrant workers to build the canal, and when it was done, many migrated to the US South and urban ports in the North. Marcus Garvey, perhaps the most famous "New Negro" of the Harlem Renaissance, traveled along these imperial labor routes, editing and publishing a biweekly newspaper that highlighted the plight of migrant laborers. The Danish West Indies that Larsen's father came from happened to be near the Panama Canal. The United States became increasingly dominant in the Western hemisphere, protecting its shipping and trade routes from perceived threats, especially Germany. In 1917, the United States purchased the Danish West Indies from Denmark, renaming them the US Virgin Islands, as it sought to extend its security state to the entire region. In 1918, already estranged from his wife and daughter, Larsen's father would have lost his Danish nationality and become a ward of the United States, if he had not already become a naturalized citizen. Perhaps this is why, writing in the late 1920s, Larsen makes Helga Crane the daughter of a Danish immigrant mother, like her own, and of an American Negro—a term that only seems to differ from her own father's nationality as a US ward. Indeed, in this way the category of Negro reveals the effort that the nation-state makes to suppress its colonial geographies. Caribbean migration proved that the boundaries between colonial, national, and racial belonging were porous and ambiguous at best. In fact, all of these categories expressed the structure of the US state's legitimate violence in the interwar years.

Moreover, the immense administrative apparatuses and institutions of civil society that developed in this period were almost entirely segregated, and African Americans were for the most part shut out of the two-party system that controlled government at both the local and federal levels. Although there was a significant growth in the number of black professionals, academics, educators, and intellectuals, they were all but irrelevant to the national professional bodies that represented these professions, established their norms, and advocated for their self-regulation. Indeed, both the rise of lynchings across the South and the urban race riots in the West and Northeast, such as the so-called Red Riots of 1919, demonstrate just how profoundly black life in this period was unevenly woven into the juridico-administrative state. White populism all too often tested its right to claim popular sovereignty by retaliatory hunts against offending black culture and communities, finding that the state— as well as many of the professional bodies—accepted the stated causes of its violence. Although black alienage and immigration entered the urban black public sphere through a highly governmentalized juridical and institutional process—making blacks acutely aware of things like nationality, passports, visas, and the related modern political struggle—black migrants' entrance into that public sphere was inextricable from these conditions of extra- or quasi-legal and nonstatist populist violence.[25]

Many black artists, writers, and producers of culture in this period sought to capture these changes, collectively devising an important subgenre in African American cultural production. Finding this subgenre in literary, musical, and visual forms, Farah Jasmine Griffin names it the "migration narrative." Less a traditional narrative than a set of linked tableaux, the migration narrative referenced the migration of two million African Americans in the 1920s from the rural South to industrial and northern cities. In literary texts by writers such as Jean Toomer, James Weldon Johnson, Jessie Fauset, Claude McKay, and Larsen, the narrative tends to register migration from the standpoint of an alienated middle-class subject. However, it uses the device of travel to connect in a single work culturally, juridically, and politically distinct geographies of violence, further fragmenting the narrative's protagonist as she or he struggles to find a unified meaning of race and blackness across these sites. Moreover, travel connects not only the disparate political geographies of blackness, but it also links traveled-through spaces to those places that are marked as treacherous and unpassable, perhaps the scene of a mob atrocity, producing a blackness that is haunted by the atrocities that can be committed against it—atrocities so cruel that they figure as the limit of the migration narrative's imagination and abilities of representation.[26]

During the interwar years, the migration narrative operated across aesthetical practices, from music and painting to literature. The narrative's appearance in literary forms like the bildungsroman marked an interruption in the genealogy of those forms and in the very meaning of the literary text. The bildungsroman was a popular literary genre in the United States during the migration-heavy interwar years. The form of that narrative, which portrays the temporal development of an individual in conditions not of his or her own choosing, became the perfect metaphor and symbol for the naturalization expected of white immigrants. Black writers in this period experimented with the bildungsroman as a literary form of representation for capturing the complexities and paradoxes of racial belonging; Larsen's *Quicksand,* of course, is one example.

By inserting the migration narrative into the form of the bildungsroman, Larsen, like other black writers in the period, frequently draws attention to the latter's contradictory status as a narrative of formation and development in relation to black social worlds. Instead of the generic characteristics of the classic bildungsroman, migration narratives emphasized the juridical limits of racialized freedom, the unrepresentable space, geographies, and violence that haunt mature identity. In the classic bildungsroman, the subject's original differentiation and alienation is a consequence of a break with family, community, or a state cultural and legal order. In contrast, in the migration narrative, the alienation is the effect of the enforced racial belonging of the individuated middle-class subject with the larger mass of the postslavery folk migrant community.

Migration narratives often stressed the limits of the *bildung* genre to capture the material conditions of African American citizenship and subject formation. Indeed, to the degree that the narrative form of the classic bildungsroman emphasizes the subject's original differentiation from a restrictive social whole, his or her gradual development into an autonomous person, and his or her willed reconciliation with the social order, it conveyed aesthetic values—such as autonomy, identity, wholeness, and synthesis—that appraised racialization, racial belonging, and black collective life as heteronomous conditions to be struggled against, negated, and buried in the subject's quest for emergence and self-development. In this manner, the *bildung* narrative itself promotes aesthetic dispositions and representational forms that not only dislocate the complexities of black collective experience—that is, the complexities of enforced racial belonging and the conditions of the racialized state— but that exclude from the very structure of meaning those historical differences that reveal the narrative of progress and development to be an inadequate form for narrating black citizenship and black alienage.

We can think, then, of the African American and Caribbean migration narrative that developed in the first quarter of the twentieth century as an interruption and intervention into the *bildung* form, one that reveals the limits of that form and the history of its function. Because the bildungsroman narrates the ethical development of the individual of European and American societies, both in its structure and in the aesthetic values it propagates, it cannot narrate the modern governmentalized and forcible production of black belonging that emerged in the twentieth century as the US state asserted a new form of sovereignty—legitimate violence—and methods of ruling through its reliance on the social scientific category of population and the naturalization of territoriality. In addition, the bildungsroman comes in contradiction with the collective practices that black cultural subjects developed as they rearticulated the very meaning of belonging, practices that often reassert and value the contingent and heteronomous character of the subject formed in the milieu of belonging. Indeed, we might read the persistent hybridization of the literary text—and even its displacement by practices of music and visuality—in black cultural and intellectual production as evidence of this negation and alternative engagement with modern experiences of contingency and heteronomy.[27] The migration narrative reveals the Euro-American bildungsroman as a contradictory cultural form in relation to the histories of race and racial governmentality. And it thereby reveals the degree to which the institution of literature that universalizes the literary object is itself active in the reproduction of political modernity, the conservation of the whiteness of the citizen subject, and the disappearance of the more complex racial modernity that exists as its ongoing conditions of possibility.

THE GENDER OF REPRESENTATION

If black citizenship and alienage offer a genealogy of the bildungsroman, they also critically engage the genre of women's fiction. And if race expresses the historically and materially produced unevenness of the social formation, then racial governmentality names the processes by which that unevenness is narrated, addressed, and managed by the state. Modern citizenship attempts to assimilate that unevenness toward its universality, promising to make all cultures part of universal culture. Yet in doing so, it doesn't ask what created that unevenness in the first place, why and how the unevenness exists, and what the implications are for inequality and structural dynamics and our sense of political society.

As race increasingly revealed its unevenness within the extant political discourses, being neither a nation nor simply a minority or complementary difference, the masculinist cultural politics of many black intellec-

tuals in the interwar years promoted within the cultural domain a universal gendered private sphere capacious enough to make race normal.[28] Yet
it was black women writers who found in the understanding of the
private sphere the ideological and discursive politics of political modernity, the centrality of racial inequality and the racialized system of inequity that are bound with and reproduced through both the concepts of
the private and the domestic as well as the schema of affect and gendered
personhood that they sustain. As Hazel Carby has argued, the female
bildungsroman so central to the way in which white and Western feminism thematized the gendered and sexual contradictions of political
modernity was itself in contradiction with the public histories of slavery,
Jim Crow capitalism, and urban racial capitalism that black women
writers sought to mediate in their literary production.[29]

However, black women's feminist antiracisms in the early twentieth
century ought not to be read solely as a critique of the racist foundations
and presumptions of white and inter-Atlantic feminisms. Rather, these
writers turn the domestic sphere into a source for materialist critique,
finding in the idealist commitments of white and inter-Atlantic feminisms the preservation of universal forms that belie the material histories, racial violence, and asymmetries that sustain gendered life. In this
way, the domestic novel is a point of departure for black women writers
along a longer trajectory of deciphering the complex relation of race to
political modernity. Thus we can read black women's critique of the
forms through which private life is realized as participating as deeply as
any other set of political movements in a critique of the racial violence
that subtends and sustains political modernity.

Black women's internationalism articulated egalitarian feminist politics as yielding divisive racial formations and sustaining the racial capitalist conditions that made Western societies and their civil and political
institutions possible. The conditions in which both leftist and liberal
feminist movements in the West promoted their agendas through civilizational discourse that affirmed white supremacy and nonwhite and colonial depravity and ignorance throughout the first quarter of the twentieth
century significantly restricted the opportunities for black women to use
the network of women's organizations or the print-based public sphere
and the corresponding civil and political institutions to which it is at-

tached, in order to engage in discourse upon the specific forms of gendered violence that black women experienced. Attempting to use the public sphere as a way to address, understand, and transform gendered social and sexual violence perpetrated not only by white men but by all men of color made it seem that black women were corroborating the outlandish discourse of black depravity that was used to justify white mob violence, Jim Crow race riots, and lynchings. To critique publicly gendered violence within black social relations risked losing not only the conferral of civilization status so central for having narrative authority and voice within the press-dominated public sphere, but also the status of autonomous person so crucial to membership in the political life that the conferral of civilization status offered. Under these conditions, black women most likely experienced various forms of gendered violence as well as forms of racialized violence, as most of the women were racialized urban women workers and domestics who could not be engaged through the larger international or transatlantic public sphere. But as many black feminists such as Patricia Hill Collins, Jacqueline Goldsby, and Jacqui Alexander have pointed out, they also experienced in this period violence that ironically was the consequence of their gaining membership, however restricted, in political society, the state, and the public sphere. Black women who attempted to engage the public sphere as a scene for their speech and the formation of their interests discovered norms and conditions for that speech that if not forcing their silence and accommodation to specific violence—making them appear to sanction that violence or making it publicly invisible through their silence—then at the very least required them to render that violence as unspoken in the public sphere.[30]

For black women as different as Ida B. Wells-Barnett and Jessie Fauset, using the public sphere to address racialized and gendered domination and marginalization, speaking through the rational forms that the public sphere sustained and extended—so crucial to verifying one's membership in political society and the institutions of the state—actually enacted specific silences around and excisions of specific gendered, sexual, and racialized forms of violence that emerge with taking up the norms of the public sphere, to keep themselves and black speakers more generally from losing access to the public sphere altogether. That is, black women encountered the public sphere, so crucial to the progressives' vision of democratically run societies, as the source of an aporia: without participation in the public sphere, they would have no chance to mobilize the state against historical forms of antiblack violence; yet in lending their speech to the public sphere, they supported the norms that give speech its authority, norms that made particular forms of violence become inconsequential or meaningless to private, public, and political life.

Yet black women intellectuals and cultural workers who had access to the racialized commercial and civil institutions of the public sphere did find other media for representing these forms of violence, if only by provisionally challenging the norms of the print-dominated public sphere. Although the blues, race records, and cabaret performances were popular media in which black women found ways to reference what could not be spoken as a consequence of entering and gaining access to the public sphere that addresses the political institutions of the state, literary discourse was a central medium through which black feminist critics sought to intervene in the institutional context and network that structured the normative form of urban modernity.[31] In the interwar years, literary discourse—most often through private literary forms, such as the novel—became a site for a number of black feminists from Nella Larsen to Zora Neale Hurston to engage the violence and norms that could not be spoken of easily in the public sphere. In literary discourse, this violence need not be mimetically transcribed but instead could be alluded to through the use of literary devices such as tropes, figures (such as the mulatta), alternative narrative structures, and all sorts of interruptive and poetic tactics. In this way, literary discourse offered a means by which black feminists could thematize both the norms governing expression and their limits, as well as what those norms construct through discourse (that is, what kinds of personhood) and what they restrict through discourse (or the contradictions in the literary institution in relation to black gendered migration).

Cheryl Wall has said of Nella Larsen, arguably the one among her cohort of black women writers who most specifically critiqued the realist narrative form and the aesthetic that governed social perception in the print public sphere: "Perhaps Larsen's most effective act of passing was masking the subversive themes that frequently shimmered beneath the surface of her fiction. Both *Quicksand* and *Passing* contemplate the inextricability of the racism and sexism that confront the black woman in her quest for selfhood."[32] Indeed, we can read the "quest for selfhood" so central to the *bildung* narrative and the popularity of its forms that Larsen's fiction engages (like the fiction of so many Harlem Renaissance writers) as the effect of the mode of social control that state formation in the Progressive Era produced, as it grew both civil-society institutions and the administrative state.

Deborah McDowell and others have pointed out that Larsen's *Quicksand*, in contradistinction to the comedic form of the classic bildungsroman, is an unnerving and caustic satire on the reigning racial and sexual social order that makes black women's efforts to gain autonomy the false promise of modernity.[33] Yet Larsen's work is clearly a critique of the realist aesthetic central to the classic bildungsroman. Akin to modernist practices that emerged in her time, Larsen disorients the realist reader, stressing the mediating conditions and the violence of modern mimetic regimes of perception that abet the naturalization of a racialized and gendered liberal individualism. *Quicksand*'s protagonist, Helga Crane, is an unreliable narrator. From the beginning, the text delivers a sustained foregrounding of the setting—Larsen casts subjects and objects equally as blurred shapes in light—stressing perspectival conditions over the mimetic values of classic realism. And character development is skewed in a direction that stresses social relations. Larsen abandons the realist focus on private interiority, focusing the reader's attention instead on characters as complex relations between social forces and psychic life, figuring her characters as caught within transindividual psychic and affective forces and structures, critiquing the classic novel's valuing of individualism and egocentric depictions of causation.

In this light, we might read *Quicksand* in a more disarticulated fashion, appreciating Larsen's efforts to throw into relief narrativity itself: by way of travel, departures, and leave-takings into radically different juridical zones—the Jim Crow South, the interracial US metropolis, the emerging welfare state of Denmark—Helga Crane's movements attest less to an enclosed and singular subject who develops her identity over time, marking instead persistent conditions of displacement, ontological instability, and temporal heterogeneity. In realist narrative, the subject itself is given a narrative form: its development is primarily temporalized, and this temporal development enables the subject to discover its identity, integrating itself through narrative time, space, and subjectivity. However, in specifically relating narrative movement to juridically distinct and unique modern biopolitical regions, Larsen's work forces the reader to recognize the gaps between the narrative scenes and tableaux; it stresses the incommensurate forms of violence that produce a subject's incoherence across places and institutions. Helga Crane migrates, shifting from being a southern mulatta, a US citizen who is a member of a racial minority in the urban capitalist city, and an exotic "other" in a European welfare state financed by colonialism and the legacy of slavery —Denmark having sold its possessions in the Caribbean to the United States in 1917. As a novel of racial, gendered, and juridical migration, the text forces us to imagine different and more complex ways in which the scenes that collectively iterate the figure of Helga Crane over the course of the narrative could be given interpretive coherence.

It is important to keep in mind that in literary discourse, the migration narrative—though disruptive of realist practices of subjectivity—was generally centered around a middle-class protagonist or focus. However, the black public sphere—through which the politics of internationalism flourished—had its own conditions of possibility in the mass migration of southern blacks to urban regions, especially those of the Northeast and Midwest. And although, as Hazel Carby writes, "this movement of masses of rural black Southern workers destined to become an urban proletariat was not immediately represented in fiction,"[34] their impact on the structures and forms of black political and cultural institutions was decisive and constitutive. Carby points out that the days in which black elites could presume that they represented their race were gone. The rise of differing black political and cultural projects—that is, a deepening of attention to differences within the category of blackness—was also an effect of a broad black popular base that spoke through its commercial, leisure, and political activity.

The heavily gendered character of the postslavery rural migration stream, in which black women originally outnumbered men substantially, was at times registered in punitive ways, for example in W. E. B. Du Bois's first sociological study, *The Philadelphia Negro*. In that study,

Du Bois noted the gendered character of the migration, the "disproportionate" and "abnormal" sex ratio among what he termed "Black immigrants" in Philadelphia's seventh ward. For the most part, the study
turned black women into ciphers for a statistical symptomology of the
racial violence of postslavery US capitalism. At other times, the gendered
migration was addressed through patriarchal ideologies of support and
duty.[35] Famously, Marcus Garvey's Universal Negro Improvement Association would not have been possible financially or otherwise without
the huge numbers of black women who joined the organization and
funded its ship line, the Black Star Line. In Garvey's vision, shared with
his heavily black female membership, the company would oversee a fleet
of ships that would transport manufactured goods, raw materials, and
produce among black businesses in North America, the Caribbean, and
Africa, creating an empowered and self-reliant global black economy. Yet
black cultural and political elites scarcely commented on the gendered
character of the migration, and the ways in which it transformed understandings of race and blackness. Instead, these middle-class thinkers
understood the changing character of black political discourse and the
meaning of race in the interwar years as primarily affected by the historically unprecedented phenomenon of what they referred to simply as
"Negro migration." In introducing the new Negro movement to the
rapidly formed but quickly established civil and cultural institutions of
the US public sphere in the academic crossover journal *The Survey
Graphic*, Alain Locke boldly condensed the complex causes of the development of new and robust forms of black aesthetic and print practices
to nothing more significant than the decisive importance of the black
"migrating peasant"[36] of the despoiled South—even if Locke overlooked
the specifically gendered character of the migration stream of racialized
labor.

QUICKSAND AS TABLEAU VIVANT

Quicksand is a novel that engages the paradoxes of black women's publicity during the interwar years. Like other internationalist writing, it
connects US modernity to the struggles of the black diaspora as well as
to African and Asian decolonization. But told from the standpoint of a

black female protagonist, it forces the reader to see the linkages between the maintenance of gender and sexual norms and the persistence of racial and colonial violence. *Quicksand* is a hybrid literary text: a coming of age story, the tale of a picaresque woman, a modernist experiment.

The novel is structured as a series of tableaux depicting the vast diversity of post-Reconstruction black publics and social worlds during the 1920s. Larsen gives us snapshots of southern normal and industrial schools, such as the one she attended at Fisk University in Tennessee and the Tuskegee Institute in Alabama, where she briefly taught and worked as a nurse; the Jim Crow trains that took hundreds of thousands of black migrants to segregated cities; the racially mixed commercial shopping districts and boarding houses in those cities; the increasingly black neighborhoods of Chicago's South Side and New York's Harlem; rent parties; black-and-tans; jazz clubs and storefront churches; the European metropoles, where hundreds of black soldiers and middle-class artists, activists, and performers sojourned and sometimes settled; and the small and impoverished black communities that developed in the rural South.

These tableaux are linked through the story of Helga Crane, a young mulatta teacher at a southern industrial school named Naxos. Suffocated by its culture of conformity and suspicion of difference, Helga leaves Naxos, traveling to Chicago, then to New York, and on to Denmark in a search for belonging and freedom. Helga is the child of a "Negro" father and a Danish immigrant mother, born in what she calls a Chicago "slum." Deserted by her father, Helga's mother remarries, this time to a white man—making her daughter's racial difference a liability in the family's quest for social mobility. When Helga's mother dies, Helga is abandoned by her stepfather and his family. She is saved by the charity of her maternal uncle, who sends her to boarding school in the South. Though her education, beauty, and aesthetic sense allow her entry in the black middle-class, Helga believes that its small and rarified circles of cultural and political elites—together with her "lewd," shameful, and mixed origins—prevent her from truly belonging to this world. She travels to Copenhagen—once again, with the aid of her uncle—seeking freedom from the racial constraints of the United States. Exoticized in Denmark, Helga finds that her hopes of belonging in European society are dashed. She returns to New York, embracing a sexuality she had been reluctant to engage—only to be rebuffed by her love interest, Robert Anderson, the former principal of Naxos. Destroyed and disoriented by his rejection, Helga impulsively marries a working-class preacher who moves them to rural Alabama. Her marriage becomes empty and isolating; her body is exhausted by domestic work and childbirth. By the novel's end, Helga's quest is a failure, her search for belonging and freedom an illusion.

The geographical structure of the novel emphasizes the role of frames in the telling of Helga's story. The novel takes place in five primary settings—beginning and ending in the southern Black Belt, a structure that emphasizes the settings' formal importance as the not-quite identical frames for Helga's narrative. Entering the opening frame, the reader immediately discovers Larsen's pictoral and tableaux style, with lush description of interiors emphasizing light and perspective. The novel begins: "Helga Crane sat alone in her room, which at that hour, eight in the evening, was in soft gloom. Only a single reading lamp, dimmed by a great black and red shade, made a pool of light on the blue Chinese carpet, on the bright covers of the books which she had taken down from their long shelves, on the white pages of the opened one selected, on the shining brass bowl crowded with many colored nasturtiums beside her on the low table, and on the oriental silk which covered the stool at her slim feet" (5). Helga appears to the reader as though in a *tableau vivant*, or living picture. Immensely popular at the turn of the century, the most elaborate *tableaux vivants* involved the use of costumed actors in elaborately staged settings that were theatrically lit. As forms of recreation that crossed commercial and private life, *tableaux vivants* ran the gamut from the extremely elaborate and ornate ones that were staged in commercial halls, theaters, and arcades to the most simple "sketch"—as if a moment in a game of charades—that groups and families put on for one another in parlors, salons, and middle-class drawing rooms. *Tableaux vivants* tended to recreate scenes from famous paintings, relying on their audiences' popular and visual unconscious to recognize the staged recreations. Incorporating theater, sculpture, photography, and the emerging silent cinema, as well as modern paintings, *tableaux vivants* were mixed-media productions that reveled in the play on modern spectatorship and subjectivity. As citations of famous works of art or photographic pictures that were often themselves stylized citations of living persons made still by the media of photography or painting, many *tableaux vivants* included as part of their staging an actor who played the artist or photographer, diligently at work.

These live, three-dimensional recreations of two-dimensional originals substituted for the image the living body—quite literally embodying the image—offering spectator and actor alike rich allegories of the modern condition. Especially in their more elaborate form, *tableaux vivants* displaced the auratic original with the human imitation, using bodily spectacle to travesty the work's aura. Borrowing an icon and citing it, only to displace it through the embodied subject, performers enacted what Joseph Roach calls acts of substitution, which are also acts of surrogacy.[37] *Tableaux vivants* spoke to a modern imperial and metropolitan "structure of feeling," to use Raymond Williams's term: the breakdown of unified time, finding the pre-emergent in reenactments of residual forms and practices.[38] In citing institutional forms and their authority only to enact changefulness, differences, and heterogeneities, *tableaux vivants* dissolved the fixed and frozen forms of society, dramatizing figures in their place. Expressing the complex play between two-dimensional and three-dimensional life, image and human, and signifier and signified—in which, paradoxically, the former term is the original—*tableaux vivants* inverted literary and pictoral art. Rather than trying to capture through literary or visual strategies three-dimensional life in two-dimensional forms, *tableaux vivants* made modern subjects imitations of two-dimensional reality. There is thus a link between the practices of the *tableaux vivants* and the new discursive condition of governmentality, which sought to organize relations of rule through the imposition of discursive categories that bodies inhabited and approximated through social practices.

Theaters that staged *tableaux vivants* displayed a series of them in a silent and sequential order that conveyed a story or narrative; making *tableaux vivants* theatrical precursors to magic lantern shows and silent cinema. Many high and low cultural forms borrowed from the *tableaux vivants*: from the folk heritage museums that conveyed the nation's history through a visual narrative to wax museums—both of which were popular in Copenhagen during the time of Larsen's visit—and the colonial panoramas that included colonized peoples as natives in their displays and that were a fixture of world's fairs, such the World's Columbian

Exposition in Chicago in 1893, the city and date that Larsen gives for her birth (although she was actually born two years earlier). Larsen uses *tableaux vivants* to stress discontinuity in narrative, as well as irregularity within subjectivity. Thadious M. Davis argues that "most noticeable in Larsen's portrayal of the contrasting cultures is her technical facility in embedding the story or narrative in a tableau vivant scene."[39]

Larsen's use of *tableaux vivants* could be read as an instance of what the critic Daphne Brooks calls black women's "Afro-alienation acts." Largely antirealist forms of cultural expression, Brooks argues, these "generically diverse and dissident, Afro-alienation acts draw from the tactics of heterogeneous performance strategies . . . in order to defamiliarize the spectacle of 'blackness' in transatlantic culture."[40] As portraits of characters, *tableaux vivants* have the advantage of using scenery and setting to enact such defamiliarizations, blending subjects and objects into a single composition and quite literally reinserting live actors or subjects back into the equalizing plane of an object world.

In introducing the reader to Helga Crane, Larsen lingers on Helga's setting before directing the reader's gaze to her seductively beautiful heroine. Helga's room is unusually spacious, filled with her private library and "furnished with rare and intensely personal taste" (5). Helga's settings exemplify her estrangement. A teacher at the fictional Naxos—an amalgam of Fisk University and Booker T. Washington's Tuskegee Institute—Helga is an eccentric element in the otherwise stifling and homogenizing community. Although at first Naxos was famous for its mission of "uplift," now "this great community, she thought, was no longer a school. It had grown into a machine." An exemplary disciplinary institution, utilitarian in its philosophy and Taylorist in its educational methods, Naxos was "now only a big knife, with cruelly sharp edges ruthlessly cutting all to a pattern, the white man's pattern. Teachers as well as students were subject to the pairing process, for it tolerated no innovations, no individualisms" (8). In this panoptic world, Helga's room is her only "rest" from the "strenuous rigidity of conduct" that pervaded Naxos. Indeed, the very arrangement of the tableau stresses Helga's diminished space for existence: "Where Helga sat was a small oasis in a desert of darkness" (5).

When the reader at last sees the novel's protagonist, the distancing language of spectatorship intensifies Helga's status as a figure among objects: "An observer would have thought her well fitted to that [her room's] framing of light and shade. A slight girl of twenty-two years, with narrow, sloping shoulders and delicate, but well-turned, arms and legs, she had, none the less, an air of radiant, careless health. In vivid green and gold negligee and glistening brocaded mules, deep sunk in the big high-backed chair, against whose dark tapestry her sharply cut face, with skin like yellow satin, was distinctly outlined, she was—to use a hackneyed word—attractive" (5–6). Next to her lay open a favorite book, the British Orientalist "Marmaduke Pickthall's *Saïd the Fisherman*," a travel tale of the Middle East set during the British occupation of Egypt and immensely popular when it was released in the United States in 1925.

Larsen's tableaux reveal the deep Orientalism that saturated commercial and popular US culture during the interwar years. Japanese masks, silk kimonos, Chinese furnishings, Oriental stage productions, and a general craze for all things Egyptian defined American modernity. In the same decade in which the political sphere and the state barred all Asian immigration, denaturalizing any previously naturalized Asian aliens and making all Asian aliens permanently ineligible for citizenship, American popular culture exalted in Oriental aesthetics that expressed the plasticity and inessentiality of modernity. As Alys Weinbaum has argued, the consumer culture's play with the so-called yellow peril and dressing in Oriental style was part of a modern aesthetics of racial masquerade, in which racial and cultural syncretisms and citations of primitivism abounded. That this coincided with the high point in the racialization of Asians as antipathetic to US modernity suggests that this frenzy for all things Oriental was part of a patently racist conception of syncretism. In the case of US women's consumer culture, Oriental dress was part of a "racially syncretic aesthetic" that actually revealed "white women's control over the racial masquerade, racial ascription, and thus their designation as members of the modern racial nation."[41] US Orientalism was not restricted to commercial and popular culture. The fields of social science that played such a crucial role in the development and ultimate passage of the Immigration Act of 1924, which included the Asian Exclusion Act, figured Asians and blacks as the limit of modernity's ability to supersede all previous social relations and communal bonds. Emphasizing a scopic understanding of race, US sociologists—most famously Robert E. Park, the preeminent sociologist of the famed Chicago School—argued that blacks and Asians were racial phenotypes that not even the forces of modernity could mask or hide, preventing their assimilation by modern consciousness.[42]

How are we to read Larsen's saturation of her tableaux with assorted chinoiserie, Orientalist novels, and yellow hues? What are we to make of Helga Crane's deep love of the Orientalist aesthetic? If the function of the tableau is to emphasize the whole composition, then it would seem that the various Asian objects—apparel, furnishings, and books— are crucial to any interpretation of the figure momentarily arrested in the tableau. In Weinbaum's powerful reading of *Quicksand*, Larsen uses Helga's Orientalist penchant precisely to show her exclusion from the racial nation, even in its modern and commercialized form. Like white women who use a racial masquerade to mark their access to the modern, controlling the racial mask they consume, Helga Crane believes that she controls the terms of her masquerade. Instead her Oriental mask, like the primitivist mask she dons in Copenhagen, is part of a series of ultimately failed acts of masquerade that reveal the actual social basis (and limits) of autonomous, individualist, and consumerist agency.

Both Thadious Davis and Cherene Sherrard-Johnson have emphasized the pervasiveness of Orientalism and its close connection to the novel's protagonist.[43] When Helga arrives in New York and sees the guest bedroom offered to her by a member of Harlem's elite, Helga is mesmerized by its interior. Rendered as a tableau, the room was "in complete accord with what she designated as her 'aesthetic sense,'" with its "historic things mingl[ing] harmoniously and comfortably with brass bound Chinese tea-chests, luxurious deep chairs and davenports, tiny tables of gay colors, a lacquered jade-green settee with gleaming black satin cushions, lustrous Eastern rugs, ancient copper, Japanese prints, some fine etchings, profusion of precious bric-a-brac, and endless shelves filled with books" (*Quicksand*, 47).

Sherrard-Johnson convincingly argues that Larsen's use of Oriental objects in her many tableaux of Helga Crane was part of a larger iconographic project that sought to challenge and substitute "the visual images of African American women then circulating throughout the culture and limiting the mobility of the New Negro woman in the intellectual and artistic communities of the 'talented tenth.' "[44] Larsen is "in effect, modernizing the mulatta figure." In an act of surrogation, Larsen replicates "the iconography of the mulatta through literary tableaux inflected by orientalist accoutrements and modern art referents in an effort to be more modernist and less New Negro."[45] In Sherrard-Johnson's careful genealogy of mulatto iconography that Larsen and others—such as the painter Archibald J. Motley Jr.—cited in their insurgent tableaux, the mulatta is a transnational and transatlantic figure. Both Motley's and Larsen's mulatta tableaux, according to Sherrard-Johnson, recall the famous 1824 painting *Aline, the Mulatress*, by Eugène Delacroix, the French Orientalist. In the case of Larsen, Sherrard-Johnson notes, the opening tableau with its "blue Chinese carpet," "black and red shade," and "Oriental silk" (*Quicksand*, 1) cites Delacroix's Orientalist interiors.[46] Like popular tableaux, Larsen's Helga Crane is a figure standing in for another figure, linking the different histories of nineteenth-century French Orientalism and twentieth-century US commercial Orientalism. Indeed, Sherrard-Johnson's history of the visual image of the mulatta suggests that Larsen's very textual choice to make Helga Crane a mulatta highlights the protagonist's Orientalist identity, further breaking down distinctions between subjects and objects in the tableau.

Read through Sherrard-Johnson's genealogy, Larsen's tableau emphasizes the interdependency and inextricability of figure and objects. Helga is less a character sitting among her objects than a figure in a tableau, a historically laden and complex citation of gendered, racial, and sexual representations. Moreover, Larsen's tableaux stress the institutional matrix that authorizes these representations and structures the visible. The Orientalized Helga reveals the dense transatlantic cultural and commercial networks of race that organized the social forms of intelligibility available to black women in the early twentieth century. And what at first appear to be objects of Helga's possession turn out to be citations and captions to her condition. Larsen's tableaux stress Helga's dependence, not her autonomy; she is less a protagonist for the reader to identify with than the object of the viewer's spectatorship. In Larsen's hands, the mulatta is revealed to be a two-dimensional category, culturally overwritten in the figure of Helga Crane. Allegorizing the conditions of black women's writing in the public sphere, Helga—sitting in an Orientalist "room of her own," to use Virginia Woolf's famous phrase—can stand in for Larsen's own critical position on the literary public sphere, a space that putatively affords black women aesthetic freedom. What can at first appear to be a definitive example of the period's black Orientalism turns out instead to be a tableau that allegorizes the limits on cultural emergence and possibility for the writers of the new Negro movement.

THE SILENCE OF OBJECTS

I would like to argue, however, that what makes *Quicksand* such a distinct contribution to American studies and ethnic studies is that it deftly interweaves these conditions of representation within the public sphere with the political conditions and types of violence that organize that sphere. Larsen's persistent and near-exclusive use of Orientalist objects to frame Helga Crane throughout the novel shows the unstable differences and continuities between US racism and European Orientalism, and between racial and colonial modes of accumulation. Additionally, in the context of US immigration politics that Larsen knew so well, the Orientalist origins of the mulatta figure suggest the complex but permeable barriers between US black citizenship, Caribbean racial alienage, and Asian exclusion, in which Asian migrants from the Pacific were assigned to races ineligible for citizenship. The use of US sovereignty to permanently exclude Asian migrants manifested a US public sphere in which migrant Asians figured not as a protected minority but as the very limit of the universal political sphere. The legal figure of the Asian ineligible for citizenship effectively barred Pacific migrants already in the United States from participation in the public sphere that addressed the state. Indeed, the same bill that banned Asian immigration in the 1910s, the Immigration Act of 1917, and marked Asians as ineligible for citizenship added a political class, "anarchists," to the list of excludable populations. These exclusions reveal the complex balance between sovereignty and the public sphere in the juridico-administrative state. Even as the public sphere normed and restricted the powers of state sovereignty, to delimit its own boundaries it ratified the use of that same sovereignty. On the West Coast, for example, white leaders of organized labor argued that Asian immigration would undercut not only the value and dignity of working men's labor, but also—in supplying monopoly capitalists with a source of labor that had no capacity for political life—would constitutively undermine the means of modern labor to access the public sphere and to use that sphere as a site for its nonviolent negotiations and struggles with the capitalists. For the racially restricted unions on the West Coast, Asian immigration meant nothing less than the loss of the public sphere and the political resolution of the battle between labor and capital.[47]

By the 1920s, US Orientalism was a more variegated project. Although the restrictionists argued that anarchism and Asian immigration would mean the end of the public sphere and the democratic nation-state, and the seizure of the liberal state by monopoly capital, new actors in the public sphere—such as the modern expert—figured Asian immigration differently. For example, for modern sociologists, such as Robert E. Park, who offered what they called scientific accounts of the structure of the social and its ailments during the interwar years, the Asian—although a racially nonwhite class like the Negro—was still an immigrant group that, unlike the Negro, could achieve modern assimilation. Rather than dangerously undermining the very possibility of an ideal public sphere, for Park, Asian immigration proved modernity's capacity to sustain that public sphere, even in spite of racial differences.[48] Yet the discourses of the restrictionists and the experts shared the racialized view that Asianness was ultimately a nonpolitical difference, subject to exclusion by the first group and assimilation by the second.

If the difference between subjects and objects, persons and settings, political life and its nonpolitical limit in the public sphere, as much as in the middle-class novel, can all be rendered as a difference between varieties of speech and silence, it is perhaps not surprising that Larsen so often presents Helga Crane in the narrative through that silent aesthetic form, the *tableau vivant*. Indeed, Helga's defining condition throughout the novella is that of silence toward the men and women, whites and blacks, and Europeans and Americans who declare her meaning. Faced with the opportunity to represent her self, interests, and desire, Helga finds herself painfully silent.[49] Within the tableaux, Helga's silence mimics that of the objects around her, stressing her equivalence with them.

Indeed, rather than offering the means for her differentiation and control of the Orientalist objects all about her, which are evidence of emergence and autonomy, their muteness in the spectatorial public sphere carries over to the figure of Helga as well. If *Quicksand* expresses Larsen's interest to write a US transnational novel on race, gendered migration, and the politics of belonging, we ought to understand the use of an Orientalist aesthetic, the littering of settings with foreign objects, as an act of substitution. Where *Quicksand* ought to suggest imbricated stories of Asian differences in the black migration novel, we find instead a silent object world of Orientalia. And if the *tableau vivant*, along with other visual techniques, is generally the way in which the racialized history of Asia and US empire is registered in the public sphere, it is a frame in which these mute Orientalist objects—a kind of material "otherness" that cannot be entirely dissolved by national consciousness—confirm the legitimacy of the development of excludable criteria. And this development orchestrated liberal state-sanctioned violences against Asians as much as against black social groups.

From the standpoint of speech, narrative, and publicity, the muteness of the objects—the fact that they present in the public *as* muteness—functions as an assurance that these racialized criteria of exclusion and publicity have no political meaning. That is, the racism of Asian exclusion and US Orientalism is, finally, the understanding that these exclusions that organize the public sphere, tying publicity to state sovereignty, do not effect, limit, or determine the development of the public sphere as that free and vital zone of infinite civil conflict and debate that makes political modernity unique.

In Larsen's novel, however, these Orientalist objects have a more ambivalent effect. For Helga Crane, visual aesthetics are central to the agency that she wields. In Chicago, hungry and nearly destitute, Helga chooses to spend her last dollars not on a meal but on a new purse in an attempt to "feed" her self-image. In New York and having decided to depart for Copenhagen, feeling caged in by the Harlem society in which she has been living, Helga chooses not words but the perfect dress, "a cobwebby black net touched with orange, which she had bought last spring . . . and never worn because on getting it home both she and Anne had considered it too *décolleté*, and too *outré*. Anne's words: 'There's not enough of it, and what there is gives you the air of something about to fly' . . . it would be a symbol. She was about to fly" (*Quicksand*, 59). In Naxos, Helga fights the utilitarian ideology of the school—expressed in the enforced dress code of "drab colors, mostly navy, black, brown, unrelieved, save for a scrap of white or tan about the hands or necks"—by frequently dressing in bright colors marked as "vulgar" (20). Believing color to be a visual signifier of black freedom, Helga found it pure hypocrisy that the dean of women forbade a female student from wearing color: "The dean was a woman from one of the 'first families'—a great 'race' woman; she, Helga Crane, a despised mulatto, but something intuitive, some unanalyzed driving spirit of loyalty to the inherent racial need for gorgeousness told her that bright colors were fitting and that dark-complexioned people *should* wear yellow, green, and red" (21). Helga wonders: "Why . . . didn't someone write a *Plea for Color?*"

For Helga, beneath its comic value, her "plea for color" is a defense of noninstitutional forms of black belonging—forms that appear but that cannot gain speech within the novel form. If Helga is for Naxos a figure of excess and perversity, whose stylized aesthetics violate the utilitarian culture of the place, the young migrant men and women who come there to get an education are figured as lack and waste, equally without value for the school. Early on, Larsen shows us Helga's strange kinship with these figures of lack. On the morning of her departure from Naxos, Helga finds herself enjoying listening to the playful antics of some young students running around and slamming doors in the hallway just down from her room, until the activity is interrupted by the "sharp sarcastic voice of the dormitory matron" (15). When the matron demands to know who among the girls is responsible for the door slamming, she is met only with their silence: "But it's just as well, because none of you can tell the truth." Sending them off to breakfast, she concludes: "And *please* at least try to act like ladies and not savages from the backwoods." On hearing this, Helga wonders if the matron, Miss MacGooden, realized "that most of her charges had actually come from the backwoods. Quite recently too" (15). Miss MacGooden is described as ugly, prim, and humorless, "with a face like dried leather," a woman who "prided herself on being a 'lady' from one of the best families—an uncle had been a congressman in the period of the Reconstruction" (16). Neither Helga nor the young girls under Miss MacGooden's charge can claim the family origins central to what Helga calls "ladyness." Family and kinship early on mark the qualities of vocal subjects in the novella, while the collectivity of young girls from the "backwoods" become voiceless background—shapes, icons, and colors that come and go. And, like Asian exclusion, the silence of the migrant black girls is "just as well" and makes no difference politically since no one can tell—or distinguish—the truth. Helga's satirical *Plea for Color* is an appeal for acceptance of these other collectivities, ones that—lacking proper kinship, origins, or family formations—are part of the constellations of sociality and historical forces that strain the very structure of narrative representation.

Unsurprisingly, when the principal of Naxos, Robert Anderson, asks Helga why she feels she must leave their community, she responds that she's miserably unhappy: "The people here don't like me. They don't think I'm in the spirit of the work. And I'm not, not if it means suppression of individuality and beauty" (23). When Anderson asks her to stay to be the voice of loyal dissent, she retorts: "It isn't pleasant to be always *made to appear* in the wrong, even when I know I'm right" (23; emphasis added). As she speaks, she notices that his "gaze was on her now, searching. 'Queer,' she thought, 'how some brown people have gray eyes. Gives them a strange, unexpected appearance. A little frightening.'" For Helga, Naxos is a disciplinary machine that cuts everyone to fit a pattern—in which speech is subordinate to the shapes of bodily order. Like the girls in the dormitory who, for Miss MacGooden, are without the capacity for truth, savages whose lack of speech fortunately does not matter, Helga's excessive individualism and aesthetic values make her the very figure of wrong, even when she's right. Crucially, it is her persistent aestheticizing —turning the occasions of her life and the contexts of her speech into images, shapes, and colors to be studied—that draws her attention to the "queer" elements in social life.

When, later in the novel, Helga takes a ship to Denmark—that country where, "if misfortune and illness came upon one, everyone else, including the State, felt bound to give assistance, a lift on the road to the regaining of independence"—it is Helga's racial difference, a difference crucial to the Danes' liberal welfare state, that dislocates her control over aesthetic expression. In Copenhagen, Helga falls under the influence of her aunt and uncle, who hang their aspirations to break into the circles of the city's cultural elite on Helga's performance of exotic otherness. Preparing to attend her first social function in Denmark, Helga chooses too sober an outfit and receives unsolicited style advice from her aunt. Her aunt recommends something brighter, reminding her: "You're young. And you're a foreigner, and different. You must have bright things to set off the color of your lovely brown skin. Striking things, exotic things" (70). Helga tries on one outfit after another as her aunt searches for just the thing to pull off her "exotic" aesthetic. In an irony that Helga will come to appreciate only later in her stay, it is Helga's "natural" and "unadorned" self that fits the bill: " 'Now that,' [her aunt] said, pointing to the Chinese red dressing-gown in which Helga had wrapped herself when at last the fitting was over, 'suits you.' " Though Helga knows her aunt could not be more right, having declared the Orientalist interior of her room in New York to match her aesthetic sense perfectly, she is disturbed and made uneasy by her aunt's willful denial of Helga's innate Europeanness. More troubling still is her aunt's elated sense of Helga's absolute identity with the Orientalist and primitivist objects that are for Helga simply elements of an aesthetic sense.

For Helga, to be the element in another's tableau takes the shine off her Orientalist performances, threatening to reduce her to the muteness of an actor in a *tableau vivant*. On a day of shopping with her aunt and admirer, the popular painter Axel Olsen, Helga's own pleasures in taking in the tableaux in the shop windows are interrupted by the constant stares of others on the street: "Their progress through the shops was an event . . . Some stared surreptitiously, some openly, and some stopped dead in front of her in order more fully to profit by their stares. 'Den Sorte' (the Black) dropped freely, audibly, from many lips" (75). Helga's very presence could turn any public place into a setting for an impromptu tableau, a spectatorial economy that inspires its viewers' speech, the audible declarations of racial recognition that resolve the meaning of the tableau.

Olsen selects Helga's new wardrobe, assimilating her to the iconography of his painterly world: "It was almost in a mood of rebellion that Helga faced the fantastic collection of garments incongruously laid out in the quaint, stiff, pale old room" (75). Olsen's iconography is decidedly Orientalist, threatening Helga's sense of self-authorization and autonomy: "There were batik dresses in which mingled indigo, orange, green, vermilion and black; dresses of velvet and chiffon in screaming colors . . . There was a black Manila shawl . . . a leopard-skin coat . . . There were turban like hats of metallic silks . . . a nauseous Eastern perfume, shoes with dangerously high heels." Gradually, however, Helga's "perturbation subsided in the unusual pleasure of having so many new and expensive clothes at one time. She began to feel a little excited, incited" (76).

At first she is sure that—"incited" to perform an exotic and Oriental difference, for which she intentionally adds a "slow, faltering Danish," deciding it "more attractive than a nearer perfection"—she can still achieve the autonomy and belonging she so craves. Yet she soon realizes that the aesthetic—its experience, meaning, and narration—belongs to the tableau's national viewers, a group from whom she is permanently estranged. Helga's time in Copenhagen is a period of intense cultural and political strife. She encounters ardent conservative nationalists who worry that Danish culture is disappearing and who seek a revitalization of its folk traditions; liberal and cosmopolitan advocates who see Copenhagen as contributing to a new European culture developing in Europe's largest cities; and modernist leftists who embrace internationalism, democracy, and oppositional cultural politics. Helga's suitor in Denmark, Axel Olsen, is a member of the middle group, his coming and goings reported in the leftist Danish paper, *Politikken*. His studio, which Helga visits frequently after agreeing to sit for a portrait, is an eccentric space located exactly opposite the city's Folkemuseum, in which can be found wax tableaux and panoramas that depict in visual narrative Denmark's folk culture and history. When it is complete, Olsen's painting of Helga is boldly modernist, primitivist, and sexually suggestive, a response to the disempowering culture of spectacle promoted by his conservative museum neighbors. Transformed into a boldly erotic and primitive shape, Helga recoils from Olsen's portrait, enraged that she must see herself through his boldly expressed perspective. Her confidence that in Copenhagen her search for belonging and freedom would finally come to an end is quickly eroded by her repeated encounters with the exoticism and Orientalism that pervades Denmark's cosmopolitan and liberal culture. She realizes that it is the very Danish cosmopolitanism and liberalism, which she has sought out, that makes her into yet another object expressive of the colonial worlds that sustains the Danish state she so admires. That is, in Copenhagen, it is Helga's racial and gendered differences that make her into an object and figure in a Danish structure of feeling, of a European nation in the ferment of change. Olsen's painting counterintuitively expresses national belonging that sympathizes with the racial differences it can so clearly see.

Helga discovers that the frames are outside of her, that her struggle for autonomy and freedom is dependent on the juridical, cultural, and political regimes of belonging. Membership in these regimes is what she feels is missing inside herself. She is ashamed, feeling that she is responsible for this failure to belong. Written out of regimes of belonging, she becomes a "silently speculative spectator," engaged in "a suspensive conflict in which were fused doubts, rebellions, expediency, and urgent longings" (85). What she wants to hide away and forget is the racial ascription that destroys the achievement of autonomy, the gendered ascription that recalls her status of being without kin and history. Unsettled again, she leaves Denmark, choosing racial belonging and championing her heretofore denied desire for the race man Robert Anderson, only to wed a preacher who takes her to the southern "backwoods" when Anderson rebuffs her desire. At the novel's close, Helga has returned to the southern state in which the novella opened, but this time to the impoverished, makeshift communities on the edge of southern cities and towns. In fact, her return migration takes her to one of those communities that make up the "savage backwoods" so despised by Miss MacGooden at the novel's beginning, where "none . . . can tell the truth" (15). At first, Helga is enchanted by her new life, feeling herself to belong precisely where, as Miss MacGooden suggests, collectivity is the "other" to literary publics and the normative, factual, and social truths of the public sphere of which literature is a part. But by the novel's close, Helga's identifications are just imaginary relations, while her body and self are progressively ruined—outside the social bond among the women in the town, left to housework and the endless tribulationstality of pregnancies and births.

Helga Crane alternates between blending into and becoming yet another one of the objects and commercial wares that litter the *tableau vivant*, on the one hand, and, on the other hand, trying to achieve the status of the subject (such as the abstract viewer constructed by the modern tableaux) through the political and epistemic control of the "otherness" caught in these tableaux. If the latter is suggestive of Marx's description of the commodity form and the rationalized and abstract social relations that commute their material particularity, then the former is suggestive of Walter Benjamin's discussion of the window and table displays of urban arcades. For Benjamin, the commercial arcade, with its global treasures for sale, creates an unexpected awareness of the strange affinities, worldwide contiguities, and material incommensurabilities that the tableau of objects in their variety and heterogeneity produce—the dream world of modern capitalism.[50] In the unpredictable mixture of these objects and cultural fragments, modernity is experienced less as a rational structure that progressively expands, homogenizing time and difference, than as a world in flux, a historical moment full of contingencies that disturb our fixed forms of description and knowing—connections yet to be made. In these moments, Helga Crane is herself a fragment or figure among incommensurate cultural fragments and commercial objects, heteronomous and part of the material differences that demarcate the excluded terrain from which subjectivity proper arises and tries to achieve the status of the subject (such as the viewer of modern tableaux) by politically controlling the "otherness" caught within these tableaux.

Helga returns to the South as a minister's wife, seeking through uplifting others to establish her status as feminine subject within the patriarchal culture that dominates the women in the black town in which she has settled—her last migration in the text. At this point, we see just how profoundly the desire to control the "otherness" within a modernity of tableaux modernity constitutes Helga in a regime of perception that abstracts her from the social world in which she lives—the world that is the limit of modern belonging. Seeking to uplift those around her— which was also the goal of Naxos, where she began—Helga mistakes rural black women as primarily objects of her power, inhabiting the panoptic standpoint of modern moral disciple, differences in need of a taxonomy. Helga's attempts to control and uplift southern women in the "backwoods" ultimately fail. Although it is her rage against the modern homogenous and disciplinary subject promoted at Naxos that drives the narrative, discipline at the end of the novel—the assimilation of heterogeneity into a taxonomy of differences—is precisely what enables narrative closure. If refusing the status of subject and recoiling from the formality of uplift, and merging instead with the "otherness" found in modernity's *tableaux vivants*, is the symbolic act that begins her migrations and journey of unbelonging, it is also the act that formally begins the text narrative. In this sense, it is formally important that it is Helga's efforts at uplifting women, a final drive to reconcile modern subjectivity with black female differences, that cause not only the end of her migrations in the text but the end of narrativity as well. Ironically, what Helga declares in the opening pages as the cause for her migration—"The South. Naxos. Negro education. Suddenly she hated them all" (7)—is nearly identical to the closing tableau, in which we encounter Helga at work at the novel's end.

Some critics position the novel as a negative narrative of migration, a depiction of failed migration. In realist narrative, the subject is made self-identical through the course of its travels and development over time, integrating with itself through narrative time, space, and subjectivity. However, I read the text's closing tableau, in which the means for narrativity (especially in its antirealist and nonnormative form) come to an end, as evidence of Larsen's attempt to critique the form of unified subjectivity that interracial marriage and uplift—and the new racialized and gendered juridico-institutional logic that they together exemplify— produce, the historically and politically created ontological uncertainty that is Helga Crane. Helga's willingness to be trapped within these regimes of power is precisely a freezing and fixing of not only racialized female migration but of the material "otherness," contingency, and discontinuities that race and racialized gender force into experience and view in a racial capitalist and global modernity.[51]

Although it is Helga's attempts to control the tableaux, to be the abstract national or modern viewer, that leads over and over again to mistaken identity and failure, it is her aesthetic sense, her embodied relation to the "otherness" to which she is bound that expresses an alternative. In the aesthetic, a different structure of feeling emerges. When Helga is inside them, she feels that these tableaux express her aesthetic. Therefore, they express affinities between the frequently mute Helga—who throughout the narrative suffers quietly the insults of non-

belonging that her intimates and companions unknowingly hurl at her—
and the Orientalist objects of the tableaux. Yet in Larsen's hands, these
tableaux of Helga's aesthetic are the point of critique from which the
narrative of belonging is observed and interrupted. The queer logic of
inclusion that organizes Larsen's tableaux not only refuses to discrimi-
nate between thing and person, animate and inanimate objects, grand
and small forces, the definitive statement and the nearly invisible gesture, but they also include as elements that are separable, if dialectically
linked, material practices and the universalizing symbolic forms—such as
citizenship and the law—that give those practices their meanings and
their force in shaping social perceptions, epistemologies, and bodily
experiences. Because these tableaux are read and not merely seen, Larsen
uses the nominating force of language to produce in a single space or
tableau both the material and immaterial forces—the contents and the
frames—that together produce liberal capitalist modernity.

Perhaps it is for this reason that when, in the middle of the novel,
Helga finds herself in a prohibition-era New York jazz club—with its
flaunting and breaking of rules, its merging of criminal and cultural
pleasures, and high and low classes—she is irritated by the spectacle
about her and her complicity with it, finding its collectivity lewd in relation to her middle-class values. Yet she is unable to suppress her aesthetic
sense, caught in the rhythms and beats of the club: "Strangled by the
savage strains of music, the crowd became a swirling mass" (61). And:

> For the hundredth time she marveled at the gradations within this
> oppressed race of hers. A dozen shades slid by. There was sooty black,
> shiny black, taupe, mahogany, bronze, copper, gold, orange, yellow
> peach, ivory, pinky white, pastry white. There was yellow hair, brown
> hair . . . She saw black eyes in white faces, brown eyes in yellow faces,
> blue eyes in tan faces. Africa, Europe, perhaps a pinch of Asia, in fantas-
> tic motley of ugliness and beauty, semi-barbaric, sophisticated, exotic
> were here. But she was blind to its charm, purposely aloof and a little
> contemptuous, and soon her interest in the moving mosaic waned. (61)

For a moment Helga is able to ask about the "Asia" within blackness and
about the alienage of racial difference. She feels what she has no "interest" in. That is, her aesthetic is not part of the modern and national

public sphere in which desire and interests, as well as bodily life and reason, align. And she leaves at the level of a structure of feeling the black Pacific that still has not emerged beside the Western black Atlantic.

To close, Larsen's use of the mulatta figure resignifies black women's citizenship as a form of racial alienage. Larsen thus remarks on the global and national functions of the state, revealing important linkages in the limits of representability within the public sphere of both gendered black migrations to industrial cities and US engagements with a transpacific modernity. Larsen once wrote in a letter to Carl Van Vechten, the white photographer and author of the sensationalist slumming novel, *Nigger Heaven* (1926): "It *is* nice to find someone writing as if he didn't absolutely despise the age in which he lives. And surely, it is more interesting to belong to one's own time, to share its peculiar vision, catch that flying glimpse of the panorama that no subsequent generation can ever recover."[52] And as Nella Larsen's work reveals, to "belong to one's own time," to find its possibilities and contingent meanings, we must be willing to forgo those fixed and continuous images of the panorama that national belonging feeds us. We must approach the institutions, forms, and sites that convey belonging—most powerfully in the United States of the early twentieth century, the institutions of sociology, literature, and the public sphere—as the contradictory formations of a racial and gendered modernity, letting our glimpse of the immense panorama lead us to this insight and inspire our appreciation of the variety of alternatives. Because we can catch only flying glimpses of this modernity without belonging(s), we will not be able to definitively separate subjects and objects, foreground and background, speech and silence, the national and the international, the citizen and the alien, or pleasure and loss. And perhaps this is the way in which we can legitimately and consistently refuse to "absolutely despise" the otherwise violently achieved age in which we live.

INTERLUDE   There is a tradition that is catastrophe.
            —WALTER BENJAMIN, *The Arcades Project*

The logic of this book's organization is to
divide my investigation of legal and political emancipation into two distinct twentieth-century periods of state formation.
As I argue in chapters 1 and 2, new forms
of state were dependent on epistemic
structures and categories, such as the social, that in turn produced and were produced by new forms and understandings
of race as well as other formations of social difference and alterity. In the twentieth century, it has been the modern disciplines of knowledge—especially the
social sciences—that have generated the
epistemic structures and forms by which
the liberal state governs in racial capitalism. W. E. B. Du Bois and Nella Larsen
are among the black intellectuals of the
early twentieth century who investigate
the terms of subjectivity and difference—
such as belonging—genealogically, connecting the epistemic forms that govern
subjectivity and self-reflexivity to the
changing structures of legitimate violence that define the formation of groups
and classes in racial capitalism.

Modern racialized gender and sexuality are part of a genealogy of race, under-

stood as the material conditions of possibility of modern social forms—including the nation form and citizenship. We might call this the paradox of race in the twentieth century, one that Du Bois argues emerges when black subjects gain political subjectivity within US political modernity. Though Du Bois's narrative resolution to this paradox is to advance an appeal for universal manhood rights, producing gender normativity and a view of black women as the bearers of tradition, *The Souls of Black Folk* preserves the ambivalences, ambiguity, and critical negativity that are an effect of the materiality of race—that is, the historical and discursive forces and social relations that produce race and inhere as its mark—and that are the basis for a dialectical critique of the forms and perceptual categories of the modern nation-state, such as history.

Gender and sexual normativity in the first half of the twentieth century was crucial to the normalization of race within political modernity, and it has been a crucial aspect of black feminism in this period to make racialized gender and sexuality the formations that yield the dialectical critiques of the perceptual forms and categories through which political modernity is experienced. Modern sociology and the modern public sphere collectively produce an understanding of civil society and the liberal democratic state that generates subjectivity as a rationale for the liberal state to employ nonpolitical violence against particular groups and social relations, most especially black poor and gendered migrants and the postslavery racial capitalist social order of which they are a part, as well as Asian migrants who emerge from the transnational politics of western Atlantic internationalism and the colonial battles, wars, and worlds it produced in the racialized transpacific.

Chapters 3 and 4 take up these conditions as they are refracted across the later twentieth century. For any student of the early twentieth century, the resonances with the last quarter of the century are difficult to miss. Perhaps most importantly for my inquiry, both eras are marked by unprecedented migration to the United States. Between eight and nine million immigrants arrived per decade in the period between the mid-1880s and the late-1910s. These numbers were unmatched until the period beginning in the mid-1980s, but from then through the end of the century, about ten million immigrants arrived per decade. In each era, US nativism confronted the strong liberal internationalism of the political and economic elites, while the academic disciplines sought to produce objective and positive knowledge about the phenomena of migration and global modernity debated and hotly contested between nativists and internationalists. Both eras were periods of vigorous state making in the context of fundamental changes in the structure of the US economy, geopolitical relations, the regimes of value, and the dominant sectors of capitalist valorization. Indeed, some scholars have come to think of the early twentieth century as the first instance of a globalization led by what became the G8 countries. This group of modern industrialized economies, each with its own colonial holdings and territories, included the United States, Britain, France, Germany, Russia, and Japan. We can think of the early twentieth century as the time of emergence of the modern industrial national economy, the development of the liberal and racial state form, and the use of the state for advancing the global commercial and economic interests of industrial capital.

In like manner, at the end of the twentieth century, the United States was in a new postindustrial period of capitalist emergence. This era is marked by a globalized industrial economy, the development of a neoliberal state form, and the use of the US state to advance the political and economic interests of financial and producer services capital through the opening of the closed economies of the Second and Third Worlds. The uncanny convergence of expressions of US sovereignty—specifically through the regulation of migration and the US colonial wars at each end of the twentieth century—is at first remarkable. In fact, it was in the first quarter of the century that US sovereignty over the rights of migration as we currently understand it developed. In the early twentieth century, immigration and US colonial wars and police actions were the basis on which new bureaucracies, institutions, technologies, apparatuses of violence, and logics of nationality, sovereignty, and the state developed. And in the late twentieth century, our experience of the twin developments of unprecedented labor migrations and US imperial wars and police actions are entirely mediated and constituted through the social and perceptual structures established by the earlier period.

Indeed, as Mae Ngai and Jonathan Inda have argued, the illegal immigrant that mediates the lives of twelve million undocumented Mexican and Third World immigrants at the end of the twentieth century is a political subjectivity invented only in the first quarter of that century.[1] Moreover, it is the racial logics, structures, and practices that produced and organized sovereignty and legitimate violence in the first quarter of the century that has generated the sets of contradictions that late-twentieth-century liberal multiculturalism has sought to manage, in spite of the pressures of counterhegemonic antiracist social and cultural politics. And as Angela Davis, Michelle Alexander, and others have argued, the genealogy of rightlessness that depoliticizes the disproportionate incarceration of blacks and Latinos in the late twentieth century returns us to the early-twentieth-century use of the Thirteenth Amendment's exemption for servitude that produced the racialized convict lease labor system on which the US Southern economy depended.[2]

There are other central reasons to link work on the first and last quarters of the twentieth century. In the first quarter, the transformations in the US economy and the rise of US internationalism corresponded with domestic transformations of the US government. US Progressives became state builders, creating the modern bureaucracies that organized governance through the form of the modern state. Not only was the modern university invented in this period, but the disciplines and interdisciplinary methods that developed were critical in organizing the state's identity, its ways of ruling, and its understanding of social participation. Within the emerging scholarly fields of history and politics, for example, sovereignty became a central point of inquiry. Woodrow Wilson's influential *The State* used the interdisciplinary methods of historical and political studies dominant in the German universities at that time to argue that the Anglo-European state is a historical ontology. This massive work traces the origins of modern sovereignty through European legal and political works, showing the various textual traditions out of which US sovereignty emerges and which it modifies. By the 1920s, the historical school of political science no longer held sway as a means of understanding the state. Instead, modern sociology—with its emphasis on positivism, abstract consciousness, and behavioral structures—became the crucial social science of state.

US internationalism in this period is governed by two differing logics. The first—liberal institutionalism—is a US-led advocacy of national self-determination, championed by Wilson through the First World War, whose colonial form in relation to non-European countries had been revealed perhaps two decades earlier in the colonization of the Philippines as what was called benevolent assimilation. The second is a form of US isolationism—or realism in internationalism—perhaps better understood as an aggressive defense of US interests globally, either through a withdrawal from international structures and relations or through the use of military offensives to promote the primacy of US security and the maintenance of its sovereignty in the Western Hemisphere. This included the occupation of Haiti till 1934, the purchasing of the Danish West Indies, and the use of military power or gunboat diplomacy in Veracuz, Mexico. US racial politics are transformed through the first instantiation of the modern state and the centralized federal government in this period. Reconstruction confronts redemption politics, and the progressive, liberal state institutionalizes retrenchment through differential practices of exclusion of racialized working peoples—including Mexicans, Native Americans, Asians, and African Americans—from so-called national democratic politics and the emerging biopolitical state.

The late twentieth century similarly witnessed the emergence of a new economic form for US capitalism, differing internationalisms—the Washington Consensus or neoliberal school, and the neoconservative neorealist school—and an intense reconstruction of the state form in its engagement with the global economy. Like early-twentieth-century liberalism, late-twentieth-century neoliberalism produced a new set of normative and dominant logics for the articulation of the state form and the expression of legitimate violence. Additionally, similar to the Progressive Era, the late twentieth century has witnessed a tremendous explosion in civil society institutions and state bureaucracies—what some have dubbed the nonprofit-industrial complex—for everything from the regulation of sexual practices and HIV transmission to the management of addictions and of refugee populations. And most importantly for my study, the close of the twentieth century has produced once more the politics of sovereignty expressed over labor migration and war as a politics of race, gender, and sexuality.

If in developing a racial governmentality that organized the state form, the early twentieth century laid the foundations for the US welfare state, then the late twentieth century can be characterized by the undoing of that welfare state. The modes, epistemes, and logics by which legitimate violence is generated and sustained at the end of the twentieth century have not only been different from those of the welfare state, they have strategically invalidated that previous knowledge. Whereas racial violence was crucial to the making of the national state at the onset of the twentieth century and the first era of Anglo-European globalization, it was central to the strategic unmaking of the national state at the close of the twentieth century in the second era of so-called postcolonial globalization.

PART II

THREE

Rights-Based Freedom
with Violence

Immigration, Sexuality, and the
Subject of Human Rights

I came to the United States from Pakistan in 1991 as a student. I had come to the
United States because I had a thought that coming out as a gay man would be
safer for me in this country. After graduating in 1995, I moved to New York City
and became a member of the South Asian Lesbian and Gay Association, SALGA. I
had realized that going back to Pakistan was not an option for me anymore. I would
not be able to do the kinds of work that I wanted to do with safety in Pakistan.
There is no infrastructure in place in Pakistan where I could obtain legal recourse if
threatened for being queer. As queer immigrants in this country are usually placed
outside immigration law, applying for asylum seemed to be the only strategy where
I did not feel that I was compromising myself as a gay man. Heterosexual marriage
and working a job I did not like for years to get a green card did not seem like
attractive choices. Choosing to apply for asylum instead of availing myself of other
options also became a political choice. Furthermore, I strongly believed in my claim
and felt that under U.S. immigration law I fit the categories of asylum. I did have a
genuine fear that if I led life as an openly gay man in Pakistan, my life would be in
danger.—SAEED RAHMAN, "Shifting Grounds for Asylum: Female Genital Surgery
and Sexual Orientation"[1]

The document is not the fortunate tool of a history that is primarily and fundamentally *memory*; history is one way in which a society recognizes and develops a
mass of documentation with which it is inextricably linked. To be brief let us say
that history, in its traditional form, undertook to "memorize" the *monuments* of the
past, transform them into *documents*, and lend speech to those traces, which, in
themselves, are often not verbal, or which say in silence something other than what
they actually say; in our time, history is that which transforms *documents* into
monuments.—MICHEL FOUCAULT, *The Archaeology of Knowledge*

This chapter builds on the understanding of the state that the first half of the
book developed: an ideal form that effects regulatory and coercive powers
within institutions. To demonstrate how

this understanding of the state continues and changes from the earlier twentieth century as the state confronts late-twentieth-century racialized migration and globalization, I would like to observe twin developments at the close of the twentieth century that organize the current epistemology and politics of sexuality. The first development, signaling a moment of legal enfranchisement, is the extension of US constitutional, or federal, subjectivity to variously queer social identities and cultural persons when the Supreme Court overturned its 1986 decision in *Bowers v. Hardwick* by its rulings in *Romer v. Evans* and *Lawrence v. Texas*, in 1996 and 2003, respectively. The second, which occurred in the 1980s and 1990s, is the institutionalization of a positivist multiculturalism across the disciplines and professional schools of the late modern university, functioning as both an ideological apparatus for the state, as Louis Althusser argues, and as the representative apparatus for the production of legitimate knowledge.[2] It has been the positivist framing, reception, and attempted acculturation of the heterogeneous politics of multiculturalism during these two decades that has repurposed those conflicts to serve the interests of what Angela Davis, Lisa Lowe, and others have termed liberal multiculturalism.[3] Together, these developments have transformed the norms that produce sexuality, yielding on the one hand a subject of sexual rights, and on the other hand a subject of queer epistemology.

The spheres of justice and knowledge both reproduce racial difference and invisibility as they are transformed by global capitalist imperatives, which are frequently articulated as the rise of neoliberalism. Here I treat neoliberalism as the ideology of rule and logic of state practice in the United States that corresponds to changing global regimes and techniques of capital accumulation in the last quarter of the twentieth century. What I understand as a neoliberal orientation of the state form in the 1980s and 1990s is marked by a legalization of the state. By this I mean that in the last quarter of the twentieth century, the state gains a legal ontology, the apparatus of a general or contractarian will. That is, in spite of the historical definition of the state produced in the early twentieth century and the modernizing definition of the state produced by the social sciences in the 1920s, the state gains a legal essence in the late twentieth century. In this later era, the state is judged by its ability to achieve fairness and neutrality in its engagement with social relations.

Connected to a politics of racial retrenchment that began in earnest with Ronald Reagan's election as president in 1980, the state has relied heavily on the judiciary as the branch most representative of the ideal of the neutral state. In the case of racial disparity, this has meant that the state addresses racism through the affirmation and protection of individual rights, while using a juridical rights-bearing subject as a means of silencing all alternative discourses and systemic accounts of antiracism by projecting them as racist.

We can speak of a neoliberal university emerging in this time that similarly promotes the contractarian and neutrality ideals of the state, especially in its functions as an ideological state apparatus. For the neoliberal university, neutrality is achieved through a positivist framework for race. Under positivism, the promotion of race as a legitimate interest of the university is defended through frameworks that, like the juridical state, avoid strong normative, systemic, or moral claims, choosing rather the neutrality ideal of diversity. Jodi Melamed has elegantly named this normative framework of race "neoliberal multiculturalism." As an epistemic and ideological formation, "neoliberal multiculturalism sutures official antiracism to state policy in a manner that prevents the calling into question of global capitalism." It has been the positivist domination of the interpretation of race that "deracializes official antiracism to an unprecedented degree, turning (deracialized) racial reference into a series of rhetorical gestures of ethical right and certainty. Concepts previously associated with 1980s and 1990s liberal multiculturalism—'openness,' 'diversity,' and 'freedom'—are recycled such that "open societies" and "economic freedoms" (shibboleths for neoliberal measures) come to signify human rights that the United States has a duty to secure for the world."[4]

The neoliberal university emerges out of the systemic racial contradictions of the modern university, which produced an epistemological system and order that was constituted through and reproduced racial exclusivity within its disciplines and practices, while producing knowledge of and for the Western nation-state that it saw and promoted as universally valid. If the opening of the university to a broader group of students in the 1970s and the establishment of a normatively postcolonial global order brought these contradictions to the forefront, the neoliberal university interpreted them as problems of diversity within the student body and the professoriate. Diversity has been the means by which the neoliberal university and its academic disciplines constructed a hegemonic consensus on the resolution of the multicultural conflicts and struggles in academe and the broader society in the 1970s and 1980s. Though some practices of interdisciplinarity in the 1980s and 1990s sought to address these systemic contradictions in the epistemological form of the university, the marginalization and ghettoization—in relation to the modern disciplines—of these interdisciplinary practices limited their force.

The neoliberal university of the late 1970s and 1980s had a student population that was more racially diverse than that of its predecessor. Less an example of the university's active efforts at transformation, this was primarily the result of the changing profile of the college-age population in the United States. Indeed, as universities admitted the members of this population, diversity quickly supplanted racial equity. Hence by the 1990s, many research universities had fewer African American students than they had had in the 1970s, even as they maintained a steadfast commitment to diversity. Diversity, then, became the way in which the neoliberal university comprehended this transformation in the national college-age population. The increase in the number of students of color, immigrants or students with immigrant parents, and foreign students prompted a systemic understanding of diversity. In nearly every quarter of the university, from the administration to individual departments, "diversity" became the hegemonic term and framework that supplanted the project of making the university meet the demands of racial equity.

Positivist multiculturalism expanded beyond the purview of modern demography, however, to constitute a fulcrum for managing the breakup of foundationalisms across the disciplines, occasioned by the rise of capitalist globalization and its attendant denaturalization of the nation form crucial to the modern division of disciplinary knowledges. Indeed, contemporary interdisciplinary identity studies—such as women's studies, ethnic studies, postcolonial studies, and gay, lesbian, and queer studies, all of which rely heavily on the humanities and were designed to address the unevenness of knowledge that such disciplinary foundationalisms created over the century—have been the sites of some of the most intense pressures to formalize their objects and areas of study through the lens of positivist multiculturalism. In this instance, "race" designates that which is not identical with the positivist concept of diversity, a remainder that haunts the institutionalization of contemporary interdisciplinary identity studies.

In other words, the incorporation of the counterhegemonic multicultural struggles of the last two decades of the twentieth century—of which the interdisciplinary politics of identity and difference were a part—into a new hegemony or state form through the regulative framework of empiricism and positivism has returned a meaning of identity and difference to interdisciplinary fields that threatens their reconciliation both to a formally abstract and seemingly value-neutral state and to the modern disciplinary arrangement of knowledge that they rose to combat. These developments are particularly relevant as we consider the impact of the modern university as the apparatus for the production of legitimate and neutral knowledge for the legal sphere and judicial practice in the 1990s. The form and breadth of contemporary positivist understandings of identity and difference in US institutions generally— and especially within judicial practice—have been an effect of the neoliberal university's management of the racial contradictions that emerged as a consequence of the movements for racial equity, the rise of postcolonial states in the Global South, and a worldwide capitalist economy.

These racial contradictions within the epistemic structure and practices of the university are central to the development of new state understandings of legitimate (and hence illegitimate) violence. They are also the fulcrum for what we might call a positivist homosexuality, which can address the state. The recognition of a positivist homosexuality within domains such as US human rights law does not resolve the racial contradictions that neoliberal multiculturalism seeks to manage, but instead forwards those contradictions to the judicial sphere. The resulting norms that rights law establishes to regulate bodies and cultural lives are the way by which the US neoliberal state disavows the figure of racialized sexuality (or queer of color formations) as the limits of its coherency.

Queer critiques of gay and lesbian identity powerfully disturb the rights-bearing sexual subject of US civil and human rights law. Particularly in its focus on norms as the contemporary mode by which capitalist social reproduction occurs, making the subject a key site of material struggle, queer studies has much to offer critical ethnic studies. Moreover—to the degree that ethnic studies has relied on empirical sociology, economics, and positivist modes of history to account for, represent, and critique racial and economic inequities—norm-based epistemologies of race, gender, and sexuality have been indispensable in ethnic studies' investigations of issues concerning social justice. In other words, an important paradox structures critical ethnic studies: although we must retain certain commitments to empirical and positivist knowledge production in order to understand and have effective accounts of systemic racial inequities, the ongoing racialization of the capitalist processes, the legal and political modes of disenfranchisement within representative democracy, and the changing global practices of capitalist accumulation and valorization in our current political context, these commitments have entrenched norms of intelligibility that preserve the positivist domination of noninstrumentalist modes of knowing, modes that address the forms of power in US society (including positivism) that regulate or efface racial, gendered, sexual, class, and historical alterities.

Engaging the politics of alterity is crucial to any project that strives not only for social justice but also for a participatory and radical democracy, a crucial aspect of the movements that founded ethnic studies. Moreover, in highly differentiated capitalism these forms of power, which are central to biopolitics and governmentality, are constitutive of and determine the social practices of accumulation, valorization, and violence. Recounting the feminist queer studies engagement with sociological positivism through a theorization of sexuality as a regulative norm can be a valuable exercise for those of us committed to the paradox of social justice, by which I mean the epistemic frameworks that organize our categories and knowledge of inequality.

Given the tensions between critical ethnic studies and queer studies, how might our transnational times suggest ways to further the methods of queer studies? Rather than restricting the field to destabilizing the norms that constitute genital sex and heterosexual hegemony, I think we can argue that when we put "sex" under erasure, what is left after is the demand to tell the history of the material detritus, the fragments and shards that are also sexuality. Queer studies has probably been the interdisciplinary field that is the most critical of the positivism that makes modern politics the violent enforcement of regulatory norms. As a critique of positivism and the positivist subject of rights, a key concept-metaphor in queer studies has been that of haunting, used to characterize both the active violence and the limits of modern movements for legal rights and other forms of political practice that seek to claim the state. Haunting has brought to the fore questions of history, archives, law, and violence. But haunting also brings the epistemological preoccupations of queer studies into sharp relief against the alternate accounts of haunting offered in critical ethnic studies, as we saw in Avery Gordon's account of haunting discussed in this book's introduction.

The epistemic battles within queer studies that focus on the question of haunting reveal both the usefulness and the limits of the concept-metaphor as a form of critique that can engage and develop alternatives to state power and legitimate violence. Thus, despite the disavowal within GLBTQ studies of race as constitutive to the object of sexuality— indeed, as its very frame and condition of possibility—we ought to observe the institutional battles in gay, lesbian, and queer studies between positivist and poststructuralist accounts of sexuality and identity (battles that have shaped different approaches to addressing the public sphere on the topic of gay marriage, for example) as a constitutive part of the racialized, diasporic, and transnational economic contradictions that generated the heterogeneous cultural and political mobilizations that shaped and were ultimately displaced by neoliberal multiculturalism. That is, we can rethink the debates within queer studies as materially determined by a late-twentieth-century politics of race, broadly conceived. Furthermore, we can advance a materialist critique of queer studies that not only avows this determination by race but that also sees the possibility of destabilizing the liberal multiculturalist account of race to discover alternative possibilities within our modernity, possibilities that affirm race in contrast to its positivist and liberal regulation and that might be as useful for queer studies and for the disciplines that it critiques. In linking these two observations—the legal recognition of homosexuality and the consolidation of positivist liberal multiculturalism within the educational apparatus—it is clear that interdisciplinary practice is currently one site where we can see the contradictions of neo-

liberal state formation. I turn now to a discussion of the law as an archive
of racialized knowledge and the structure of legitimate violence.

NEOLIBERALISM AND ITS CITIZENS

The sexual history of Asian diasporas is being written across nations,
institutions, and their publics. But what kind of history of sexuality is
being written in this collision of diasporic groups and US space?[5] For
nearly two centuries, this collision has produced a genealogy of sex for
both the US nation-state and the modernized diasporas. The Chinese
prostitute who was the focus of the Page Act of 1875 and the Chinese
bachelor featured in legislation from the Chinese Exclusion Act of 1882
through the Chinese Exclusion Repeal Act of 1943 are just two of the
most famous figures to emerge from this collision.[6]

Here I set my sights on one of the newest figures to emerge from the
annals of the sexual history of the Asian diaspora. This figure, like his
counterparts in previous historical periods, is to be found in legal texts
and supplementary genres, such as works in public health, anthropology,
and psychology. The figure is named the gay Pakistani immigrant, and he
is found in immigration proceedings, court cases, and legal journals.
Though murmurs of his existence were heard before, and debate as to
whether or not he was real continued for a number of years, he crossed a
certain threshold of reality in the mid-1990s and emerged onto the legal,
cultural, and social scene with an attire and voice fully suited to his
claims of equal personhood and a seat at the table. Like his predecessors,
he continues to have his juridical and discursive constitution defined by
US immigration law. The epigraph with which this chapter begins offers
a representative example of his speech, as it has been produced by and
deposited into the annals of law. The epigraph comes from the narrative
testimony of Saeed Rahman, a gay Pakistani immigrant, and was recorded in the pages of the *Columbia Human Rights Law Review* in 1998. A
gay South Asian immigrant living in New York City, Rahman successfully
petitioned the government—through what was then called the Immigration and Naturalization Service (INS)—for asylum based upon his claim
of belonging to a persecuted social group.[7]

Only a few hundred applicants have convinced the US government that their sexual orientation—in Rahman's case, his homosexuality—qualified them for membership in a social group. And Rahman's discourse marks a certain liminality within both normative diasporic formations and the nation-state, each of which is dependent upon the racialized institutions of kinship and family. The very site in which Rahman's homosexuality is recorded and protected by the law is also a site partially deterritorialized from the nation-state. Although US asylum law was until 2003 under the authority of the INS, the judges who preside over these administrative cases are generally considered exempt from some of the mandates of national immigration law that otherwise determine admission into the United States. Instead, these judges' rulings are governed by broadly defined standards of international human rights, established by the 1951 Convention Relating to the Status of Refugees. Hence, as the globalization scholar Saskia Sassen has argued, asylum law is one instance by which nonnational or global forces are creating a de facto immigration policy, one that—far from reinforcing the universality of the nation—is beginning to break the links between sovereignty and the nation-state in important ways.[8] In this way, asylum cases represent anomalous states from the perspective of national right, marking instead the emergence of supposedly new capitalist social formations that are parasites on the modern institutions of the state and its forms of power. If Rahman and the few hundred successful applicants like him enter the nation through the law and the institutions of the border, such as the INS courtroom, their entrance betrays a transformation of those very institutions. Indeed, Rahman's designation as a homosexual within the legal record is a symptom of the contemporary forms and forces of capitalist globalization.

The juridical appearance of the gay Pakistani immigrant must be situated within the context of the neoliberal restructuring of state power. Examining the broader discursive and material reorganization of US immigration policy in the 1990s through the Immigration Act of 1990, moreover, we can see that the reconstitution of state power through the deployment of the concept of "family" constitutes the conditions of possibility for the juridical recognition of the gay Pakistani immigrant. As a figure at the limit of national law, this immigrant marks an important and constitutive tension within the national record and the practice of governance that it subtends. The gay Pakistani immigrant, like the earlier Chinese prostitute and Chinese bachelor, is produced in the conflicts and contradictions expressed by the state. This critique requires us to situate that more recent immigrant figure within the context of neoliberalism—the name for the contemporary mode of capitalist accumulation and the logic that, broadly speaking, organizes current political practice and social rules, enfolding the discursive practice of the family.[9]

Although neoliberalism elaborates a world historical context, its relation to the nation-state differs between the Global North and South. In both regions, neoliberal economic policies and programs that began in the late 1970s have stressed the opening of markets, the financialization of currency regimes, the privatization of the public services sector, and the commodification and capitalization of biological life. Neoliberalism has most powerfully affected the imagined relation between the state and civil society, disorganizing the image if not the actual operation of the so-called closed welfare economies that were dominant during the period of neoliberalism's emergence. As Gayatri Chakravorty Spivak writes in an essay examining the politics of diasporic studies in our transnational times, "within the definition of an ideal civil society, if the state is a welfare state, it is directly the servant of the individual. When increasingly privatized, as in the New World Order [of neoliberalism], the priorities of the civil society are shifted from service to the citizen to capital maximization."[10] Yet, although "the undermining of the civil structures of society is now a global situation," Spivak suggests that: "A general contrast can be made: in the North, welfare structures long in place are being dismantled. The diasporic underclass is often the worst victim. In the South, welfare structures cannot emerge as a result of the priorities of the transnational agencies . . . Political asylum, at first sight so different from economic migration, finally finds it much easier to re-code capitalism as democracy. It too, then, inscribes itself in the narrative of the manipulation of civil structures in the interest of the financialization of the globe."[11] As Spivak argues, the particular structural economic constraints on Global Southern countries—the postcolonial and decolonizing countries—continue to effect a dismantling of the state and the national economy as agencies and sites for social redistribution. Under such constraints, the national citizen as a figure of recent decolonization is by necessity separated from the state. This citizen then operates as a persistent reminder of the state's inability and failure to achieve security for its citizenry against the ravages that daily accompany neoliberal capitalism. Importantly, the seizure of citizenship discourse by the new social movements in the Global South remains a compelling catachresis in the globalized fight for a just life, in part because it necessarily foregrounds the splitting of nation and state from their modernist configuration as the nation-state, due to the pressures of neoliberal capitalism.[12]

Yet, as Spivak reminds us, immigrant advocacy and social justice projects in the Global North that make their appeals to the state are implicated in the very structure of global inequity that continues to separate nation from state in the Global South. In the Global North, Spivak shows, the citizen remains consonant with the state, not despite but precisely because of neoliberalism. We must therefore ask how the promulgation of a politics of citizenship—most often expressed as the desire to partake in civil society and the social safety net designed by the welfare state—might further the ends of neoliberalism rather than thwart them.

Indeed, this observation suggests that we redefine what has colloquially been understood as the contemporary dismantling of the welfare state in the United States. In actuality, neoliberalism has not precipitated the state's complete dismemberment or the erosion of its social safety net. Rather, it has entailed the reorganization of the state through two mutually linked processes. The first is the consolidation of a welfare state for US citizens and professionals who hold green cards in the lower middle through the upper classes. This consolidation promises not social redistribution of wealth but rather the distribution of entitlements and the security to wield and exercise them in a newly internationalized civil society. In this process, the redistributive functions traditionally associated with the welfare state are indistinguishable from the social reproduction and growth of capital. In other words, although the welfare state is organized to reproduce labor power and simultaneously regulate and capture labor, the current postwelfare state is organized to produce wealth through the freeing or releasing of capital. The privatization and public investment of retirement funds and the growth of the 401(k) capital investment sector are cases in point.

The second process is the state's revocation of this welfare structure and of social rights for the racialized poor and the noncitizen class, also in the name of the security of the citizen. Since the mid-1990s, this has become a particularly salient phenomenon. The passage of the three linked federal laws in 1996—the Welfare Reform Act, the Illegal Immigration Reform Act, and the Antiterrorism and Effective Death Penalty Act—worked to politically and economically disenfranchise the noncitizen and simultaneously to redirect capital's surpluses back into the economy. Each of the acts was facilitated discursively through practices of security. Moreover, these acts specifically denied immigrants the basic rights of all workers at a time when the immigrant category was primarily composed of Latino, Asian, and Caribbean people. In another example, the ending of legal affirmative action in wealthy states such as California and Texas coincided with the buildup of the prison-industrial complex in these very states.[13]

In both cases, the political and economic disenfranchisement of the racialized noncitizen immigrant and the racialized poor citizen is devised in the name of securitizing civil society for its entitled subject, the citizen as capitalist. In addition, the current wars in Iraq and Afghanistan, originally justified as protecting American lives, has extended this disenfranchisement, clarifying that the so-called quality of life and standard of living that we attach to US citizenship is, like reporters on the battlefield, embedded directly in the machinery of the neoliberal imperial state, in the occupation and destruction of the fragile but still active infrastructures of Afghanistan, Iraq, Venezuela, North Korea, and any other non-European or non-Zionist country that challenges US policies in its region. The current war has only magnified the conceit that to occupy the place and logic of the US citizen is to willy-nilly situate oneself structurally within an imperial neoliberal state and social formation.

If these latest acts of international war and violence by which the citizen becomes the subject of both neoliberal and imperial forms of power are retroactively coded as a defense of American life, that coding has solidified a discourse of security in which the terrorist is figured as the racialized and sexualized "other" of the citizen.[14] Within the binary that organizes this discourse, the terrorist is indistinguishable from any formation that seeks to contest the welfare rights of the US citizen (as a bearer of capital), in whose name the state survives. Through preemptive defense—the practices that are metaleptically founded on national security—the state has relied on the logic of racial discourse to suture imperial and American multinational corporate endeavors. The US citizen—even and especially as the liberal multicultural subject—is in fact a racial figure on the global scene.[15] By splitting the totality of populations for which the US state operates as a tactic of rule into the bifurcated categories of the citizen or the "international" subject of civility and the varieties of nonnationals and non-citizens whose imperatives to redirect the state as a figure of redistribution and social difference designate them as terroristic, the US state has made security an aspect guaranteed almost exclusively to capital. Under such conditions, the keywords of modern political life—"democracy," "citizenship," "civil society," and "rights"—become the very terms by which the liberal and now the neoliberal representative state legitimates imperialism and racial exploitation as a social good.

And if the construct of the US citizen, and more broadly the subject of international civil law, ratifies the current mode of production—a mode of production for which the state is both a facilitator and destabilizer—that construct in the postwelfare state inaugurates the very opposite of what it ideally represents. That is, the citizen's freedom requires the reduction of the immigrant worker to the state of impermanence; democracy designates military order; and the protection of civil rights ratifies the torture of the enemy combatant. Or, as Marx wrote of the French Empire under the rule of Louis Bonaparte during the era of monopoly capitalist colonialism, "only *one thing* was needed to complete the true form of this republic . . . the [president's] motto, *liberté, égalité, fraternité* must be replaced with the unambiguous words *infantry, cavalry, artillery!*"[16]

We might say that the US citizen subject has become the twenty-first-century version of the "conservative peasant" of whom Marx spoke so scornfully.[17] Petty in his or her interests, heterogeneous to the formation of social classes on the global scale, and resistant to being politically and socially represented by the global proletariat on whose back society prospers, the US citizen under neoliberalism is not a figure of reflection and enlightenment. Indeed, the regulative discourse of citizenship, which continues to operate as the bearer of capitalist rationality, deconstitutes the positions and locations from which a US-based subject might grasp the world historical context of neoliberalism, and the order by which she or he is both ruled and sustained.

FAMILY RIGHTS AND THE REUNIFICATION OF THE STATE

The current conditions suggest that it is imperative for us to refuse the figure of the citizen as the subject of knowledge and as the trope of unity. Moreover, in the context of US asylum cases, as Spivak argues, a narrative that promotes the desire of the racially and sexually excluded to enter US civil society while failing to situate that desire within the context of other desires (of the gendered subaltern, for example) that are structurally foreclosed, violently refused, or made impossible by the fulfillment of the former desire in neoliberal times risks producing current struggles as alibis for exploitation. It also risks foreclosing and forgetting the critical disruptions and radical possibilities that these struggles open up. In order, then, to develop a critical reading of Rahman's testimony, I want to suggest an examination of the conditions that produced it but that are not directly visible in the text in which that testimony appears. That is, I want to explore how family as a regulative formation in the current governmentality organizes the conditions for gay asylum. Hence, we can resituate that supplementary figure as the site for a critique of the regulative function of family.

In a series of pieces about the rush of gays and lesbians seeking marriage licenses from the San Francisco County bureaucracy, an article in the *Los Angeles Times* included the following testimony: " 'We are already a family,' said Mara McWilliams, a 34-year-old health worker from San Jose, as she waited in line for her turn [to receive a marriage certificate] in the clerk's office Sunday morning. Her 8-year-old daughter Serena, clutched her leg . . . 'This is to show the world we are already a family. We're normal professional people. We're not here with our freak on.' "[18] In the contemporary United States, we are witnessing a certain recrossing of what Foucault has named the "deployment of alliances" with the "deployment of sexuality."[19] These different historical currents have once again found their point of convergence and intersection in the space of the family. Moreover, this domain of family, whose centrality to the current governmentality is as indisputable as it is unstable, is also the effect of new articulations of race and sexuality, articulations whose investigation poses specific challenges and critical opportunities for those of us working in queer studies.[20]

In *The History of Sexuality*, Foucault argues that the relations of sex that were organized by a *"deployment of alliance*: a system of marriage, of fixation and development of kinship ties, of transmission of names and possessions" (106) were gradually transformed into the deployment of sexuality, a new set of apparatuses whose object is the individual body. Although both deployments have a constitutive relation to economy, the deployment of alliance arranged the relations of sex to definite statutes in order to direct the proper transmission and circulation of wealth. In contrast, the deployment of sexuality, Foucault argues, "is linked to the economy through numerous and subtle relays . . . proliferating, innovating, annexing, creating and penetrating bodies in an increasingly detailed way, and in controlling populations in an increasingly comprehensive way" (107). If the deployment of alliance waned in importance due to shifts in the mode of production by the late eighteenth century, Foucault argues that its main institution—the family—was preserved and even extended by the new deployment, which emerged from within the peripheralized apparatuses that subtended the previous system of sexual relations. Since then the family, in the West, has remained "the interchange of sexuality and alliance: it conveys the law and the juridical dimension in the deployment of sexuality; and it conveys the economy of pleasure and the intensity of sensations in the regime of alliances." This incorporation, in which alliance is sexualized and saturated by desire, is also the mode by which a new form of power links the state and the family.

Our current moment—in which representations of same-sex marriage reconcile homosexuality with the family—shows that the state has emerged as a central locus by which certain nonnormative sexualities have sought to make it a terrain of freedom, destigmatization, and normality. Sexuality has thus once again become, quite powerfully, organized around questions of legitimacy and illegitimacy, intensifying the libidinal attachments to legal figures and subjecthood, and displacing many of the diverse knowledges and practices of sexuality whose aims and modes of existence are in excess of or relatively autonomous from concerns about legal ratification.[21]

It would appear that the current moment requires us to think also about the ways in which the deployment of sexuality subtends and is anchored by the contemporary capitalist mode of production. In the United States, that mode of production continues to rely on nonnational differences (of gender, race, and sexuality) to expand the proletarian class. Diaspora and migration have increasingly come to define and restructure these differences, subtending new formations of nonnormative sexualities.[22] How might we enter the "focus on family," to use a term of the US Christian Right, in order to pursue an inquiry into the functions of capital, the US state, and contemporary strategies of accumulation? In particular, what might be the different functions of family in the current elaboration of racial and neoliberal capitalism?

In 2004 the Audre Lorde Project, a queer people of color organizing center in New York City, completed a report on queer immigrants of color and the politics of immigration.[23] The report reveals that since the 1980s, the US state has actively worked to produce a racialized and gendered labor migration through the rubric of family reunification. Designed to assess the ways in which current immigration policy creates the conditions for a certain homophobia within immigrant communities, which remains unaddressed by both gay and lesbian and immigrant rights groups, the report and the broader organizing initiative behind it seek to reveal how the depoliticization of certain social forms—such as the family—deployed by the state at the current moment has become the means by which the state racially stratified immigrant communities in relation to the broader citizenry and actively organized a social structure for global capital in the city while appearing to be pursuing a neutral and even just social policy—a policy that corrected historical exclusions.

Since 1990, a large number of low-wage immigrant workers have come to New York City. Though many scholars have suggested that the major factor in favor of immigration in the 1990s was a shortage within the United States of workers, especially those in the domestic, low-wage services and in unskilled labor markets, the Immigration Act of 1990 capped the number of immigrant visas for so-called unskilled workers at a paltry 10,000 visas each year, while it increased family-based immigrant visas to 480,000 annually beginning in 1995. Although family immigration obviously includes minors and seniors who are either legally or functionally unable to enter the labor market, family-based immigration offers by far the largest pool of immigrant visas for unskilled workers.[24]

In other words, although immigrants are attracted to places like New York City by the number of entry-level jobs in the service, industrial, and informal sectors of the economy, the federal government continues to recruit such workers through the language and networks of family re-unification. The effect of creating economic factors to pull immigrants in, while at the same time using bureaucratic categories like family re-unification to code that migration as essentially produced by the petitioning activity of immigrants already living in the United States, is to meet the country's need for immigrant workers while projecting the state as either a benevolent actor that is reuniting broken families or as an overburdened and effete agent that is unable to prevent immigrants' manipulation of its democratic and fair laws. In either case, the recruitment of low-wage workers—who make up the majority of the immigrant of color populations in New York—is removed from the state's sphere of responsibility and returned to the immigrants themselves. In this manner, the state is absolved politically from having created and expanded the conditions of noncitizen life within the borders of the United States and at the same time, distinguishes itself as the apotheosis of Western democracy by achieving the status of depoliticized neutrality.

Indeed, since its original passage of the Immigration Act of 1990, the state has increasingly elected to make the petitioning families responsible for the welfare of all new immigrants arriving through the provisions of the act.[25] In a rather stunning move that has effectively bypassed the redistributive function of the state in a managed economy, the state has mandated that petitioning families must absorb the welfare functions of the state with regard to immigrants, in the context of the state's continuing bid to dismantle the welfare economy—a move that means it is now the role of the poor to absorb the social costs of poverty and a so-called healthy unemployment rate. The state has effectively managed to increase the numbers of immigrants, as the economy continues to demand low-wage noncitizen labor, and at the same time use immigration as a vehicle to dismantle its welfare responsibilities.[26]

In addition to the benefits that the state accrues through coding the recruitment of labor as family reunification, these governmental practices also engender conditions within which the family unit is now willy-nilly a site and apparatus of state regulatory and capitalist power. For immigrants recruited through family reunification, patriarchal, and heterosexual mandates have often become prerequisites to gaining family or welfare support. With the effective dismantling of welfare benefits for noncitizen racialized workers, workers brought in through family reunification have increasingly been forced to depend on family ties for access to room and board, employment, and other services, such as healthcare, child care, and what amounts to workplace injury insurance. In other words, federal immigration policies such as family reunification extend and institute heteronormative community structures as a requirement for accessing welfare provisions for new immigrants by attaching those provisions to the family unit.

In sum, the new federal structure has increased immigrants' exposure to and structural dependence on heteronormative and patriarchal relations and regulatory structures. Many queer immigrant interviewees spoke about the impossibility of being gay in a context in which their dependence on family—broadly defined—is essential to living as an immigrant in New York.[27] Although this problem is commonly spoken about in progressive circles, even there the typical reaction is to immediately assume that the supposedly more homophobic nature of immigrant cultures in comparison to American culture, or the extraordinary willingness of queer immigrants to accept homophobic silencing and closeting, is responsible. Such culturalist arguments only further mask the role of the state in engendering and enforcing the homophobias that many Americans claim immigrants have brought from their home countries. Both the intensity and specificity of homophobia in the lives of queer immigrants of color are founded on local conditions in the United States (and not because of the culture of the immigrants' countries of origin, as so many scholars are quick to suggest) and are produced at the intersection of the state's immigration policies and its fixation on the hetero-patriarchal family unit. In fact, the category of "gay" presumes a particular liberal order of family, civil society, and the state that is discursively and ideologically impossible for queer immigrants because it reduces the queer of color to the status of the nonnational, at the limit of civil society.[28] More pointedly, the liberal isomorphism of family, society, and state requires as its condition of possibility that the queer of color immigrant be seen as a nonindividuated, non–rights bearing subject, whose conditions of existence confound that isomorphism.[29]

In addition to the state's official immigration policy, federal and state governments since the Clinton administration have also been empowered to shift the delivery of services away from public and private nonprofit secular providers and toward religious organizations and groups. In New York, rising numbers of church organizations petition for government money, and an increasing number of immigrants use religious groups as their primary service providers. Again, the dislocating of the state's function as a welfare agent has exposed queer immigrants of color in particular to remarkable hetero-patriarchal coercion and has produced the disproportionate enforcement of hetero-patriarchal relations within immigrant of color communities.

Some scholars have pointed to what they believe is a potential silver lining in the end of the traditional welfare state: the diminishing importance of the state in the private and social lives of citizens and residents.[30] However, the erosion of the welfare state has not only been manifested in the withdrawal of economic and social resources from working-class and poor people. In addition, the continued deterioration of the welfare system will not result in the withdrawal of state power from the lives of immigrants of color—particularly queer immigrants of color—but instead will foster the expansion of social regulation through a growing reliance on social forms that are circumscribed or sponsored by the state, such as religion and the family. Moreover, the state's dependence on these forms for social regulation and political economic reproduction suggests that the forms will increasingly be burdened and restructured by the state's interest and demands, distancing the forms from their historical social forms and compelling them to conform to the state's representation of their limits, functions, and modalities.

Recruiting and socializing labor through the category of family reunification enabled the state to extend its regulatory power while at the same time disestablishing a welfare state for immigrant communities. Moreover, by posing the denial of family reunification as historically a racially restrictive and ascriptive state practice that denied equal citizenship to immigrant of color communities, the state was able to produce a racialized and gendered differentiated class of workers via its pursuit of equality and supposed racial redress. The state's recourse to the family as the means by which to recruit noncitizen labor and simultaneously distance that labor from social rights became the very condition for a state-enforced heteronormativity that projected immigrant communities as antiliberal and sexually conservative. Lastly, through asylum law—in which gender and sexuality were recognized as membership in a social group—the state began in the 1960s to treat US citizenship as a formally protective apparatus against patriarchy, homophobia, and supposed illiberal cultures. In other words, family reunification enabled state power to create hetero-patriarchal relations for the recruitment and socialization of labor while simultaneously justifying the exclusion of immigrant communities from state power through a liberal language of US citizenship as the guarantor of individual liberty and sexual freedom.

HOMOSEXUAL ASYLUM AND THE CRITIQUE OF LAW

Returning to Rahman's testimony at the beginning of this chapter, I would like to use the preceding discussion of neoliberal political economies of the family to pursue a queer of color critique of his petition for asylum. In *Aberrations in Black: Toward a Queer of Color Critique*, the theorist Roderick Ferguson argues that the sexual, as the expression of racially gendered relations, has emerged in the United States in the conflict between capital and the political state, especially protracted since the twentieth century. Although industrial capital, Ferguson argues, seeks labor, regardless of its origins, the political state qualifies its body politic through a set of racialized and gender ideals that it narrates as fundamental. Ferguson writes: "Capital is based on a fundamentally amoral logic. Capital, without pressures from the state or citizenry, will assemble labor without regard for normative prescriptions of race and gender."[31] Yet "the modern nation-state has historically been organized around an illusory universality particularized in terms of race, gender, sexuality, and class, [and] state formations have worked to protect and guarantee this universality."[32]

Such imperatives come into conflict with one another as capital tends toward the accumulation of heterogeneities, disrupting social hierarchies, while the state tends toward heteronormativity, multiplying racial, gender, and sexual differences and particularities as it seeks universality within the material conditions of heterogeneity. In this way, industrial capital also disrupts modern political ontologies of rule: "While capital can only reproduce itself by ultimately transgressing the boundaries of neighborhood, home, and region, the state positions itself as the protector of those boundaries."[33] Reading sociology as an archive of the arts of governance, Ferguson argues that this tense contradiction is expressed in the rise of certain stock figures in the archive across the twentieth century, such as the "transgendered mulatta," the Negro as the "Lady among the Races," and the "out-of-wedlock mother."[34] These figures, among others, constitute the genealogy and limit of " 'community,' 'family,' and 'nation.' "[35]

The gay Pakistani immigrant extends that genealogy as industrial capitalism is reconstituted by transnationality, neoliberalism, and the dominance of finance capital in our contemporary moment. In particular, working through Ferguson's framework, we might suggest that the figure of the gay Pakistani immigrant offers a genealogy of family within the contemporary United States. Indeed, the gay Pakistani immigrant as produced by the law is a supplement to the discourse of family and kinship as the state seeks to survive in a "post-state class-system."[36] Hence, I would like to take up a queer of color critique of the current US social formation and place that critique in opposition to citizenship, particularly as that practice is organized by the discourse of security for free capital. Situated within the shift from the welfare to the postwelfare neoliberal state, such a reading eschews an interpretation of Rahman's petition as seeking the security of US citizenship to protect gay liberty or sexual freedom, as well as an interpretation that poses the emergence of the gay Pakistani immigrant within the legal text as a victory for gay visibility in the archive.

Rather, this critique discovers and names in the legal record the strategies of repressive management that seek to define for its own ends what is knowable and thinkable about the figures that are ensnared in its web. It reads against the grain of the national archive we call the law— whose regime of truth demands the daily conquest of multiple pasts— and of the historical differences irreconcilable with that regime. And it reads the figure of the gay Pakistani immigrant as formed in the contra-

diction between heteronormative social relations mandated for immigrants of color by the state's policies and the liberal state's ideology of
universal sexual freedom as a mask for growing these social relations. In
the annals of the sexual history of the Asian diaspora, we might name
sexuality as the materialization of the conflict between an emerging
governmentality and the state's desire to perpetuate itself beyond its
point of expiration, in which family is their site of intersection.

If, as Ethne Luibheid has argued, the US nation-state has historically
ascribed sexuality to its populace through the technologies of the border,
then asylum law both extends and breaks with that historical practice.[37]
In this case, the set of logics, discourses, regimes of truth, and imperatives that establish and identify homosexuals as a social group and the
gay Pakistani as a victimized member of that social group, available for
the nation-state's protection, is paradoxically the expression of a transformation in the contemporary governmentality. That is, the figure of the
gay Pakistani immigrant is both a symptom of globalization and the
transnationalization of US capital and a new formation developed in the
interstices of the nation-state. This figure emerges in the breach between
the nation-state and the political economy.

Returning to Rahman's narrative, we see certain complexities. On the
one hand, it names the legal and civil infrastructure of the United States
as a protective space in which it is possible to freely conduct work or
pursue private enterprise—work and enterprise that presumably connote
homosexuality or that subtend a homosexual existence. On the other
hand, these very notions of freedom and security are negated or denied
for Rahman by the same legal and civil infrastructure that, through the
immigration apparatus, denies queer immigrants permanent access to
the civil and legal infrastructure of the US nation-state. If his application
for asylum resolved that contradiction, it also became a point of politicization, one whose trajectory he does not give an account of here. In this
way, Rahman's politicization is appropriable for a number of groups and
interests. For example, it could be used by gay and lesbian human rights
groups to claim the importance of sexuality as a human right, and of
human rights as incubators of political subjectivity, a precondition for
full personhood. It could be used by so-called gay and lesbian civil rights
groups in the United States, such as the Human Rights Campaign, to
expose the unfairness of immigration laws that deny gays and lesbians

equal rights as citizens.[38] Alternatively, it might be appropriated by Asian American political and cultural groups to establish the authenticity and legitimacy of queer Asians.

How else might we read this statement, this racialized and sexualized figure of speech? In asking this question, we pose the law as more than a terrain on which pressing social relations and the asymmetries and inequalities that subtend those relations are structured, adjudicated, and resolved. Instead, we situate the law—by which I mean more broadly the legal sphere—as an archive, in this instance an archive of racialized sexuality. That is, we approach the legal sphere as one site where the nation's official records are maintained and reproduced, giving those who seek identity through the law a history of their kin.

By naming the law an archive, I mean to observe the way in which the law seeks to be the record of the confrontation of social groups with the universality of community and the state posited by liberal political theory and epistemologies. Not just the law of record, the textuality of the law is also the expression of the law as record. And, as an archive or mode of record keeping, the law seeks to produce an account of social differences that preserves the conditions for universality. In other words, historical and social differences (of gender, race, and sexuality, among others) are subjugated by the law as a precondition of their entrance into the national record, and forced to preserve the liberal narrative of universality on which the legal sphere bases its notion of justice and on which the nation is said to be founded. As an archive, the law organizes social and historical differences in ways that promise both membership and knowledge of difference. In this way, the law as an archive is not a dispassionate or disinterested space of records. Rather, it is the privileged ledger by which knowledge, idealized as dispassionate and disinterested, paradoxically is made coincident with community, idealized as nonalienated experience—producing that peculiar epistemological affect associated with the citizen.

Like all archives, the law—and the broader textual legal sphere—as an archive is not simply an institutional site for the recording of the past and of historical and social difference. Rather, it is a framework that, ironically, promises its reader agency only through the perpetual subjugation of differences—a subjugation that targets not only the past but also the future. Indeed, the law as an archive addressed to the citizen or potential subject of civil society seeks, above all, to be an archive of the future. If, as Foucault argues, the archive must be construed as "the law of what can be said" in a particular social formation, then what we understand as the law in a more limited sense is an archive of how the state has come to be organized necessarily upon and within that broader social and material formation.[39]

Hence, the archive is not a passive domain in which differences—such as the gay Pakistani immigrant—can be found, extracted, and restored to their fullness, if necessary. It is the active technique by which sexual, racial, gendered, and national differences from both the past and the future are suppressed, frozen, and redirected as the occasion for a universal knowledge. It is the technique by which the modern US state promotes the citizen as a universal agent through that knowledge production—to women, queers, people of color, and so forth—demanding that we take up its framework for difference (both historical and social) as a prerequisite for a validated agency. As a differentiated social formation, US capitalist society is mediated by the law, which operates as the regulative structure and archive for that very differentiation. The legal archive subjugates pasts and futures in the name of recording what is supposedly difference and community.

Contending with the law as an active archive, or technique of self-making and the making of selves, as I do here, requires that we not simply accept its narrative and framework. Instead, we need to ask how regulation marks its interest in difference. Asking this requires reading figures like the gay Pakistani immigrant against the grain of the archive, situating that archive within and against the social formation—the forces and relations that constitute it—that bourgeois law cites but that it cannot comprehend. In other words, we need to read these figures as the limit of the archive, the point at which the archive's own conditions for existence might be retraced.

QUEER STUDIES AND THE POLITICS OF LEGITIMATE VIOLENCE

I would like to return, then, to queer studies and to the question of how transnational and critical ethnic studies of sexuality might take up such figures of the archive. Sexuality is regarded as an indispensable domain of study for all modern disciplines—including sociology, psychology, biology, statistics, anthropology, English, philosophy, and the arts—as well as professions such as law, social work, public health, and medicine. Indeed, significant aspects of each discipline's and profession's foundational knowledge and methods have been established, interrogated, and reestablished through research focused directly on the topic of sexuality, as that term is understood within each field.

The interdisciplinarity of queer studies, then, is defined not simply by its fusing of distinct disciplinary methods and knowledges—for example, those of the empirical and interpretive sciences, or those of law, medicine, and public health—the importance of such work notwithstanding. Rather, queer studies is a vibrant intellectual field ranging across disciplines and professions that has attempted, first, to theorize our contemporary epistemological predicament and, second, to collect these theories into a shared domain of inquiry. Queer studies has emerged out of and sought to engage two related issues. First, if our disciplinary and professional ways of knowing sexuality are neither value neutral nor unrestricted in terms of the scope of social subjects they encompass, but are inextricably tied to the epistemologies of their respective disciplines, how do those of us who think with, through, and for our disciplines gain knowledge of what these disciplines logically do not allow us to think with, through, or for in the domain of sexuality? And second, how do we gather and name the emerging body of exciting and cutting-edge scholarship developed to represent within the disciplines the meanings, expressions, and possibilities of sex and sexuality generated among sexually nondominant and historically excluded social groups, often by scholars who come from sexualized nondominant social worlds, without recourse to a unified sex or sexuality? Such scholarship has produced some of the most important methodological, theoretical, and practical contributions to advancing their—and our—disciplines and professions beyond the limits established by their Western, twentieth-century formations.

At its core, queer studies must be defined by its specific interest in studying those social worlds that have been excluded, delegitimized, violated, or silenced as a consequence of the modern disciplinary and professional need to know, manage, restore, value, and—at times—repair sexuality. We must address and represent these intellectually deauthorized and normatively defunct sexualized social worlds within the disciplines and the professions that remain—necessarily so, if they are to be workable and broadly meaningful—committed to a norm-based sexuality as a defining attribute of social life. For example, HIV/AIDS has complicated global health (a crossdisciplinary social-scientific, medical, and public health endeavor). Yet even as scholars in global health have tried to define sex and sexuality in a uniform way in order to gather empirical data on and establish metrics for transmission of HIV/AIDS and population demography, they have discovered that their very attribution of a norm-based sexuality to populations has contributed to a failed prevention policy against transmission, especially in politically, socially, and economically nondominant communities and regions. Queer scholarship in nonnormative and nondominant social worlds has revealed that the replacement of gay or bisexual designations, once seen as cultural, with new designations—such as men who have sex with men (MSM), men who have sex with transgenders (MST), and men who have sex with women (MSW)—seen as scientific, has in fact only made it more difficult to generate effective prevention protocols or a useful metric of transmission rates and vectors among social groups for whom such practices are enacted through different regimes of meaning and embodied selfhood, and within differing systems of social and political rule.

Queer studies has been at the forefront of theorizing and institutionally representing those groups that are sexualized and marginalized by the norm-based constructions of sexuality—whatever designations they use—work that is indispensable for developing the tools through which we gain valid assessments of the HIV/AIDS epidemic. In other words, it provides scholars with the training to not only assess the legitimacy or validity of norm-based views of sexuality but also to use those norms in their own work, even as they seek to open institutional representation and epistemological debates to the nondominant social groups that are obscured by the drive to develop a homogeneous or norm-based sexuality within different disciplines and professions. Over the last twenty years, innovative scholarship in queer studies across a number of fields has forced a reappraisal of the concept of the sexual in various disciplines and professions. Indeed, this scholarship has often made sexualized social worlds visible to other fields, whose formal methods at best inadvertently pass over (as inconsequential) and at worst constitutively efface the social meanings of the sexual. Queer studies does not seek to offer students simply a new nondiscriminatory and pluralistic understanding of sexual practices, meanings, and forms by which to define a new norm of sexuality for the disciplines. Instead, it offers an important reassessment of knowledge from within the disciplines and professions themselves, often by scholars and practitioners who are introducing new interdisciplinary methods into their fields.

This work has not only changed field-specific understandings of and engagements with sexuality, it has also frequently led to new and more broadly relevant disciplinary methods. Queer studies has been an important catalyst and tool for such work. Usefully, the field does not have its own separate institutional or disciplinary home. Rather, it functions as a transdisciplinary space that immerses students in the methods and knowledge that can teach them the impact—on knowledge, institutional practice, society, and communities—of critically representing within their fields nondominant and nonnormative sexualized social actors and social worlds. Queer studies has acted as a critical supplement to the intellectual and professional system, in which discipline-based normative accounts of sexuality and knowledge more generally are crucial and currently indispensable—as anyone who has trusted a doctor with his or her bodily well-being can attest. Queer studies offers training aimed at producing not a new transdisciplinary discipline of sexuality, but at a cadre of scholars across disciplines and professions who are attuned to the ethical, political, social, and epistemological impact of societies organized, protected, managed, enhanced, and healed by discipline-based knowledges of human sexuality.

Determined in its own moment by, on the one side, an AIDS pandemic that is responsible for the violent extinguishing of relations, intimacies, lives, and histories at a shocking pace and, on the other side, the institutionally momentous engagement and transformation of the disciplines by feminist scholars and activists, queer studies has focused on the politics of livability as a primary cultural and political inquiry. One main scholar of queer theory, Judith Butler, has termed this "precarity."[40] This has often resulted in figurations of the social through the metaphor of haunting to stress, as argued earlier, the limits of positivist methods for its account. Haunting here describes the set of foreclosed signifiers, relations, and historicities that constitute, as Butler puts it, "the excluded and illegible domain that *haunts* the former [social domain] as the spectre of its own impossibility, the very limit to intelligibility, its constitutive outside."[41] Therefore, the work on haunting emphasizes the set of formations that limn the borders of intelligibility. By doing so, the work gains a political charge in that its disruption of intelligibility can also be a change in the terms by which intelligibility is decided. As in my reading of the gay Pakistani immigrant, the project of haunting investigates the link between social identity and the norms that give the political sphere the appearance of neutral representation. Such haunting formations can constitute a change, that is, in the norms that determine the spaces, domains, and matter of politics even before and while political struggle is waged.

This queer methodology maintains the productive tension between, on the one hand, politics understood as submitting to and engaging with a distinct political process and, on the other hand, politics understood as the material elaboration of cultural forms and subjects. The first understanding of politics relies upon universalized norms that threaten to extend the political subject and its epistemes to those constitutively excluded domains of life that were necessary for the development of political modernity. This can take on a particularly racialized and sexualized charge, for including constitutively excluded formations within the universality of political modernity while attempting to maintain the validity of the norms crucial for that universality requires figuring as nonpolitical or unpolitical any cultural difference in the forms of livelihoods, social relations, and modes of embodiment that shape the contingency and historicity of those norms. The second understanding of politics mobilizes cultural forms, practices, and meanings as enactments of alternative social possibilities within normative and hegemonic social relations, possibilities that cross the line between what is socially possible and what is socially knowable and validated. That is, it reveals that what is socially known and institutionally recognized of a social formation does not exhaust the existing social possibilities of that formation. This erases the line that marks the boundary between politically meaningful life (as life that is known) and life that has no consequence for meaning.

Cultural politics is always the dangerous supplement to the modern political, figuring originally as evidence of the preservation of and re-spect for the right of particularity (the rights of cultural difference) that the modern political supposedly affirms and protects through grounding in universal norms. Yet racial and sexual culture becomes the remainder of those norms, that which cannot be integrated into current norms without their forcible reappraisal. These remainders, which are figured or aestheticized as cultural difference, can become the sites from which to mount a dialectical critique of the ideal of neutrality that is inherent in those norms. Some scholars find in the category of cultural difference noncongruent epistemes and forms of sociality, the basis for developing a variety of syncretic and incommensurate alternatives to the universality promoted by political modernity. As I demonstrated in my discussion of the figure of the gay Pakistani immigrant, I have instead approached this remainder that is aestheticized as cultural difference as the basis on which asymmetrical racialization can proceed. I have also argued that this remainder can be the source of a genealogy of state forms and the mode of liberal political thought upon which those forms rely for the coherent integration. Rather than uphold the coherence of the national state (even as it undermines itself) that cultural difference promotes, these remainders can be the basis for a narration of the incoherence of current state practices. In displacing the coherence of the state—upheld in our time, for example, by sexual norms such as gay or homosexuality—we can reveal other forms and constructions of power, such as those that reproduce transnational capitalist social relations, which the nation-state thwarts and screens from inquiry. In so doing, we expand the horizon of political life, transforming our relation to the modern category of the political and the subject it promotes. These remainders are the historical and material nonidentity of social practices and relations to the norms and idealism central to the legitimacy of the modern liberal state.

POLITICAL RIGHTS AND THE QUEER UNCONSCIOUS

If we are not to idealize queer theory, it is necessary to discover the contingency of which it is a part. That is, we need at least to attempt to understand why it became such a powerful critical discourse in the 1990s. As I have argued here, it is perhaps because queer theory has emphasized and theorized the violence of neutral norms—of the misrepresentation of figures as rational categories of social reality—that this mode of critique and critical project has felt so compelling and important in our time. As the US neoliberal state as a regulatory form and apparatus of violence has become a synthesis of its administrative and juridical institutions, it has relied on the neutrality ideal as the primary way in which it can reconcile the deepening of asymmetrical social relations— increasingly reproduced through violence and force—with a state form that continues to rely on the discourse, institutions, and structures that stress rights and equal political representation as the meaning of modern freedom and the only basis for legitimate violence.

The dominance of positivist and social-scientific *techne* within the university in the 1990s that promoted the normative neutrality of norm-based knowledge, and for which diversity became the tool to manage the political and racialized limits of its knowing, is crucially linked to the shift in the liberal state from a welfare to neoliberal security apparatus. The coupling of positivism with diversity became the dominant logic and form that linked and integrated the differing divisions of knowledge within the university. This coupling also made the university an important ideological apparatus for the state. Queer theory developed at the time of the extension of positivism through the category of diversity to the nonpositivist humanist disciplines. Queer theory and the positivist social sciences are part of a single dialectic that emerged in the material production and contestations of the neoliberal state and the racialized growth of its apparatuses of violence.

More recently a strain of queer theory influenced by this work—yet critical of its political orientation, its negotiation with and for state power—has pushed the critique of sociality to an apparent limit, arguing that if the modern political sphere is the domain in which cultural citizens and others are regulatively determined and mystified to themselves as a positive being or socially authentic, then the politicization of the critique of sociality is at best an oxymoron, and at worst the usurpation of a powerful tear in the social by variously meretricious supplicants who go by the name of "public intellectual." Variously identified with Lacanianism and formalist and universal aestheticist theories of subjectivities, these critiques have issued primarily from English departments and other disciplinary formations.[42]

To the degree that this strain suggests a political motive for its mode of critique, it perhaps reveals the links between a so-called progressive politics and the liberal political emphasis on modernity as the achievement of personal freedom. Both supposedly deny the alienation and structuring of subjectivity, its repressive violence and determination, and its eschewing of the so-called real—understood as nonrepresentational particularity, whose excess in the realm of the social reveals the gap between what Lee Edelman terms "real liberty" and its regulative simulation as political liberty under modernity. The following claim by Edelman, whose book is felicitously titled *No Future: Queer Theory and the Death Drive*, is representative of this type of critique:

> The signifier, as alienating and meaningless token of our Symbolic constitution as subjects (as token, that is, of our subjectivation through subjection to the prospect of meaning); the signifier, by means of which we always inhabit the order of the Other, the order of a social and linguistic reality articulated from elsewhere; the signifier, which calls us into meaning by seeming to call us to ourselves: this signifier only bestows a sort of *promissory* identity, one with which we can never succeed in fully coinciding because we, as subjects of the signifier, can only be signifiers ourselves, can only ever aspire to catch up to whatever it is we might signify by closing the gap that divides us and, paradoxically, makes us subjects *through that act of division alone.*[43]

For these scholars, politics is the site in which the struggles of meaning around terms like "equality," "citizenship," and "freedom" are at best deferrals and at worst ruses that continue to advance the transparency of the social, evading recognition of the false plentitude that modern subjectivity promotes in its quest to expand regulatory power.

There is a cultural and political vanguardism to this position, despite its elegant critique of the narrative logic that organizes and sustains the phantasmatic experience of political freedom in liberal political societies. For Edelman, queer is a figure that exposes the limits of the regime of meaning by which we are transformed into subjects of the signifier, and only the Lacanian ethical subject—which is also an aesthetic subject— interrupts, breaks, exceeds, and foils liberalism. All other subjects, as subjects of politics, only ever dupe themselves into affirming liberalism by their constant need to resignify norms, produce new meanings, or claim their legibility and value. My criticism of this view is that it entirely stabilizes the domain and category of the political in order, paradoxically, to argue for a resistance to the enforcement of the social order. In Edelman's account, the subject comes to have an unrelenting attachment not just to the intractability of the law, or the symbolic order, but to the imagined unity and universality of that order (generated through a selection of cultural texts) and to what is understood as the universality of the subject, its architecture of experience within that order. The effect of such an attachment is the erosion of any plural historicity to the implacable logic that the psychoanalytic subject is seen to be in opposition to.

As a critique of liberalism, this account generates an epistemology that gravely underestimates the variety of contradictions threatening the dissolution of a liberal order by what has been made into its constitutive outsides. This variety matters because it expands the sites in and through which we can mount a politics of nonidentity and pursue ethical critiques of the modern political sphere. In addition, and most important to my discussion here, this variety reveals a social formation that is heterogeneous and always in flux, made up of what Louis Althusser and Etienne Balibar call a mixed mode of production, of uneven and incommensurate historical conditions, trajectories, and formations, that trouble and make unavailable the very cultural homogeneity of the symbolic order on which Edelman ultimately relies.[44] The point is not that the discourse of the child and futurity hides the appalling treatment that both the US political state and US liberal political thought have inflicted upon actual youth of color. Indeed, Edelman powerfully argues that one reason the child is such a crucial ideological figure in US liberalism currently is that it inspires the violation and even death of racially, sexually, and gendered different children, who are then saved or mourned as children they never were nor could ever be—the child makes development and livability within adulthood the limit of these children's already precarious existence. Rather, my concern is focused on the way in which Edelman's critique of the political or the "Symbolic" implicitly conceives of the contemporary United States as a white social formation (to be sure, including liberal multicultural differences).

And yet Edelman's account of the child as the spectacle of an imaginary wholeness toward which political society supposedly strives trans-

forms US political space into one that is exclusively constituted by whiteness, marked by a cultural archive that ranges from the musical *Annie* to
the films of Alfred Hitchcock. This cultural archive rapidly becomes a
regulatory filter, privileging the texts and forms of textuality that only
extend the previous examples—dissimulating their actual exemplarity—
even when they might be used to undo and supplant those previous
texts. More important, this cultural archive is further normed by a reading practice that installs a particular implied reader or consumer of the
cultural objects used as the examples in a psychoanalytic reading. In
Edelman's case, this implied reader, viewer, or cultural consumer is a
white citizen subject, presumptively the only—or at least the primary—
addressee of the political sphere of the nation-state.

Thus the formalism of the psychoanalytic argument against the social
can never fully disassociate itself from the cultural archive and texts
through which it makes its argument, including the cultural text of Lacanian psychoanalysis. And here what appears to be an ethical critique of
the Western political sphere and liberal political epistemology becomes
in fact the means by which the ethical regulates and seeks to determine
what we understand to be political life, what cultural formations will and
will not appear under that category or in that domain. And so, unwilling
to disclose its own political status, and arguing that politics is its antithesis, the ethical critique controls the understanding of political life, reify-
ing that which it figures as a limit. That is, the boundary between ethics
and politics breaks down. A formalist ethical critique of nonidentity
becomes the means by which, once again, an unmarked political operation installs itself within social and political life—within the histories of a
social formation that matter—and ethics betrays itself.

My criticism is not that Edelman reserves for the white male queer
an ethical radicalism that he names the "sinthomosexual" and that he
doesn't extend this radicalism to the terms "black," "Asian," "Latino,"
"prisoner," or "diaspora." This may be true, but there is nothing in Edelman's argument that wouldn't allow one to suggest that all kinds of
embodied cultural formations could be sinthomosexuals. Indeed, Edelman argues that as homonormativity becomes more the rule than the
exception, the sinthomosexual is not absorbed but displaced onto other
cultural subjects and figures—two that come to my mind are the illegal

alien and the so-called Muslim fundamentalist. Surely one meaning of queer ought to be a figure that reveals the corrosive vitality of the death drive that coincides with the establishment of a universal social order. Yet if we restrict the meaning of that term, so that using it in any other way is a capitulation to the values and order of liberalism, then we reinstall a singular historical and cultural formation and subject in the very process of advocating for an alternative and radical ethical critique of political life. Both the masculinity and the whiteness of the categories of queer and queerness go unremarked, assimilating diverse historical formations within national space to the historical predicament of the institutionally enfranchised white male queer (as a requisite identification) who elects unintelligibility. And this problem is not solved if we simply find examples of racialized and gendered subjects within this single definition, or substitute for it the sinthomosexual of reproductive futurity.

Yet what if we remind ourselves that political modernity in the United States regulated not only citizens and whiteness but racial aliens, alien citizens, black citizens, tribal citizens, the undocumented, and the racialized formations those categories mediated? Have these formations not been subjects constituted by disidentification and the negativity Edelman argues that we need to ethically embrace as normative? What should we make of the fact that for each of these formations, inclusion within citizenship has been frustrated by the longer and public histories of existing within political society as present detritus, meaningless for political futurity or historical time? What might we find as a meaningful critique if we take these other cultural subjects as the point of departure for our inquiry into the normalization and estrangement performed by political discourse? Again, my point is not to criticize Edelman for failing to include these other cultural formations and figures in his book; that would be an unfair and senseless criticism to make, as of course no book can "do it all." Rather, I am trying to stress how a methodological formalism that neither seeks to enunciate the limits of that formalism nor attempts to offer an account (however inaccurate and inadequate) of its historical determination produces an epistemology that has no need to ask about those social and cultural formations that exist as the limit of its critique. I am asking why and how such exclusions can appear legitimate, and what this might tell us about the racialized limits of certain modalities of queer critique. And I not only ask to make a claim about who and what this style of critique cannot think about or address; I seek to claim that in failing to address multiple and linked cultural subjects and formation, which figure as despised metonyms for the negative through which the social is constituted, Edelman's polemical critique ultimately fails to grasp power in its contemporary operation. The affirmation of difference and even non-identity that characterizes late modern power and that operates through highly differentiated modes of regulation within the nation-state needs no ultimate coherence for the political to be constituted. Though it announces itself as a radical and impossible critique of the political, Edelman's project only corroborates the fantasy of the United States as an archetypical European nation-state in a modernity already sublated by contemporary racial capitalism.

For the racialized groups constituted by US political liberalism and universal citizenship, their historical conditions suggest that the terms of Edelman's reproductive futurism—futurity, politics, the child—can and will signify differently in a normative sense. The terms will not just signify normatively as plentitude but also always as loss, a cutting, a gash in viability. If this is the normative condition for racialized subjects of the US public sphere, then we cannot confidently assert that we know that any and every appeal to futurity, the child, and politics means that liberal politics has just won again. If racialized conditions are as normative in the United States as the white social formation of reproductive futurity, then these formations are the basis by which other discourses inhabit the signifiers—in themselves meaningless—that Edelman associates with white reproductive futurism. Futurity, for example, will not be the basis by which a narrative temporality of freedom elides once again the awareness of the abjection that is constitutive of the social. Rather, it can name a premonition of a new and irregular reproduction of the racialized subject, a subject for which abjection and disidentification as constitutive to each and every iteration of that subject is normatively, if at times painfully, avowed.

Such projects must undertake an enquiry into the geohistorical and racialized heterogeneity that political modernity at once engages, constitutes, produces, and regulates. It must come to see as meaningful to its project the noncitizen racialized and gendered subjects that US political modernity has also produced and hailed in uneven ways—not as derivative copies of the normative citizen subject, but as distinctly regulated subjects and objects of the political sphere. For what formations of modernity does futurity signify normatively as a regulative idealization that sutures the gap between identity and the subject of subjection, or between meaning and the arbitrariness of the signifier? And on what authority do we decide that modern power is best understood through those formations, rather than the formation for which normatively the political term of "futurity" and the rational public sphere have, for much of modernity, signified destruction, abandonment, even death.

My point is simply that, unwilling to think, name, and theorize its own historicity, queerness—that otherwise remarkable anti-identitarian elixir —becomes the means of making institutionally dominant, though not hegemonic, whiteness as coincident with the space of national politics and culture. Because Western liberalism has been a political epistemology that has mediated and produced a racially divided and stratified national social formation, its terms, categories, and cultural forms have—since the moment of racial inclusion and enfranchisement—always been ironic and contradictory in relation to those racialized groups and formations that have been the US nation-state's conditions of possibility. Racialized political actors and cultural producers have engaged the forms, language, and terms of liberal political modernity as instances of catachresis (terms that, in having no proper referent, announce the figurality that mediates and constitutes social reality), just as the most institutionally validated racialized actors have disavowed this truth.

When the US political state can construct the otherwise oxymoronic term "alien citizen"—a category that describes the specific social status and legal conditions of US-born and naturalized people of color during the twentieth century—it would be difficult to believe that the normative discourse of the US public sphere or the normative subject of political life is exclusively and singularly the white multicultural citizen subject of reproductive futurism. Instead, we need to understand US liberalism as mediating a multiplicity of regulated subjects, each inhabiting different locations within a social order. These locations inflect the way in which different subjects experience, understand, and relate to the conditions of nonidentity within a single social order or liberal political society. If we affirm this broader spectrum of public subjects that US liberalism has mediated and sought to regulate, then we need to ask some rather simple questions. For whom is the homophobic violence that Edelman so elegantly and powerfully reveals and dissects constitutive of their status as subjects? Does homophobic violence operate differently for subjects who must normatively avow their nonidentity in the social order and in politics? Does the critique of futurity that Edelman offers in recalling the death and memorializing of Matthew Shepard ring at all true when thinking of the death of Sakia Gunn in 2003?

Perhaps the media that publicized Shepard's terrible death failed to find Gunn's gruesome murder of national interest not so much because lesbians of color are less valued national spectacles—an effect of being regulated by the discourse of the racially unmarked child. Maybe the deeper reason was the way in which a poor racialized community in Newark that campaigned for justice for Sakia threatened to make the child a signifier of the very historical particularity of that racialized community—threatening the very colorblindness that makes terms like "heteronormative," "negativity," and "queer" so compelling, useful, and desired. That is, when this community organized politically to speak up for a future in which a death like Sakia Gunn's would not occur, its residents were not trapped by the dominant symbolic and liberal political order that it would have been in their interest to refuse. Rather, for a moment they made "the child," "futurity," and "politics" all metonymic signifiers of social worlds normatively addressed in antimimetic forms of discourse—the world of poor, racialized "aggressives" and girls of color. They revealed a dense material particularity and world that liberalism could not translate adequately without showing its remainders—without, that is, revealing the violence of its translation, the arbitrariness of its order.

I do not mean to suggest that there is some kind of politics that can overcome the constitutive fact of the subject's domination by social relations and the linguistic order. Quite the contrary. Rather, I mean to argue that the ethical figure in Edelman's argument is, in the final analysis, a political project. And it is one that in denying its own historicity and restricting the political to everything but itself, perpetuates a silencing of the postliberal and antihumanist histories we have yet to institutionally engage or know. I am also trying to stress that a modern liberal social order is always mediating a mixed mode of production. Lacanian critique stresses the power of the "one" and domination through identity, equality, and mimesis. Yet racial capitalism, as I've argued, is more heterogeneous, proliferating necro-political subjects that are normatively distinguished, differently controlled, regulated, and killed. Late modernity in the West may ultimately be significant for the way in which power—which is always created through institutions—has overcome in some ways its restrictions by the order of the "one" and classical hegemony even if our institutional critiques have not.

There is never just the social and its binary antithesis—antisociality, negativity, the real. Rather, that antithesis is only one of the forms of difference and figures of alterity that the US social order has been founded on and that have simultaneously been subject to ongoing institutional or state counterviolence. When the Europeanist discourse of poststructuralism or Lacanianism is taken as a general account of alterity as such, it is ultimately only more aligned with the liberal order and historicity that it seeks to seemingly undo. We must understand that, far from breaking with history, every claim for asociality regulatively conserves a particular genealogy, and that even advocacy for antifuturism can be among the most authoritarian claims on futurity by seeking to delimit in advance who or what speaks through the signifier of futurity. Only then can we use the form of negative critique advocated by Edelman in the US academy without reproducing racial divisions and dominations through these accounts of alterity. (Indeed I can't think of a more social act than making a Lacanian critique of sociality—through academic discourse, in academic journals, following and mastering the protocols of US academic writing and the citational structure, broadly construed—necessary for its effects as the means by which to engage alterity.) Otherwise, queer studies is the vehicle for a whiteness that seeks to construe the nation as a homogeneous social and economic form, rather than as the name for a space that goes beyond a single national form.

Whereas Edelman's antisociality relies on individual particularity and the human animal as the site from which a social order is constitutively undone, over and over again, I have suggested that it is the public histories of racialization that interrupt the very national social order that depended upon, included, and reproduced those racializations. As historically excluded racialized sexual formations enter institutional domains and political life, inevitably forcing a future resignification of the norms that organize those domains, they reveal the limits of the historical and social discourses that seek to tame or hide their disruptive and non-analogous elements. As these discourses seek to translate what they necessarily excluded into their own terms, that translation leaves a racialized remainder. Though these remainders are subject to immense institutional and social violence, since they threaten the veracity of a present social order, they are also what haunts the felicity of inclusion. To accept this haunting, this upheaval of speech and rationality, is to accept the demand to imagine and develop our collective abjections and negations.

FOUR   Moving beyond a Freedom
with Violence

The Politics of Gay Marriage in the Era
of Racial Transformation

Only that historian will have the gift of fanning the spark of hope in the past who
is firmly convinced that *even the dead* will not be safe from the enemy if he wins.
And this enemy has not ceased to be victorious.
—WALTER BENJAMIN, "Theses on the Philosophy of History"

There is no contemporary discourse that is free or independent of the itinerary of
the concept of race.—NAHUM CHANDLER, "Originary Displacement"

The 2008 US election produced both the first African American president and the defeat of so-called universal marriage rights in California, the country's most populous and racially diverse state. These electoral decisions occurred in the context of two unpopular US wars and failed neoliberal epistemes and policies for the management of the globally deregulated and finance-dominated economy. In many ways, the votes return us to the problem of knowledge in capitalist modernity where knowledge is crucial to the government of that modernity. Although in response to these failed policies, some scholars have once again advanced the nation-state as the normative and exclusive apparatus for the government of modernity, contemporary conditions of globalization and the transnationalization of societies have threatened the validity of that view. This is nowhere better illustrated than in the state of California. The 2008 election might seem to be a paradigmatic instance of the persistence of the nation form of modernity—the national people may be most present as a single causative will in electoral practice—but in fact it would be better to see the election as the transnational disorganization of national interests. This chapter pursues the conversation on race, modern violence, and the politics of knowledge by offering an account of the current drive to place—or, more properly, to reorganize—sexuality within the political economy of California. That drive has sought to situate sexuality within the purview of the state. I understand the state as an ideal form that authorizes regulatory and coercive powers within and through variously designated institutions for the protection—in our time—of society, economy, and markets. Recalling the recent cultural, legal, and electoral battles over Proposition 8, known more colloquially as the marriage amendment—intended to codify copulation as heterosexual in California's constitution—I want to ask what possible social and political meanings and modes of inquiry can be applied to this moment by those of us in queer studies and critical ethnic studies. In other words, I want to consider how we might address the ongoing legal, legislative, institutional, and cultural movements and interests for so-called universal marriage—more accurately, gay marriage— in a manner that disrupts liberal identitarian and homophobic politics, as well as the current state form to which those agonistic politics lay claim.

In discussing California's recent election cycle, my goal is not to offer a comprehensive analysis of state politics or a sociological account of the legal movement for gay marriage. Instead, I take California's passage of Proposition 8 in 2008—the same time when the country elected its first president of color—as an opportunity to meditate on the complexities of racial, sexual, and transnational politics in our current moment. Califor-

nia's 2008 election results disorganized the understanding that many of
us had of progressive politics. Supporters of the proposition seized on
the results as proof that the movement against gay marriage was not
simply a top priority of a small religious constituency, but a widely
popular concern of Californians who had also voted for the first African
American president. Meanwhile, media pundits and many progressive
gay and lesbian organizations and their supporters in the state explained
this conjunction, not surprisingly, as the result of the political behavior of
California's African American communities. Despite constituting a mere
10 percent of California's electorate, African American voters were sin-
gled out as the responsible party for once again undoing the citizenry's
social and cultural progress.

Though it was common in the aftermath of the election to hear again
that a mythic "black homophobia" was the cause of Proposition 8's
success, this claim has since been disproved. Indeed, the easy and sweep-
ing use of the term "black homophobia" became a screen for how little
the media or gay marriage advocates really knew about what Melissa
Harris-Lacewell calls the "black counter-publics" in California.[1] Instead,
black homophobia became the means by which the media, the rest of the
public sphere, and the institutional marriage movement could disavow
their lack of knowledge of the actual social and political context, social
meanings, and worldviews that determine blacks' (or others') electoral
choices. No one asked what specific social meanings organized and were
expressed by the casting of a vote, choosing instead to locate meaning
exclusively in the numerical interpretation of aggregate results whose
frames were never commented upon.

Most striking was the near-uniform reliance of gay progressives and
the media on this explanation, despite the fact that, if only in the form of
a disavowal, it could reveal the persistent racial inequities in California's
political process. That is, this explanation, like any stereotype, threatened
to reveal the racialized unevenness in our knowledge of the meanings
expressed by an electoral choice. To be sure, the continued reliability of
antiblack racism, especially in mass media domains, can go a long way
toward explaining why those who chose this explanation seemed absolutely unconcerned that it revealed the racial and economic fault lines
that organized the gay marriage movement and the media coverage of

the political process. That something called black homophobia could pass as an explanation only reveals how much the media and the institutional political process are central apparatuses for the continued marginalization of the many distinct alternative political ideologies, institutions, and groups that organize political life and activity within communities of color.

If few reporters or proponents or opponents of gay marriage appeared disturbed by the resort to racist explanations for the outcome of the election, even fewer asked why such racism had been suggested in the first place. What were the epistemological frames that allowed the vote for Proposition 8 to become a crisis that needed explanation? Why was it so apparent to all those who turned to this explanation that it was the intersection of gay and black politics that marked this election? Why was the conjuring of this intersection such an available frame for engaging the election results? And finally, why was this intersection perceived as a crisis for and disorientation of progressive politics? As I noted in the last chapter, we might use this moment of apparent incoherence within contemporary electoral politics as the means of pursuing an inquiry into the epistemological frames that enable us to analyze this crisis state.

HISTORY AND A POLITICAL ANALOGY

On June 12, 1967, the US Supreme Court unanimously struck down Virginia's Racial Integrity Act of 1924, which declared marriage between a white and "colored" person a felony offense.[2] Coming three years after *McLaughlin v. Florida*,[3] which invalidated laws against interracial cohabitation, *Loving v. Virginia* is credited with invalidating and abolishing all remaining state-based forms of racial discrimination in marriage contracts. The fortieth anniversary of *Loving* in 2007 might have passed unnoticed by all but legal scholars and a few constituencies still caught in the aftereffects of modern US antimiscegenation laws, but for the fact that the issue of gay marriage has drawn *Loving* into an expanded arena of meaning and application.[4] Most Americans would have seen in *Loving* nothing more than another chapter in the nation's racial morality tale, which began with the US Supreme Court's decisions in *Brown v. Board of Education* and *Bolling v. Sharpe*. That *Loving* might be related to social relations and forces that determine their own lives would surely not have been in the forefront of Americans' minds in the twenty-first century except for the emergence of gay marriage as a central issue in both state and national electoral politics and judicial culture.

All of a sudden *Loving* became a touchstone of comparative history, politics, and identities. What were the legacies of *Loving* for homosexuals? What are the analogies between racial and sexual differences? Is racial discrimination in marriage contracts arbitrary, while sexual orientation discrimination is moral? And are both forms of discrimination necessarily invidious? Questions such as these have been preoccupying scholars, historians, and lawyers, including—to name just a few—Janet Halley, Andrew Sullivan, George Chauncey, Evan Wolfson, and Randall Kennedy. Trying to understand how we remember *Loving*, and why we remember it at all, might be as interesting an endeavor as answering the questions I just listed, in part because such an investigation would help us see some of the animating field of force within which those questions are posed, comparisons are made, and answers are sought.

Janet Halley has argued convincingly that "like race" analogies abound in legal discourse, especially in antidiscrimination claims—in part because nearly every equal protection claim cannot avoid citing the race-based jurisprudence for which the Fourteenth Amendment was crafted.[5] This can explain to some degree the reason for *Loving*'s popularity at this moment. As gay marriage advocates press their claims in the courts, they cannot help drawing analogies to race-based claims of discrimination made in the context of the Fourteenth Amendment. Indeed, these references have generated what Siobhan Somerville calls the "miscegenation analogy" in legal communities, policy circles, and media culture, an analogy that argues that sexual orientation discrimination in the form of sodomy laws and in the restrictive recognition of heterosexuals by the state only in marriage contracts constitutes, like antimiscegenation laws, an indefensible exclusion of a suspect class.[6] Both the similes and analogies with miscegenation, then, propel *Loving* into the public light for the purpose of revealing not ongoing racial discrimination by the state or the failure of legal equality to result in substantive equality, but rather the invalidity of state-based homophobia and sexual discrimination.

It is important to note here that the desire to remember *Loving* at this historical moment in the interest of furthering such causes as gay marriage is ultimately circumscribed by that interest in the marriage cause. This interest analogizes the discursive productions of sexuality and race in the law—and in the broader social formation for which this law was devised—reducing and effacing the specificity of each production as well as their linked and related production of each other, as Halley and Somerville each separately argue. Indeed Somerville, like Darren Hutchinson and Mary Eaton before her, is particularly acute in revealing how this desire for the "miscegenation analogy" effaces and occludes gay, lesbian, and queer people of color, in particular, as a compound class with distinct experiences of domination and subordination not captured, comprehended, or articulated by prevailing legal and cultural epistemologies founded on so-called single-issue oppression or suspect class subordination.[7]

In addition, Somerville argues, analogical thinking—of the sort promoted by the miscegenation analogy—also effaces the linking of the nonequivalent histories of stigmatized homosexuality and formal racial equality within the law that *Loving* actually tightened during the era of the decision. Examining the legal codification of homosexuality as a legitimate ground for exclusion in the 1950s and 1960s, in domains such as citizenship and immigration policy, as a precursor to the affirmation in *Loving* that the individual's right to marriage cannot be constrained by state-based racial restrictions, Somerville argues that what's significant about the intersection of race and sexuality is not their analogical relation but rather the manner in which the former depends on the latter for its normalization.[8] To the degree that US law, through the *Loving* decision, universalizes in its domain the virtue and right of marriage for everyone without restrictions of race at the very same time that the law stigmatizes homosexuality as a legitimate ground of exclusion from membership in the state suggests that analogies constructed between miscegenation and homosexual marriage promote the omission of this heterosexualization of race and the racial construction of homosexual practices that *Loving* helped advance. Somerville writes: "What activists fail to see when using *Loving* as a precedent for same-sex-marriage rights is that the case is not parallel to a history of homosexuality as it is represented in the law; rather, it is embedded in the same history of sexuality that has determined the status of gay men and lesbians as the excluded others. By establishing a fundamental right to marriage regardless of race, the federal state in effect shored up the privileges of heterosexuality through a logic that was on the surface antiracist and anti-white supremacist."[9] Following Somerville's insight—that formal equality generated a new organization, rather than the abolition, of structuring power in the lives of those interpellated by the law—perhaps we can ask a different kind of question about those who today seek, indeed desire the acceptance of, the miscegenation analogy. It appears that this desire among activists and other advocates for gay marriage rights is ultimately a desire for formal equality before the law, one that in being withheld constitutes an assault on their dignity for lesbian and gay citizens.

Yet here we run into a paradox: if it was formal equality—the mode by which the state addressed, absorbed, and sought to neutralize the disruptive demands of the civil rights movement—that strengthened the law's power to delegitimize GLBTQ lives, what enables the current faith in that same formal equality as a solution for gays' and lesbians' subordination, inequality, and cultural domination not to strengthen still further contemporary forms of illegitimacy in the law? Might we see in this desire for formal equality not just hopes for better terms of living and intimacy but for an identity in the law itself, one that places gay rights at the leading edge of formal equality? And what of the forms of illegitimacy that formal equality not only refuses to address but surreptitiously further estranges from rights itself? I venture to suggest that even the most single-minded gay marriage right advocates have not been immune to these questions. Rather, I see in the promotion of the miscegenation analogy the symptom of the advocates' wrestling with these questions. In fact, the analogy becomes the form by which the symptom is temporarily resolved. Indeed, is there not a second analogy desired by those gay and lesbian advocates who promote the miscegenation analogy, one that seeks to supplant the miscegenation analogy in the near future with something like the gay marriage analogy, to be used by others seeking to emerge from the shadows of legal illegitimacy that the assertion of formal equality at this moment casts?

To be concrete, the current demand for gay and lesbian marriage rights as a means of gaining formal equality before the law has intersected, for example, with broad demands by undocumented immigrants; Latino and Latina, Chicano and Chicana, and Asian immigrant communities; and their supporters for citizenship and an end to the legal delegitimation, harassment, violence, incarceration, and criminalization that afflicts twelve million undocumented workers in the United States. How have advocates for gay marriage rights engaged with this demand—one that interrogates the moral basis of citizenship exclusion by breaking a law they cannot but break as evidence of their moral degeneracy that excludes them from citizenship—at the very moment that gays and lesbians seek inclusion into the moral universalism promoted by the law, which is supposedly founded on the fundamental right of marriage? Based upon the above argument, we should not be surprised by statements such as those made by Los Angeles resident Jasmyne Cannick, a lesbian writer and member of the National Association of Black Journalists. In appraising the demands and the public debate constituted by the unprecedented immigrants' rights marches, Cannick argued in a widely circulated essay for the online edition of the *Advocate*, a gay and lesbian magazine, that gay marriage rights must be achieved before US citizens, their representatives, and the Left champion the rights of undocumented workers. Cannick suggests that although the justice claims of "illegal immigrants" might be compelling—conceding that it "might even be the *next* [emphasis added] leading civil rights movement"—this new claimant for rights needed to wait until "we . . . [have] finished with our current civil rights movement." She "recognize[s] the plight of illegal immigrants. I do. But I didn't break the law to come into this country. This country broke the law by not recognizing and bestowing upon me my full rights as a citizen." And she concludes: "Immigration reform needs to get in line behind the LGBT civil rights movement, which has not yet realized all of its goals."[10]

There is much to say about such symptomatic language—about the way in which rights are construed as goods, the nation as recipient of its subjects' labor and lives, and the state as little more than a disperser of those desired goods. But permit me instead to focus on the blurred analogy that is being constructed here. Cannick's discourse fuses two different ideologies. One represents the law as unfaithful to its own principles, whereby gays and lesbians now stand as the representation of that breech for which African Americans once stood; the other sees the law as appropriated by a neoconservative ideology that rhetorically effaces the worldliness of the civil rights movement by turning it into an American exceptionalist drama of the nation's repeated betrayal of black equality. In this latter ideology and rhetorical argument, that betrayal is most often manifested and figured as a contest between immigrants and African Americans for social mobility in civil society, but this contest is shifting to one for legal recognition between gays and immigrants in the domain of law.[11] Cannick's statements gained widespread popularity, not only because of her analogy between black civil rights and the so-called gay and lesbian civil rights movement, but also because of her turn to analogy itself as the narrative and logical form for discussing, reasoning, and thinking through the multidimensional crisis and conflicts that—far from being resolved—seem only to reappear as new contradictions.

It is worth remembering that, as a class of metaphor, the legal definition of analogy is the creation of resemblance or likeness between unlike subjects that is permitted by their "govern[ment] by the same general principle."[12] In the law, analogy expresses an "identity or similarity of proportion, where there is no precedent in point."[13] If analogies draw their rhetorical, affective, and apparent logical force from the resemblance or likeness they constitute between unlike subjects, they also regulate what we understand as the essential matter and meaning of those subjects by their reduction to the "principle" supposedly shared between them. Each subject is vulnerable to the principle that supposedly constitutes them. But equally, in linking unlike subjects through a single principle, that principle must cut off anything that is irrelevant. Hence, the principle is also vulnerable, in the form of a failed analogy, to the accumulating forms of unlikeness not just between the subjects compared, but also between each subject and the principle to which that subject is reduced. In this way, far from stabilizing both historical and contemporary contradictions—in this case, those of the civil rights era and those of our contemporary moment—analogies such as Cannick's risk multiplying the unlikeness of subjects not only to each other, but also to the seemingly stable principle that they must represent.

Analogy, as a form of legal reasoning, generates its own vulnerabilities, ambiguities, and instabilities. Perhaps this is why Cannick must use appeals to affect and interest in order to fuse the imperatives of the civil rights movement and those of the gay marriage movement. Yet in doing so, she must weaken the links between the civil rights movement and the immigrant rights movement, promoting the principle that will relate the likeness of the former comparison (gay rights and civil rights) while simultaneously making it impossible to relate the likeness of the latter comparison (civil rights and immigrant rights). To the degree that she makes appeals to the civil rights subject (African Americans)—via discourse most closely associated with that subject, as when she says, "This country broke the law by not recognizing and bestowing upon me my full rights as a citizen"—she reopens rather than resolves the contradictions generated by the state's attempt to neutralize and rearticulate the meanings of the black freedom movement.

If analogical reasoning such as that of Cannick and other gay marriage advocates has import for the law and legally constituted subjects at this historical moment, that is because those advocates posit a fundamental identity between unlike subjects that are otherwise incommensurate. The advocates promise to reduce the terrain of conflict to a single contradiction (the principle found within the analogy), and they promote the resolution of that contradiction as resolving not just the tensions of the present but also those of the past that continue to roil our present and the law's legitimacy within it. Analogy screens off incommensurability and heterogeneity, positing instead a principle to which each contradiction constitutes a more or less identical segment of a single line—in which immigrants must get in line behind the other segments. For Cannick, if the law is to remain legitimate, it must prosecute the nation, like any other offender—just as it did before, in cases such as *Loving v. Virginia*. And while the nation must suffer this prosecution from the law, Cannick's analogy offers it the status of principle or framework to link—indeed, to combine into a single line of continuity— the unlike differences that threaten the transparency and self-evidence of that framework.

In the case of analogies like Cannick's, it is the nation and its ties to liberal law that is supposed to be the deep principle connecting the unlikeness of each claim. Indeed, in making immigrant rights the next civil rights movement, behind the gay marriage movement, Cannick argues that putting gay marriage first in line for rights promises the limitless continuity of the nation as analogical principle. It is marriage equality that realigns our past (the civil rights era), present (gay rights) and future (immigrant rights), with that first person plural possessive representing nothing less than the nation form. That is, the nation form —while critiqued for its transgression against the law—is simultaneously offered the chance to rise again, if it accepts this indictment and recognizes its accuser. And to the degree that both national law and the nation form are at this moment particularly vulnerable to displacement, inquiry, reduction, and reappraisal, we may see here the appeal of gay marriage for both representatives of the law and cultural nationalists. It might come as a surprise that not only do many gay and lesbian groups ally themselves with cultural nationalism and liberal legalism at this moment, but the fact that these groups and ideologies find gays and lesbians— whom they have so recently reviled—now to be cherished comrades provides a shock of recognition that some believe we seek with our coining of the terms "homonormativity" and "homonationalism."[14] However much these groups might look like strange bedfellows for gays and lesbians, perhaps we are now in a position to grasp analogy as the very form that enables these coincidences. In fact, to drive the point home we might say that in our contemporary modernity, analogy is the logic upon which the nation narrates its relation to the differences it constituted, but which now threaten the revelation of its own incoherence. Seeing the nation-state as the promise of analogy between forms of difference reveals its incoherence, its struggle to remain the principle of differences.

Keeping this vulnerability of the liberal nation in mind, we can better grasp the promise that advocates of gay and lesbian marriage make to remember *Loving* through analogy as compelling to cultural nationalists and liberal rights advocates precisely for the way in which it reinstitutes the bond between the nation and liberal rights at the very moment when they are especially threatened by an irrevocable sundering. But I hope I have also explicated to some degree how this homonormativity reveals in fact the precariousness of the very vehicles—cultural nationalism and liberal rights—with which their proponents seek to identify themselves. In fact, we might be in the position to ask something other than why gays and lesbians desire formal recognition from national law.

Rather, let us ask why US law in this historical moment desires gays' and lesbians' desire for recognition. Why does it solicit this desire? What vulnerabilities and instabilities are created when national norms such as the law desire GLBTQ desire? And lastly, we might see in these vectors of desire—between the gay and lesbian subjects' desire for formal rights and the norm's desire for that desire—a nonequivalence such that the latter does not merely have the status of something that can fulfill or thwart the former's stated desire, but rather that both are vulnerable to the incompletion and exposure that desiring can produce.

To understand why national norms might desire GLBTQ desire for formal equality through marriage, permit me to return again to the current interest in *Loving*. If we suspend the desire for the miscegenation analogy as the import of *Loving*, what other stories might we tell about this decision and its historical value? Of the many legal decisions delivered by the Supreme Court around the middle of the twentieth century, *Loving* may be the only text in which the Supreme Court declared in writing that the norms to which state marriage laws assented prior to the suit were those of white supremacy. The Supreme Court of Virginia upheld a lower court's decision that the Lovings broke Virginia's anti-miscegenation laws by citing its own decision in *Naim v. Naim*, which upheld a lower court ruling voiding the marriage between a white woman and a Chinese immigrant—who had married outside Virginia but later moved to the state—as a violation of the state's Racial Integrity Act.[15] Although the immigrant defendant in *Naim*, subject to deportation after the voiding of his marriage, appealed to the US Supreme Court, that court declined to hear the case. Hence, in its reversal of the Virginia Supreme Court's decision in *Loving*, the US Supreme Court directly made reference to the Virginia court's own citation of its position in *Naim v. Naim*, a position the US Supreme Court had implicitly shared, or at least allowed to stand, just a decade earlier. The US Supreme Court writes in *Loving*: "In *Naim* the state court concluded that the State's legitimate purposes were 'to preserve the racial integrity of its citizens' and to prevent 'the corruption of blood,' 'a mongrel breed of citizens,' and 'the obliteration of racial pride,' obviously an endorsement of the doctrine of White Supremacy."[16] What had compelled the US Supreme Court to write that, when it had refused to give Naim a hearing?

The ruling in *Loving*, as a document, enacts a performative representation of racism legalized by the United States and the nation-state's own invalidation of that racism and its transformation into state-legalized antiracism. How did a nation-state that once used its Constitution to uphold antimiscegenation laws now find in that very document the means not only to invalidate that text—the Constitution—but to uphold it as well? To what did the law turn, and how did it present itself in such a light that it could uphold and invalidate itself in the same act?

Loving is part of a historic shift—what Howard Winant refers to as the "racial break"—in which the state apparatus moved from being officially white supremacist to officially liberal antiracist.[17] And yet, as critical race theorists and historians of the civil rights movement have argued, it is only a willful forgetting of the past to remember and hear race-based social movements' claims and demands against US racial capitalism as synonymous with the legalized formal remedies to racism that the capitalist state offered as an address and response to those demands.[18] That is, as the state shifted from white supremacist to officially liberal and antiracist in this period, it distilled from the changing and unstable meanings of both race and racism—generated by a society rife with antiracist contestation—meanings specific to its framework. In particular, race is analogized either as a private particularity or as a mark of membership in a group—like nationality or religion—both of which are protected from invidious state action. Indeed, *Loving* produces an account of race that seeks to organize the meaning of race and racism in a manner consistent with the state's liberal theory of individual liberty, formal equality, and right of property.

Gay marriage advocates who repeatedly interpolate *Loving* into the public sphere—producing similes with race and analogies with miscegenation in their pursuit of marriage contracts—ironically only affirm the *Loving* decision's original and unstable analogizing of race itself as a mark or visible sign of membership in a social group. In affirming *Loving* as the basis for their claims, gay and lesbian advocates either deliberately or inadvertently further extend a state-based juridical analogy of race, displacing the contest of racial meanings produced by the civil rights movement and other social agents contemporary with the *Loving* decision. In reopening the decision, then, we might seek instead to observe the way in which the legal understanding of race and racism is in fact a performative act, one that attempts to win the social contest over racial meanings produced at that historical moment in US society.[19]

COMMEMORATING DESIRE

What enables the law to succeed in such a strategy? Only through temporalizing racial experience into a past, present, and future can the state both invalidate itself and maintain its legitimacy. For gay marriage advocates who commemorate *Loving*, legal victories—whether in the context of the antimiscegenation laws of forty years ago or of the contemporary legal codification of marriage as exclusively heterosexual—indicate less the arrival of a particular social group, either African Americans or homosexuals, into hegemony than they do these groups' efforts to free modern norms and the state produced by those norms from the petty restrictions and blockages that prevent the norms' development. In this view, to remember *Loving* is to reconnect with the goals of the era's antiracists—to see in those goals the image of a modernity, both originally and presently constricted—and to prepare oneself and others for battle yet again, perhaps for one last battle to unshackle the norms already at our door. Indeed, if the writings of William Eskridge, a legal advocate of gay marriage, can stand as an example of this mode of commemoration, both *Loving* and contemporary gay marriage struggles are merely protracted stages of cultural development in the full expression of a specifically US nation-state liberalism. Eskridge writes:

> Liberal premises do not require the state to recognize any two people's marriages, nor to attach legal obligations and benefits to such interpersonal commitments, but once the state has made a policy decision to recognize and even encourage marriages, the state may not arbitrarily deny that recognition and bundle of regulations. For example, the state presumptively cannot give marriage licenses to same-race couples but deny them to different-race couples. The United States Supreme Court elevated this liberal principle to a constitutional rule in *Loving v. Virginia*, which held that the state could not bar different-race marriages . . . Today, the Court's liberal jurisprudence considers sex a quasi-suspect classification, namely, one that is presumptively arbi-

trary and requires strong justification when deployed by state policy . . . By analogy to miscegenation, state recognition of same-sex
marriage is required by this liberal sex discrimination jurisprudence:
just as it is race discrimination for the state to deny marriage licenses
to black-white couples because of the race of one partner, so it is sex
discrimination for the state to deny marriage licenses to female-female
couples because of the sex of one partner.[20]

Here, Eskridge defines the contours—relevant to his argument—of a
specifically US liberalism, one shaped by active state participation in the
social definition and recognition of marriage. In his normative reading,
Eskridge argues that it is this specifically US-style liberalism that generates the contradictory force of both *Loving* and the contemporary gay
marriage movement. Eskridge offers no hypothesis for why the US government became involved in or continues to involve itself in the regulation of marriage.[21] Rather, he seeks merely to suggest that the unity of
national culture with liberal universalism requires the substantive equality of homosexuals, defined for him by the universal extension of marriage rights to same-sex couples. To commemorate *Loving* in accounts
such as these is to commemorate a future in which the law, signified by a
state founded upon liberal precepts, is unified with American culture and
social life, which in turn is signified by the apparent historical choice to
involve the state in the recognition of marriage. If *Loving* is an event that
is firmly in the past, it is still worth remembering because it signposts the
origin of a substantive American liberal modernity.

Commemorations can also house a second position, seemingly opposite from the one taken by Eskridge and many gay marriage advocates
in relation to the anniversary of *Loving v. Virginia*. The second position
has been voiced most powerfully by scholars, activists, and historians
interested in remembering the social and cultural history of specific
oppressed social groups, whether they be African Americans or homosexuals. These scholars and others argue against using commemorations
to universalize or normativize a single political position or perspective,
particularly one determined by present needs or desires. They argue that
such a mode of memorializing misrepresents the uniqueness of social
histories of difference that intersect at one point or another with the law.
In contrast to the attempt by Eskridge and others to remember the past

as a milestone in the gradual development of a singular, quasi-liberal legal subject of US modernity, this position advocates making social histories of difference the subject of commemoration.

For this group, then, to remember *Loving* is to remember the history of African American struggles for equality and dignity in all spheres of life, including intimacy, as well as the contributions of the African American civil rights movements to the meaning of equality and dignity that we have inherited as a newly revamped modern society. It is through an engagement with this social history that we can ethically conduct important political comparisons between African American civil rights struggles and the legal movement for gay marriage.

Randall Kennedy's "Marriage and the Struggle for Gay, Lesbian, and Black Liberation" is emblematic of this important mode of commemoration. Remembering *Loving* in our contemporary moment, Kennedy says, requires an engagement with the current drive for gay marriage, a drive against what Kennedy terms "the heterosexual—'straight'—majority." Yet he cautions against what he and others term the "Loving analogy," which argues that "prohibitions against interracial marriage and prohibitions against same-sex marriage are the same."[22] And he concurs with the social historian George Chauncey, who notes that doing so "does no justice to history and no service to the gay cause."[23] Moreover, Kennedy argues, such analogizing tells us next to nothing about why heterosexual majoritarianism persists or—more important for his concerns—why there are traces of that heterosexism in African American communities as well, despite their formal position in the law as historically oppressed and against majoritarianism. Kennedy argues that instead, we must look in the domain of "American history" to discover repeated instances of "victims victimizing,"[24] so that we might work against both our and the previous victim's complacency and righteousness. Hence, commemorating *Loving* by remembering African American social history can help us better understand both past and current forms of oppression, racial, sexual, and otherwise. Indeed, it is through the encounter with and remembering of African American social history that we might: "Remember that history unfolds in mysterious ways that are difficult (if not impossible) to anticipate. The ugliness of the reaction to *Brown*, the Civil Rights Act of 1964, and other progressive racial reforms helped to awaken the country to the need for a larger, more determined, and ongoing confrontation with past and present racial injustices. A similar chain of events may assist in prompting society to confront and overcome its deeply ingrained oppressions of gays and lesbians."[25] Here, remembering actual African American social history through *Loving* commemorations enables the important understanding of history—not, as Eskridge would like, as a normative schema. Rather, social history reveals the power of unexpected (from the perspective of the norm) agents of society. Social history from below—of the type that Kennedy, Chauncey, and others advocate—repopulates political life with minoritized social actors and their collective efforts, which are left out of the normative accounts such as those produced by the *Loving* analogy and often excluded from the privileged domains of the political sphere and policy-making. A related point is that engaging African American social history during *Loving* commemorations enables the use of history to repress acts of African American homophobia coded as righteousness, as well as serving as evidence for gays and lesbians that the confrontation against dominating norms, however difficult and apparently failed in their own time, can serve as a moral beacon for a future generation—one that, unlike the current one, is not immune to the brutalizing agency of exclusion.

For those who hold this position, commemorating *Loving*—like in the previous position—is an act of remembering an event that is firmly in the past and fully completed. This past is more or less knowable—at least, what is important about it is—for the subject who seeks to commemorate it. And, most important, it is an event with vital meaning for the present. However, unlike the former position, the past—in this case the social world that *Loving* merely represents—is seen as distinct from the present. Precisely because we are the inheritors of that past, despite its seclusion from our present, commemorations—for those who adhere to this position—promise to remember the past that brought us here but that is no longer, no matter how many of its remnants or repetitions persist in the present.

To commemorate *Loving* in this sense is to spotlight the apparent difference between our contemporary society and that of the past. We must remember this past not merely because it can serve as an important negative example for contemporary subjects of society, lest we are destined to repeat the mistakes of the past—though remembering the past certainly does perform this function. More important, we must commemorate this past because of a moral commitment to remember the victims of the society to which we belong.

Whereas from the standpoint of norms and normative accounts of society, such as the one offered by Eskridge, the past is merely an early and primitive moment of national development, this second position— although not entirely contesting that view—grips the past also in order to remember the social histories of the groups that had once been excluded from the norms and normative society of which those who remember are a part. Within this temporal logic, commemorations are tools of memory, non-site-specific monuments to the past that settle for us—in the sense of placing, revealing, and representing—the "otherness" of the past that is both produced and threatened by our desire for and experience of modernity as the universalization of once-exclusive norms.

This is demonstrated most vividly by the numerous injunctions of social historians and legal scholars of all political stripes to remember the past correctly, with its warts and all. Such activities for the modern citizen and historian demonstrate the historical and ethical capacity of the modern subject to appraise the past just as it was, suppressing the apparent modern or postmodern desire for identity, affiliation, congruence, or even juxtaposition and contiguity.[26] At stake is the valuing of those others, now firmly lost for the present, whose lives and meaning could be grasped by the subject who seeks to remember them through the practice of history. For this subject, to commemorate *Loving* is to gain the opportunity to once again remember fellow citizens subject to and violated by racism and state-based forms of segregation, and specifically to remember African Americans, the group particularly ravaged by such legal and extralegal violence. However, central to the logic that upholds this mode of commemoration and memory is the notion that the historical subjects of the past are themselves whole and unique, sharing a positive essence. Hence, within this logic of commemoration, emphasizing differences—of gender, sexuality and so forth—within the group of African Americans is beside the point, for such differences are merely an expression of the organized plurality within a unified and positive (in the sense of empirically real) black human community. It is this community that is commemorated, and it is its struggle for survival and equality in the face of repeated material and symbolic violation and subordination that is remembered and honored.

This latter mode of commemorating *Loving* has importantly revealed the real disregard for African American history that many advocates of gay and lesbian marriage who supposedly seek to commemorate *Loving* evidence. As Kennedy has pointed out, the antihistorical legal formalist mode of comparison and commemoration that many of these advocates pursue when they remember *Loving*, tends to ignore or forget critical differences. For example, while gay and lesbian marriage is not legally recognized, it does not constitute the criminal offense that interracial marriages like that of the Lovings did in their time. That is, the desire for state recognition by gays and lesbians misremembers or forgets not only gay history before the US Supreme Court ruling in *Lawrence v. Texas*,[27] but also the history of African American survival and struggle precisely against the state, which was then formally white supremacist. Indeed, seen in this light, a more historicized formalist analysis of *Loving* would suggest that the genealogy of which it is a part is definitively not gay marriage rights, with its proponents' desire for recognition by the state, but rather something like the contemporary disproportionate sentencing guidelines for crack cocaine possession that further swelled the disproportionate incarceration of black and Latino men and women in the United States over the last two and a half decades. In both cases, de jure in the former and de facto in the latter, "the criminality of an act depend[s] upon the race of the actor," to cite Justice Potter Stewart's concurring opinion in *Loving v. Virginia*.[28]

Additionally, gay and lesbian historians, such as Chauncey, have argued that the drive for gay marriage must forgo the logics of dehistoricized comparison with *Loving*, lest we forgot the unique and specific historical forms of discrimination that lesbian and gay people experienced for most of the twentieth century. Just as African American history, to be commemorated on the anniversary of *Loving*, remembers a people's past, so too gay and lesbian history must be a memory of a people's past. Although the latter is neither experientially nor historically separate from the former—as Chauncey argues, the segregated logics that produced Harlem also made Harlem a refuge of survival and space for self-expression for a number of black and white gays and lesbians in the early twentieth century—each tells the story of a unique people and identity, however racially or sexually plural each people and identity might be.[29]

We see that in the case of Eskridge, commemoration suggests a past continuous with our own time, although in the case of Chauncey, the past is sequentially and chronologically linked, but nonetheless discontinuous with the present. It is the place where some of the kin of our generation are now lost, but not forgotten. In the first case, the substantive difference of the past is denied in the interest of establishing an identity between the past and the present within a single continuum of modernity. In the second case, the difference of the past is preserved and engaged to some degree; indeed, modernity—with its care only for the present and the future—is diagnosed as a generative loss not of historical consciousness as such, but of a certain people's history as their future and present kin are otherwise absorbed into the singular and continuous modernity from which they were originally excluded.

Commemorations, then, in this latter model, offer an opportunity to remember not just the past but, more important, a previously excluded people in their wholeness, people who are the historically important subjects of this past. Indeed, remembering these people operates as a reminder that our modernity—understood as singular, continuous, and expansive in its contemporary promise of near-universal inclusion—can easily inspire a letting go of the past that has nothing to tell us about who we are in the present. But that letting go has devastating consequences for remembering the lives of those originally excluded from that modernity. This latter model appreciates the disheartening irony that people who have been victimized by a particular modernity—as African Americans were in the making of an American modernity—must not be forgotten, lest they suffer yet another injustice, however inadvertent, this time at the hands of a new national unity for which they become the unremembered "other."

The two modes of commemoration share a sense of modernity as singular and continuous. Both divide time into units called past, present, and future. And both seek to remember the murky origins and "discontinuities" within modernity through that very prism of past, present, and future.[30] While the former commemorates the past as the beacon of a liberalized modernity that is still incomplete, promising oneself for the completion of that modernity, the latter commemorates the past as the figure of an "otherness" no longer with us, committing oneself to a vigilance directed toward the modernity of which one is a part but that historically denied the belonging of some of our past kin.[31] The latter mode of commemoration acknowledges what the former is anxious to deny: that American modernity, particularly that produced by the nation-state, has had the dual tendency to, on the one hand, both recognize and include certain forms of difference and, on the other hand, to violently exclude other forms—namely, racial difference. In the latter model, however, commemorating *Loving* as the means to remember black survival of hyperexploitation and violent subordination by the nation is if not atonement, at least a gesture of reparation, one that inserts in the space and time of commemoration—perhaps a conference, a special issue of a journal, or a social history—a people to remember and study.

In the case of the former mode, history is little more than formal memory, a pure means of revealing the demanding truths of a developing universal norm, such as the universal recognition of marriage as a fundamental right. In the case of the latter, history is a revered site of social agency, one triggered by cultural memory but irreducible to the particularistic attachments associated with memory. This is in part what the gay social historian George Chauncey means when he says that, in using the *Loving* analogy to pursue its agenda, gay marriage advocacy "does no justice to history."[32] For those who adhere to this position, history is not simply a means of representing the past. It is in fact the only means by which the we who share a modern set of norms—a normative modernity —can address and reconcile with the ghostly otherness that haunts the borders of those norms, those "others" among us who were not, in the past, fully included in those norms. In the case of the former mode, historical memory is merely the reinforcement of an already developing abstract norm, such as the universal right to marriage. In the latter, historical memory, in the form of producing and receiving social history, is a central aspect of the work we do to make the universality of the political sphere just. In contrast to the former position, in the second view, history is not merely a means of viewing the norm at work, embracing all forms of difference, whether by apparently universal or universalizing character and capaciousness. Indeed, if we must take care to do justice to history, this is because history has a central role in the making of a just society, governed by legal norms that were once exclusive but are now universal.

History has both a redemptive and an explanatory force in relation to the legal norms that were once exclusionary. It is redemptive in the sense that it is a promise not to forget those communities that were once excluded from the very norms to which the remembering subject belongs, lest the injustice of their historical exclusion be redoubled by the injustice of their erasure within social memory. And it is explanatory in the sense that it details the specific social relations that denied a people protection and recognition by those norms. But it is also explanatory in the sense that it relates the distinct meanings encoded in those norms by a people or marginalized community originally excluded from those norms—such as the right of marriage—in such a way that the norm is itself, in our present moment, a sort of monument to the once historically excluded community or people. The irony, of course, is that the social history of the excluded community is now dependent for its conditions of representational existence on the popular affirmation of the norm from which it was excluded. In addition, what is socially remembered of that community is governed by the framework of the norm or norms, which means that the social history of the excluded people is told only through the prism produced by that norm or set of norms.

The norm, such as the right of marriage, becomes both an abstraction universally valid for members of present society and simultaneously a metonym in the present for the past exclusion and the people excluded—so that the perpetuation of the norm is now paradoxically the very means by which a society promises never to forget the historically excluded just when the norm is supposedly cleansed of its social and cultural heteronomy. That is, at the very moment when the norm, apparently cleansed of its heteronomy, makes that promise it is freed from social history, from the need to historicize itself. Ironically, then, society redeems itself and its norms from their exclusionary origins, paradoxically through the universal extension of those norms. To the degree that the norms exist, and present themselves as transhistorical, and promise temporal perpetuity, the "other"—the people excluded from the norms—will always be the face of those norms. Identifying the historically excluded "other" with the very norm from which it was excluded generates a certain ambivalence from the standpoint of the excluded subjects. If the memory of the excluded community—of its "otherness" in the present—depends on the perpetuation and universalization of the very norm from which they were excluded, then any desiring of the norm must also be the desiring to remember the history of exclusion. This ambivalence makes any articulation of the norm by either descendants of the excluded community or by contemporary communities also denied recognition by the norm necessarily difficult to decode, for it is unclear if what they desire is the norm or the face—the historically excluded people. There might even be a contemporary subject who possesses both rage against and desire for that norm.

It is only through history, the careful work of representing and remembering the particularity of the past, that the universalization of the norm in the present is made legitimate. It is only through social history that the excluded are made an inextricable part of the norm from which they were originally and otherwise severed. Hence, to the degree that US legal norms are foundationally exclusionary—in particular, of racialized communities—those norms must have for their faces the social histories of the excluded, as the governing precondition of their abstract universality and universalization. Yet, if the representation of these histories of exclusion is constitutive for the contemporary extension, circulation, and universalization of these norms, they are also regulated by the framework of the norms to which they are constitutively attached. These norms powerfully shape what we seek to know when addressing the excluded face of the norm, and how we apprehend that excluded face, as well as what gives that face its unity and representational coherence for us. To the degree that the norm has this regulative force in shaping the excluded face, it has been difficult to desire that excluded face—the histories of the excluded and marginalized—without also and simultaneously internalizing the norms that both preserve the excluded past in our present and define what we desire from this past. If the norm mediates our access to the excluded past that haunts our present, to the "otherness" of the past, it also powerfully shapes both us and that past. Hence, we might ask what it would mean to remember *Loving* in a way that did not ignore the mediating function of the norm, a way that sought out the particularity of the norm that wishes to distinguish itself both from us and the excluded history that is now the face of that norm. How might we do this? From what location? And what might that kind of commemoration look like?

Walter Benjamin reminds us that "there is no document of civilization which is not at the same time a document of barbarism,"[33] and that the historian's task is to retrieve the past for contemporary struggles, lest the past be surrendered as yet another of the victor's spoils: "Even the dead will not be safe from the enemy if he wins. And this enemy has not ceased to be victorious."[34] Indeed, as Benjamin argues, "the danger [of oblivion] affects both the content of the tradition and its receivers. The same threat hangs over both: that of becoming a tool of the ruling classes." He reminds us that a social history shorn of its cultural remainders, of the historicity that disrupts formal comparison, jeopardizes the social struggles of both the past and the present, producing instead representations of both that operate in the interest of the victor. It is only those of us willing to fight in the unrefined, underdeveloped, and crude spaces present in our ambiguous times who might seize hold of the past as it flits by in the empty, homogeneous time of our present.

QUEER OF COLOR CRITIQUE AND THE POLITICS OF GAY MARRIAGE

What I'd like to do, then, is put the question another way: What are the other legacies of *Loving* for our contemporary moment? Or, perhaps more appropriately, what legacies of *Loving* does our moment make available—legacies that can be used to overcome the victors' histories? What kind of past is opened up for collective memory in this moment? And what kind of legacy is *Loving* within this condition? What I would suggest is that *Loving v. Virginia* is not just the record of the break in the racial state away from miscegenation, one of a number of precedent-setting cases in the state's transformation into an officially liberal, nationalist, anti-white-supremacist state. It is also the record of the way in which that emerging order sought to incorporate substantively black life into its legitimate domain. Katherine Franke has written articulately about the first abortive attempt of the state to do that in the aftermath of the Civil War, in the short period we know as Reconstruction. And in many ways *Loving* is part of a genealogy that might include the numerous petitions for cohabitation rights that Franke unearthed brilliantly as an archive of forgotten and perhaps nearly unrecognizable intimacies among African American slaves, both during and after slavery.[35] Engaging *Loving* as a genealogist, then, or as a Benjaminian historical materialist, we might read it as the anniversary of the beginning of both the end of the white supremacist state and of our new times, of the norms that replaced white supremacy as the new forms of socially and ethically acceptable violence. Let us turn for a moment to the decision. In a rather remarkable quote, the majority opinion begins its reversal of the *Loving* decision handed down by a Virginia trial judge by quoting that judge: "Almighty God created the races white, black, yellow, malay and red, and he placed them on separate continents. And but for the interference with his arrangement there would be no cause for such marriages. The fact that he separated the races shows that he did not intend for the races to mix."[36] The majority opinion cites this rationale only to replace it with the emerging dominant reason or foundation of the state: liberal racial humanism. Citing *Korematsu v. United States*,[37] the court averred that Virginia's antimiscegenation statutes could not prove that the state had an abiding interest in racially regulating marriage. Arguing that such regulations could not pass muster under the "most rigid scrutiny" review demanded by the Fourteenth Amendment and affirmed by *Korematsu*, the Supreme Court struck down Virginia's Racial Integrity Act as violating both due process and equal protection rights.[38]

Note the way in which the knowledge of difference as a social and economic force had been understood comparatively through racial typology by a Virginia judge. In refuting Virginia's argument that preventing interracial intimacy was a compelling state interest, the Supreme Court issued the following proclamation—perhaps one just as outlandish as the one that the Court refuted, but one that I fear would be passed over as little other than "reason" and hardly as the anachronism that we clearly now consider the state judge's opinion. Here is the Supreme Court:

These statutes also deprive the Lovings of liberty without due process of law in violation of the Due Process Clause of the Fourteenth Amendment. The freedom to marry has long been recognized as one of the vital personal rights essential to the orderly pursuit of happiness by free men . . . Marriage is one of the "basic civil rights of man," fundamental to our very existence and survival. To deny this fundamental freedom on so unsupportable a basis as the racial classifications embodied in these statutes, classifications so directly subversive of the principle of equality at the heart of the Fourteenth Amendment, is surely to deprive all the State's citizens of liberty without due process of law. The Fourteenth Amendment requires that the freedom of choice to marry not be restricted by invidious racial discriminations. Under our Constitution, the freedom to marry, or not marry, a person of another race resides with the individual and cannot be infringed by the State.[39]

What is remarkable about this quote—and what makes it just as much a historical curiosity as the state judge's wording—is that racial typology and its comparative logic of racial differences is preserved and even extended in the very decision founded on a new liberal state humanism.[40] What we see here is that even though the Supreme Court justices, the late modern descendants of agrarian industrialists and the modern industrial elite, provided a new rationale to refute that of the state judge, the modern descendant of the slavocracy, the representatives of two different modernities share a larger racialized and gendered modernity, one defined by the organization of social differences into racial typologies. Indeed, that modernity is both made ambiguous and reaffirmed by the majority opinion. It is made ambiguous by the fact that racial typology is apparently invalidated as proper science—that is, as legitimate knowledge for the production of state reason. As the court avers, racial classifications are "so unsupportable a basis" for state action that such knowledge is "subversive" to equality, making Virginia's action a violation of individual liberty. Yet the negation of racial classification is not, as the *Loving* decision shows, the destruction of racial typology. Rather, racial typologies are preserved—in the opinion's discussion of white men, black women, Indians, and so forth—and made coincident with both equality and liberty through the legal subsumption of heterosexual marriage, through heterosexuality and heterosexual gendering as the metonym for marriage—through, that is, marriage as a right.

Further, we could say that the late modern subsumption of marriage into a form or right is simultaneously the cultural production of race and gender as both the remainder and, paradoxically, the formal units used in the state's notion of abstract equality and personal liberty structured through marriage. It is also, then, only through marriage as right that the ambiguities present as race and gender are deferred in the perpetuation of a singular modernity, of which the US modern state and its juridical liberalism are a part. As a consequence, we can also say that marriage as right—which demanded heteronormativity at its time, but may not need to do so now—is the means by which racial typology is preserved despite the ambiguities generated by a state science founded on that typology, named here as racial classifications.

Indeed, it is this longer modernity that is refashioned and advanced in *Loving* and that is now operated through a rational state liberal humanism, where it turns out that marriage (that most modern of things) is in fact one of the "basic civil rights of man" (who knew?), fundamental to the very existence and survival of an "orderly" human kind. And it turns out that the freedom to marry or not marry a person of another race (and let's just note here the sad fact that we are indeed almost at the point where we will need to be able to exercise the right to "not marry") is in fact presumed by that long modern political document we call the US Constitution. Indeed, it was precisely this right to marriage upon which modern US suburbia was founded—with the promise of marriage, real property, and commodities a plenty; the shifting of the welfare state's resources to the production of suburban infrastructures like highways and on ramps, which devoured the almost emancipated urban racialized neighborhoods; and the creation of the single largest threat to the natural environment, the American middle-class nuclear family, with its 2.5 children. To say this is to say as well that race and gender are the critical cultural remainders of a modernity forcibly made ambiguous and temporarily resolved through the substantive subsumption of marriage into a right.

It is the history of the severing of white supremacy from liberal property that *Loving* is a part of, and that activists for gay and lesbian marriage rights now champion. Indeed, whatever other legacy *Loving* might be, it tells those of us trying to catch the past—as it flashes up in this moment of danger—that the universalization of the right to marriage is the very means by which the law forecloses other, perhaps more radical, articulations of antiracism. Perhaps we can read in the desire to further extend marriage as a right the preservation of a modern feeling of personhood founded in racial typology. To this degree, we could say that the desire for the universal right of marriage is above all the preservation of an episteme that has outlived its usefulness, its capacity to describe the current "what is."

This is particularly true as we turn from the politics of commemoration to the struggles mediated by gay marriage in the present moment. If we were to use a queer of color framework for thinking about gay marriage as well as about the political conjunction of the victories of Barack Obama and Proposition 8, how might we proceed differently? I argue that this framework can help us think of gay marriage and the proposition as symptoms and projects within a transnational, rather than a national political contest. Economic globalization and the emerging and at times stunningly violent regimes of accumulation that it denotes are what we might call the political unconscious of the gay marriage debate, including the struggles over Proposition 8. This approach shows how the proposition and gay marriage more generally are caught between two conflicting and historically heterogeneous expressions and understandings of the state form that have emerged in the late twentieth century.

The first understanding, deployed by advocates for Proposition 8, developed in the era after the Second World War, as the United States sought to curb labor radicalism.[41] It figures the state as an apparatus for the creation of a safety net for national citizens against the forces of the market, with its cruelties, tendencies to contract and expand, and its irregular almost-pathological episodes, if not its total meltdown for protracted periods, as we have recently experienced. This is what goes by the name of the welfare state. And it's important to remember that historically that state excluded black, Asians, Mexicans, and Native Americans from most of its protections. Currently it excludes from full protection the majority of the racialized twenty million people in the United States who are not citizens. And it continues to produce a gendered racial and racist discourse, particularly against black and Latina women—who are often presented as variations on the stereotype of the welfare queen and used to represent the dangers to the moral vision of the independent and autonomous person that the state creates when it supposedly over-extends its welfare provisions. This gendered racist discourse has been the means by which the welfare state has retracted the size, scope, and meaning of safety net for all citizens, as evidenced in the rising cost of public healthcare, education, and credit, even as the state has expanded the base of racialized poverty.

The second vision of the state, often advanced by advocates for gay marriage, emerged in the 1980s, a period of racial retrenchment against the state form discussed above. This vision of the state is also based on a theory of market universality but is more classically liberal. It describes the state as an apparatus for respecting and defending the private liberty of individuals, in particular through the enforcement of contracts irre-spective of national, social, or private differences and particularities. This is what we term the neoliberal security state: it addresses market capital-ism as the only universally true mode of sociality and hence can legiti-mately use force to penetrate markets across societies irrespective of national borders, if necessary in cases where people are subject to the irrationality of nationalist states and their leaders—as in the case of the revised justification for a US war in Iraq. The welfare state takes market capitalism as its fulcrum; it treats the state as the representation of the essential unity of society and human universality, a unity in which we all thrive like the distinct parts of a whole that is greater than our sum, and a universality only discoverable in the context of modern individuation. The neoliberal security state makes no similar moral claim. Rather, it positions itself as a guarantor of the rights that organize egoistic life in civil society, most especially the right of contract and the rights and privileges of recognition that come from making, sustaining, and existing through contracts. And, contra the welfare state, the neoliberal security state is less the means by which society addresses and corrects the cruel rationalities, errors, and breakdowns endemic to market-based forms of sociality and human social development than it is the means by which both the use and threat of force to enforce egoistic social relations are ratified as legitimate violence or force. The Bill of Rights has, in this view, transmogrified from the rights of the states against the federal government to the rights of the egoistic person of civil society against an externally imagined state, described more colloquially in our time as "individual rights" or "individual civil rights."

The legal and policy elite that organized the first phase of the gay marriage movement—a movement that I would argue began in the early 1990s and continues today—were doctrinally neoliberal in this sense, as Lisa Duggan has eloquently pointed out, arguing that the rights of contract and the moral universality of private egoism found within a civil society that contracts represent are universal values currently suffocated by an archaic and provincial national-religious welfare state.[42] Ironically, many members of the legal and policy elite are embedded in institutions like Lambda Legal and the National Gay and Lesbian Task Force, which began as institutions attached to and seeking to engage the exclusionary contradictions of the welfare state. That is, the legal, policy, and electoral initiatives for gay marriage have transacted the business of and expanded the neoliberal state within the very institutions that had their historical horizon of possibility within the contradictions elaborated by the welfare state. The racial, gendered, and sexual exclusions of the welfare state enabled the rise of the neoliberal security state, in which virtuous citizenship is understood as nothing more than equality, and equality is understood as nothing other than the equal right of each to egoistic pursuits in civil society, and to the support of the institutions that affirm and reproduce that pursuit, such as marriage. At the same time, for racialized and immigrant queers, the neoliberal security state has only intensified the contradictions of racialized inequality originally found within the welfare state. In both its political and economic definitions, the contract grants the right to make contracts for that which queers of color do not have—such as inheritance, patrimony, property, autonomous personhood, and land—while withdrawing their very means to survive and speak against the social forms that the contract institutes and reproduces in the arena of daily life.

For many queers of color, the horror of seeing the history of social movements, grass-roots activism, neighborhood and other public actions, alternatives to the protection and policing rackets prominent in gay and racialized ghettos, makeshift shelters for GLBTQ of color throwaways and runaways, and so forth presented now as a struggle first for cultural recognition and second for recognition of marriage as the boundary between a meaningful and supported existence and remaining subject to others' intentions and worldviews feels of course like a betrayal of the very histories, practices, and knowledges that were invented to survive, comprehend, and combat material modern homophobic violence. From this perspective, gay marriage is little more than the theft of collective history, the usurpation by elite and middle-class homosexuals of the material conditions and expressions of homophobic violence of poor, racialized, immigrant, and diasporic communities of color. These conditions and expressions are then repackaged as an assault on individual dignity, a private injury, and a problem of cultural citizenship, all matters supposedly alleviated by the recognition symbolized in the extension of universal marriage rights to everyone, regardless of sexual orientation. That is, advocates for gay marriage have a theory of homophobia that sees it being overcome only through the marriage contract, and a theory of contract that directs their comprehension of homophobia and its violence. Queer of color critiques continue to unsettle the beliefs that we know what homophobia is, and that it can be annihilated by the marriage contract. These critiques continue to ask why the homosexual was invented in national modern times?

For many white gays and lesbians who are US citizens, the gay marriage project actually brings together the two differing visions of the state: the welfare state and the neoliberal security state. Advocates for gay marriage often speak of marriage as a distributional right—extending access to the so-called safety-net—while at the same time characterizing the right to marriage as involving neoliberal fairness and equality. These advocates believe that gay marriage will change the state discriminations that deny them the status of autonomous person in civil society, capable of making and entering contracts, and they criticize the imposition of the parochial heterosexual morality of the political state on civil society. Similarly the Mormon, Christian fundamentalist, and so-called religious right opponents to gay marriage justify the restrictive codification of marriage through positions that affirm at once both the welfare and the neoliberal security states. At times, the opposition constructs heterosexual marriage as a central and crucial institution for the cultivation of the moral citizen of the state, justifying the discriminatory functions of the state as falling within the purview of its police powers—those broadly defined powers the welfare state possesses to interrupt personal and communal liberty in the interest of protecting the moral development of society as a whole in domains like hygiene, health, education, and public life.

At other times, the opposition espouses a worldview in which the state is positioned as a neoliberal security apparatus. In this instance, judicially recognized gay marriage is figured as the overextension of the state into civil society, forcing state belief upon private life and experience, and fundamentally breaching the right of privacy in civil and personal life that gives the security state its primary source and cause of legitimate existence. For advocates as much as for religious opponents, gay marriage has produced the means of wedding the capitalist welfare state with the neoliberal security state—both of which have had distinct racialized impacts of dispossession and disposability on communities of color. That is, gay marriage has disorganized traditional political oppositions between the so-called Right and Left (both of which talk like each other), between Republicans and Democrats, between progressives and conservatives, and between those who see there is a clear political victory and those who detect an equally clear loss in any of the recent events in the struggle over gay marriage. Gay marriage has disorganized these modern political categories, even as it has affirmed nationalism and the market system of social development. Its staying power in the national debate, media, and policy institutions appears to be an effect of its function in transacting this new hybrid of welfare and neoliberal security state, to which both the supporters and opponents of gay marriage have been beholden.

We are now in what I would call the second phase of the so-called "gay marriage" movement. It is no longer exclusively an institutional movement of lawyers and policy makers who seek to get the members of their groups behind their efforts. It has also become the means by which differing popular groups (the members) have asserted themselves in the corporate media–dominated public sphere. After the results of Proposition 8 were announced, the streets of Los Angeles were filled with outraged queers, many of them queers of color and immigrants. This is, I think, the most valuable contradiction of the gay marriage moment: it has become the vehicle for incredibly heterogeneous expressions and histories of queerness and race to announce their social and bodily presence in the public sphere again. Unlike traditional marriage, which is affirmed for transacting uniformity and sameness in both bodily and moral speech, gay marriage in this new popular, noninstitutional iteration that we saw briefly in the streets of Los Angeles is transacting heterogeneity and difference. And I believe it is our responsibility as institutionally affiliated intellectuals to take up the challenge of representing this heterogeneity as materially determined and historically produced, and to think through the consequences of that representation.

This brief eruption into the public sphere—dominated by institutions and the media—is not about the universality of marriage, a common norm among differing groups and social worlds, but is suggestive of the permanent foundation of material heterogeneity within political life and the cultural subjectivities that heterogeneity produces as the source and economic fulcrum of the national community. Gay marriage in these moments reveals something more than and something entirely different from what it was intended to do: it is disorganizing the national public sphere by inserting into social life the material cultural heterogeneities that the institutions of the nation-state are designed to suppress. And it is yielding voices and representations that it does not know how to address or entirely suppress by its formalizing drives of equality, rights, and identity. If we are to affirm this contradiction, we need to think of gay marriage not as part of the winning back of the dominant (white) national popular community from the religious right, but as part of the transnational popular community's revealing itself, through the mediation of nation-based institutions, as a new source of the critique of national sovereignty in a critical reclamation of state power from both the welfare and neoliberal states. And California's Proposition 8 campaign is an event in which we can see these sources of the transnational popular community making a claim to state power and normative constraints.

PROPOSITION 8 AND TRANSNATIONALITY

Let us close by focusing more explicitly on the example of Proposition 8. Its advocates argued that Californians should vote for the referendum because marriage is an essential institution of society. And it was on this basis that its supporters made their second claim: without a constitutional delimitation of marriage, gay rights legal activism would change the meaning of marriage. We must presume that the proposition's supporters felt that society would break down in that case. Hence, we would need to ask ourselves what is this society, its identity, boundaries, shape, scope, and role? I suggest that we approach a number of other questions as symptoms of globalization and capitalist transnationalization. To speak of society—for which marriage is a fundamental institution, the identity of which is codified and protected under the state constitution— is at once to register the social forces within and by which California is produced and sustained. Even as the proposition was put to state voters, it was restricted to California citizens, and it is clear that the proposition's advocates had chosen to introduce it in a state in which noncitizens, the undocumented, and diasporic groups constitute nearly a third of all residents. The referendum also appeared within the same election cycle that witnessed the forcible opening of the legitimate public sphere to the "speech" of transnational Latino undocumented workers, who—in May Day marches and protests, student walkouts, and work stoppages and strikes in industries, services, and private residences— demanded a political and moral response to their daily living conditions of intimidation, violence, and economic theft by the collectivity of citizens; the stealing of their surplus value; and their transformation into disposable life through their political categorization as a criminal class. Voting was in this context a response to such speech.

The transnationality of Californian society extends beyond its demographic conditions. With an economy larger than all but five national economies in the world, the state has an economic form and practices that are more intimately and intricately tied to Korea, Brazil, Qatar, and South Africa (the last of which is the only nation to include gay and lesbian rights in its constitution), than to Iowa, Connecticut, or Maine (all states where gay marriage is legal). As urban geographers and sociologists such as Edward Soja, Ruth Wilson Gilmore, and Saskia Sassen, have explained, the natural and built environment of the Golden State— with the vast agricultural lands of its central valley, the vineyards tucked away in the rolling hills that protect California's majestic oaks and other native species, the coastal towns along the mighty Pacific, on the one hand, and, on the other hand, the endless arteries of interstate roadways, arid suburbs, abandoned couches on urban asphalt playgrounds, and the freeway catacombs that shelter some of the state's nearly 200,000 racialized unplaced, as well as the country's largest share of the chronically homeless—are constitutive effects of global recessions and transnational capital's drive for profit maximization. For example, Japan's deep economic recession in the 1980s, along with the fall of real estate values in the wake of California's slow recovery from the oil crisis, made California the main recipient of all direct foreign investment coming into the United States. This share was so large that by the beginning of the 1990s, California had made the country the largest recipient of direct foreign investment in the world, surpassing China, India, and the so-called emerging economies.

Indeed, Gilmore has brilliantly revealed that until now, lodged between global and local processes, California's government has not had a deficit crisis or cash-flow problem, but a surplus problem, of how to appropriate its vast surplus from these global forces in ways that maintained a national and state hegemony in the domain of politics. As Gilmore explains, the state's solution included a complex history of racial and class realignments that led to the stunning expansion of the state's punitive apparatus, yielding a prison-industrial and policing complex like no other in the world, save for Texas. That is, the success of the state's integration into transnational and global capital circuits depended upon the industrial caging of black and brown people, precisely the demographic limits of the national and state encompassment of the political.[43] Not only has this had the effect of the racialized disappearance of and political ignoring of nearly two million members of the US public sphere, it has entrenched the state within a form that Gilmore terms the "anti-state state."[44] That is, the growth of the prison-industrial complex through government appropriations as the solution to California's surpluses in the global economy of the 1980s and 1990s established a precedent that has been hard to dislodge even now. The prison-industrial complex has become the state's main policy lever for morally equilibrating and managing California's globally dependent and globally realized surpluses and deficits. And it has transformed the state's coercive apparatuses from an enforcement of police powers, which were in theory for the development of society as a whole, into apparatuses of pure security, in which law is nothing but a tool for the workings of a civil society lacking a moral subject, project, or fulcrum.

It is in this context that we can understand the 2008 election cycle as a transnationally dependent social event, disorganizing a national comprehension of present modernity. And it may be useful to consider the outcomes of Proposition 8 as not just a moment of despair or hopelessness for a progressive politics that sadly appears to be California's last priority. Rather, understanding the passage of the proposition as a moment within a transnational chain of events might actually afford the sexual progressive the possibilities of liberating the question of sexuality from its regulation by the nation-state, opening other horizons of political and collective agency that until now did not exist as a normative social possibility. For example, the Mormon church attempted to court communities of color and immigrant communities, not only by suggesting that they shared an identity as a unified homophobic constituency (ultimately a poor basis for a coalition) but by acting as an institution within the public sphere that could mediate immigrant communities' emphasis on family rights as foundational rights that precede and ground the identity of the state. If we remember that it has been precisely on the terms of family rights that groups of undocumented Latinos have sought to counter their depiction as a criminal population—by arguing for family reunification as a moral virtue or right that all states and citizens ought normatively agree with—then we see that one meaning of the passage of Proposition 8 has been that various nonnational popular constituencies have sought to argue for a relation to state power in which they are not its expropriated object but in fact the ground for the state form. (As an aside, would the movement against Proposition 8 have succeeded if it had used the racial and immigrant political argument that "no family is illegal" against the state determination of moral legitimacy and criminality?)

This is a moment in which, as Foucault argues of modern power, the state originates from below—is appropriated by subaltern groups, no longer entirely or exclusively in subalternity, for their own interests.[45] We are witnessing the possibilities of transnational public sources and cultural heterogeneities for remaking state power against both the neoliberal and the welfare state, and toward a transnational state of articulated differences and nonsublatable cultural heterogeneities. This is not about rights, equality, or identity—it is about the speech of bodily groups that are the material foundations of the US nation-state. And although we don't yet know the complex content of this speech, we are becoming aware of its multiple voices and forms.

Don't Ask, Don't Tell

There is no document of civilization which is not at the same time a document
of barbarism. And just as such a document is not free of barbarism, barbarism
taints also the manner in which it was transmitted from one owner to another.
A historical materialist therefore dissociates himself from it as far as possible.
He regards it as his task to brush history against the grain.
—WALTER BENJAMIN, "Theses on the Philosophy of History"

Freedom with Violence is a study of race,
knowledge, and the violence that saturates the normative movements of US
modernity. It takes as its point of departure the current popular and academic
understanding of twentieth-century US
political modernity as at once liberatory
and uneven, the result of both reflexive epistemologies and attempts to narrate the shadows cast from the previous

century as modernity's historical and material conditions of possibility.[1] Slavery, empire, territorial occupation and annexation, racially restrictive admissions and naturalization, and imperial sovereignty—all are cited and their ongoing effects detailed within the hegemonic accounts of the onset of twentieth-century US modernity. These prior political and historical formations and social practices produce the uneven topography of liberty that characterizes US liberal modernity caught—whether or not it chose to be—upwind of modernization.[2] In such accounts, twentieth-century egalitarian struggles emerge as the progressive, even dialectical, elimination of the unevenness in the meaning of freedom. And the general tendency has been to write histories and political accounts that attribute this unevenness in meaning to the aforementioned social, political, and military practices that were the material conditions of possibility of the twentieth-century American nation-state. Few scholars at this point take up the jingoistic perspective of official history— which sees the nation's past, its conditions of possibility, that have disfigured the scope of freedom and its uniquely American provenance, which Thomas Jefferson dubbed the "Empire for Liberty."[3] Yet like official history, hegemonic historical practice has sought to render the above practices as responsible for a racially ascriptive tradition within the territorial nation-state. Some accounts, seeking to register these conditions of possibility—the practices of slavery, empire, and wars of annexation as the material foundations of twentieth-century US society—emphasize a declension or even absence of the modern subject to explain the ethical and moral failures of the US citizen to fulfill the promise of universal liberty.[4] In contrast, others argue that the racially ascriptive tradition within American modernity is a modern ideational construct, the legacy of the deliberate and juridically constructed racial foundations of American society, its cultural life, and its political system.[5]

But whether the unevenness is attributed to a failure to extend American modernity universally or to an unwillingness to forgo the racially ascriptive tradition that saturates civil and political society, these accounts both attribute to race—with different degrees of emphasis—the cause for the polysemy and disorganization of American or egalitarian freedom. That is, these positions maintain the nation-state as the exclusive totality for the synthesis of political practices, and thus both impose a priori regulative conditions for the investigation of race as US modernity's conditions of possibility. Perhaps a hallmark of contemporary scholarship on race is the fact that even scholars who champion an understanding of race as part of the conditions of possibility of political modernity produce the concept of race as exclusively the direct material, practical, and ideological foundation of the nation-state; without such a foundation, they argue, American political modernity would not be possible, and yet because of this foundation, political modernity continues to be fundamentally uneven. Mired in the epistemic structure that subtends and upholds liberal egalitarian citizenship, the form of US modernity that these accounts relate is, then, often against their authors' wishes, an unshapely, cumbersome, and inelegant linking of modern freedom with violence.

In contrast to dominant practices of history, sociology, politics, literature, and the law, I have attempted throughout this book to explore alternative approaches to race as part of the conditions of possibility for US political modernity. The introduction began by exploring the Western egalitarian or statist political standpoint, an epistemology that uses either liberal-individualist or republican-nationalist perspectives to rationalize the failures of universal liberty and the errancy of historical progress. In the subsequent chapters, I surveyed various epistemologies that have either disavowed (and hence incorporated), or have sought to control, the relationship between race and the global conditions of the nation-state. I argued that gendered sexuality is currently one important mediation of that relationship and thus is crucial to our current struggles for social, political, and epistemological transformation.

Taking up literary, legal, and social-scientific discourses of the twentieth century, *Freedom with Violence* has argued against accounts of race that reduce it to an explanation for the uneven development of universal liberty that twentieth-century social struggles sought to rectify. Race is not reducible to its presentation as a function or an instrumentality, no matter how sophisticated and systemic these accounts get. Taking a critical ethnic studies approach, this book has treated race as constitutive of social form. In other words, it has treated race as both an immanent contradiction of political modernity and the disruptive limits of that modernity. Issuing from women of color and Third World femi-

nisms, queer of color theorizations, antiprison scholarship, and diaspora and empire scholarship, critical ethnic studies at the beginning of
the twenty-first century understands US modern sovereignty as that
which establishes the terrain for freedom as legitimate violence. From
these critical locations, US political modernity is revealed as the means
for increasing domination and the legitimate force relations of the racialized liberal state, even as current global capitalist practices to which
this state contributes undermine the liberal thesis of territoriality by
which universal equality is promised for all modern subjects. That is, collectively epistemologies generated by critical ethnic studies suggest that
our contemporary moment is one in which the conditions of freedom
and violence—or liberty and slavery, freedom and empire—constitutive
of nineteenth-century racial modernity, and upon which modern citizenship is founded, cannot be resolved by epistemologies that see violence
as a means or an instrumentality that can be dissociated from the ideals
that organize political life. Whereas liberal egalitarian epistemologies
argue that the termination of such violent conditions is a matter of self-
willing—whether the self is that of the institution, collective or individual
—critical ethnic studies returns to Frantz Fanon's critique of the limits of
Western-inspired understandings of revolutionary violence for historically colonized and racialized groups.[6] Indeed through critical ethnic
studies, we can have a different understanding of revolutionary formations within political modernity and the limits of the nation form and the
politics of knowledge. These alternative understandings demand that we
focus on the continual reemergence of racialized cruelty and extreme
violence within egalitarian political and social formations. A genealogy
of juridical equality and state-based and state-enforced freedom, critical
ethnic studies reckons with slavery, empire, wars, land seizures, deportations, and racialized immigrants as not so much contradictory as immanent to the US exceptionalist state formation. It is a genealogy that
reveals state-based freedoms as conserving even as they produce anew
the racial and gendered inequalities that US egalitarianism has been
dependent upon and been an alibi for.

From the genealogical perspective that critical ethnic studies affords
us, this book reveals how the state form in the second half of the twentieth
century sought to address race by including it in the juridical and liberal

forms of egalitarian freedom and its apparatuses. From the genealogical perspective that critical ethnic studies affords us, this book reveals how the state form in the second half of the twentieth century sought to address race by including it in the juridical and liberal forms of egalitarian freedom and its apparatuses. As I've argued, race has historically been rendered as the original violence that demands from the liberal political state an ethical counterviolence. The progressive institutionalization and formalization of race within the meaning of the state during the second half of the twentieth century has done little to abate this structure. Rather, the state promotion of racial equality within US capitalism, most markedly in the so-called multicultural decades of the 1980s and 1990s, has contributed to an expansion and made more complex racial and racialized gendered inequalities. It has done this while growing the apparatuses of legitimate violence that do the work of securing and reproducing those inequalities. Indeed what we find by the late twentieth century, in ways that repeat the onset of the twentieth century, is a braiding so thorough of the repressive and ideological state apparatuses within the institutional sites, occasions, and acts that ensure racial inclusion that it is nearly impossible to demarcate their boundaries. As juridical equality mediates the grossly uneven distributions of history, meaning, and value that constitute racial capitalism, practices of racial inclusiveness are indistinguishable from what Ruth Wilson Gilmore calls the racialized workfare/warfare state that promulgates the structured asymmetries and divisions of contemporary racial capitalism.[7]

Critical ethnic studies, then, renews the conditions for a contemporary and materialist politics of knowledge. The chapters of this book have pursued a materialist method, one that seeks to account for our relation to the material conditions for epistemology, as well as for the social relations produced across universities, public spheres, literary texts, legal archives, and social movements. I have tried to demonstrate how our disciplinary modes of knowing have contributed to a certain acceptance of the fact that the resolution of racial modernity through modern citizenship is the limit of a politics of race. And to the degree that contemporary citizenship has been determined by the defeats as much as the successes of the struggles against persistent racial inequality and domination and colonial and imperial politics, the modern experience of race is neither an overcoming of violence by freedom, nor simply an extension of violence through freedom, but rather an ambiguous contemporary modernity as a racialized freedom with violence—every expression of contemporary racial transformation is at once conjoined with substantively modern forms of violence. In *Freedom with Violence*, I promote a critical rupture with the resignation that contemporary modernity seems to foster, either in relation to the failure of racial transformation or to the restricted victories of a pragmatic modern citizenship in overcoming racial modernity. If we presume a freedom with violence as both a normative and descriptive point of departure, we might think of the present as offering us the occasion for an engagement with the structures of legitimate knowledge that—as much as any other set of social forces—have identified the problem of contemporary modernity as precisely this ubiquitous form of violent freedom.

To demonstrate the stakes of this epistemological intervention and to return to the politics of gendered and racialized sexuality as the locus for the contradiction between historical and persistent racial and US global practices of accumulation and contemporary egalitarian politics, I would like to return here to the legislative case with which I opened this book. In 2009, President Obama signed into law the $680 billion National Defense Authorization Act of 2010, which included the Matthew Shepard and James Byrd, Jr. Hate Crimes Prevention Act. As I explained in the introduction, this second act expands federal hate-crime law to include crimes motivated by the victim's gender, sexual orientation, gender identity, or disability. I will now return to the political standpoint used to comprehend this legislative moment, but this time I will explore the specific epistemologies of violence and modernity that these legislative acts produce. In so doing, I will reveal the contradiction hidden within those epistemologies, turning to the military policy of "don't ask, don't tell" to reveal the contradictory demands of racial and sexual citizenship when articulated through state egalitarian epistemologies of violence. This analysis develops the philosophies of violence of thinkers such as Walter Benjamin, Frantz Fanon, Jacques Derrida, and Giorgio Agamben but refracts them through US racial modernity, looking beyond the nation-state to show how an epistemology of legitimate violence tethered to the nation-state creates and relies upon modern race wars. By reading the logic of sexuality that the military used to institutionalize "don't ask, don't tell" in the context of the 2004 revelations—or, more properly, snapshots—of its practices of sexual torture at Abu Ghraib, I try to show how national sovereignty comes to generalize military power both within and outside the nation-state, rather than curbing it.

US liberal egalitarianism is, as I argued in the introduction, fundamentally tied to the logic and sustenance of the nation-state. For liberal reformers, the state's assertion and use of its right of force is always as a counterviolence, what I term "legitimate violence," which importantly is from their standpoint not symmetrical in any way with the violence that occasions its appearance or demands its assertion. The reformers read the law, ideally, as a resolution or counterviolence to a seemingly discrete condition of original violence—figured, for example in my discussion in the introduction of the 2010 National Defense Authorization Act, as anachronistic hate violence. Whereas the phenomenal character of original violence—against which and for which the modern state is a counterviolence—is that it is or at least aspires to be unmediated violence, legitimate violence is fundamentally mediated violence. The state, here, is an abstract name for a complex and only loosely integrated set of institutions and the practices specific to them. The modern state is composed of institutions that make up a division of labor that ranges from law making to law preserving. And this division of labor comes to have determining force in the state's philosophy and epistemologies of legitimate counterviolence.[8] Indeed, as Robert Cover has argued, legitimate violence within liberal-democratic states is produced through a material division of labor between modern institutions—such as courts and legislatures—that formulate a legal decision, on the one hand, and institutions—such as police forces and prisons—that perpetrate acts of state violence, on the other hand. This division of labor is necessary for the achievement of legitimacy and produces a context in which the latter institutions—those possessing the material and physical means of domination—produce constitutive constraints on the former that go to the very heart of what kinds of legal, moral, and social interpretations, statements, and meanings are possible. So too the law-making apparatuses produce regulative constraints—such as the determination of conditions for the use of force—on the institutions of violence that are effective in alienating, anaesthetizing, and protecting the agents of violence and pain from moral, ethical, and legal culpability.[9] This division of labor, which combines in a particular historical moment a set of institutions by which the state form is produced, is key to the kinds of practices we associate with the state as well as with the legitimacy of the violence it asserts. Yet it is also this division of labor that produces conflicts within and among elements of the state, as well as unevenness across the institutions responsible for the production of its form.[10]

As Cover elegantly argues, the material conditions for the achievement of liberal-democratic societies, in which theoretically everyone is equal before the law and is equally subject to the law, include a division of labor in which courts and legislatures make the law and other institutions—prisons, police, interrogation centers—enact the violence of that law in the interest of preserving the sovereignty of a singular and universal rule of law within the nation-state. Those who make law, if only in the form of giving a judgment or pronouncing a sentence, as judges in a criminal court do, produce interpretations, or a hermeneutics and epistemology of the law, in which their discourse, logic, worldview, and standpoint must conform to the requirements of universality. They must imagine, for example, the judge and the criminal defendant as equally bound by and to the law's universality within its jurisdiction. Yet it is only in the enforcement of that universal against the will of the criminal defendant, when he or she is requested by armed officers to return to prison, jail, or the asylum, that the limits of legal hermeneutics and the boundaries of the universal are constituted. In that moment, it is the law's universality that is protected and maintained through the application of disproportionate state violence (of officers, guns, shackles, chains, and cages) against those who (such as the criminal, who like the judge, possesses nothing other than his or her body and voice) manifest as a particularity that cannot be universalized, or as the immediately established and enforced limit necessary for the preservation of universality. Once again, we see here, as I argued in the introduction, that universal law (ground in a liberal ethics and morality) cannot include within itself the violence on which it is predicated; for it to be universal law, it must first think without recourse to or the use of disproportionate violence. It is, then, that the material relations constituted in the violent margins of the law are and always remain (in the logic of liberal and state egali-tarianism) heterogeneous and nonidentical meaninglessness from the standpoint of universal law. Universality defines liberal law as the "other" to violence, as that which thought must give up—or, more properly, as that which is within the law as meaninglessness when pursuing the enquiry into universality or the hermeneutics of meaning. This founding exclusion quite literally makes violence meaningless in and for the prac-tices of thinking, making. and enacting universal secular law. Yet none-theless it is in the defining margins of universality that this meaningless-ness of thought, this meaningless violence, conveys the law it serves.

These margins of universality are the material relations whose shadow a legal hermeneutics seeks to dissipate. They are among the material elements excluded from and heterogeneous to meaning that meaning nonetheless must absorb within itself—attempt to render and norm within its universal terms—to the point where meaning attempts to absorb its materiality, its excess to signification. It thus attempts to transform the materiality of violence into nothing but an element of difference within its universal discourse. And in this way, the material force relations are incorporated into the discourse of the law and come to shape that universal discourse—though not as a negative, but rather in the form of a difference (such as the representation of violence through and as professional policing institutions) in the identity that is the uni-versal law. This transforms the materiality of violence into a form of namable difference within the order of meaning of the universal law. One example of this can be found in the naming of violence as a mere functionality, the responsibility of specific and delimited institutions that together exhaust the meaning of the violence of the state. The law names "violence" as a certain element (force, power, or strength) that can be located in a specific set of institutions or as a specific subset of an institu-tion in the hopes of making invisible the materiality (that is, the vio-lence) on which it is dependent but that it originally excludes from and for the production of meaning. The law's nonidentical violence remains then—like the gun that needs a bailiff, if it is to enter and serve the judge's court—as the trace of the material relations and the division of labor in the production of violence that appear within and finally inter-rupt every pronouncement of universal or settled meaning.

So the state as an ideal form or as expressing and bestowing meaning upon social relations is always cracked and interrupted by its own dependence on what it nonetheless originally excludes as the negativity of universal meaning. In this way, the state reveals its seams, manifesting as a concrete assemblage of distinct institutions arranged in a division of labor whose meanings are fundamentally nonidentical but bound together. This incoherence and gap inside the state, between the institutions charged with making laws and those charged with preserving or enforcing them threatens the reformist vision of the liberal-national state as fundamentally egalitarian. And in this sense the division of labor that produces a state practice such as the law, like the general division of labor that produces bourgeois society, is part of the material conditions of the state that produce the contradictory ideal forms of the state and of society.

Returning to the context of the Shepard-Byrd Act—which passed as an amendment to the National Defense Appropriations Act of 2010— and the broad approbation that its passage received in US progressive quarters, we need to investigate how the hate-crimes act conserves for itself the material social relations and their historically produced violence and relations of force, while elaborating epistemic structures that seek to occlude these founding conditions. In this regard, national GLBTQ and civil rights reform movements have trouble sustaining the egalitarian terms by which legitimate violence is figured both logically and ontologically as counterviolence to an original, immediate, and arbitrary violence with which it is by definition not symmetrical.

Indeed, conservatives and conservative libertarians argued that hate-crimes legislation, like all antidiscrimination policy in their eyes, makes the state party to arbitrary and illegitimate violence by overextending its reach and abilities, positioning itself as capable of gleaning the thoughts and motivations of the perpetrators of violence. For libertarians, this can lead only to an improper growth of the state in which its ungrounded and ultimately unprovable decisions about what thoughts motivated the perpetrators of violence are in fact arbitrary, a result of the disproportionate authority possessed by and granted to the state that passes itself off as based on reason or legitimate methods of investigation.[11] Indeed, for conservative libertarians, antidiscrimination laws since the civil rights era represent a confusion of the contemporary judicial state with the human itself, attributing to the former capacities and an authority distinct to the latter. For libertarians—whether of the conservative, liberal, or radical variety—decision making is an attribute of the human, that universal person whom liberalism both protects and promotes. It demonstrates the sovereignty of human will, which is irreducible either to mechanical characteristics such as strength or force, or to institutional practices founded on knowledge, rationality, or logic—all of which are crucial to the redistributive practices of the state.

Therefore, and contra the views of Straussian thinkers such as Paul Wolfowitz, a former US deputy secretary of defense, decision making is here both the source and sign of individual sovereignty—which is the only true sovereignty—from which the state gains both its legitimacy and its authority to rule. Because an individual's decisions, represented in his taste, choice, and private discriminations, are ultimately without prior causative determination—which is precisely what makes both baseless and dangerously authoritarian the juridical state's claim to be able to determine through the use of secondary evidence the thought motivating a violent crime—they are autonomous acts free of any prior authority or set of conditions that causatively determine the will's decisional agency. According to the libertarian perspective, this will that acts without prior authority is the ground from which all other forms of authority are produced and to which these forms of authority, including that of the modern state, must appeal if they are to be legitimate. When the judiciary—and, more broadly, the juridical state of the post–civil rights era—creates forms of state practice that deny the existence of, or even criminalize, the sovereignty of autonomous will, either through attempts to control and legislate thought or through a juridical determination of causative thought, they institute an authoritarian state, termed by conservative libertarians since the Second World War a totalitarian state. This is considered a ruse to make what is in the end an arbitrary state decision, backed by sheer force and strength, appear dispassionate and legitimate. Worse, for libertarians, these policies and judicial practices represent a false sovereignty, a statist sovereignty that legitimates the state's authority only by erasing real sovereignty, which in libertarian philosophy is individual sovereignty. In doing so, libertarians argue, these state practices criminalize what is definitional to the human: its ability to produce unconditioned thought. That is, when this illegitimate state acts, it does so on the condition that the human is robbed of his or her very humanness. For conservative libertarians, then, the processes of judicial deliberation, decision, and judgment that are stipulated and provided for in the hate-crimes law are each moments and expressions of the state's disregard for—indeed, violence against—the universal human, making these processes in name only.[12]

In contradistinction, the supporters' approval of the passage of the Shepard-Byrd Act was predicated on the beliefs that the state is primarily an apparatus of egalitarianism (whether liberal, republican, or communal), and that the protection against institutionally sanctioned bias is at the very core of the federal state's identity. Indeed, the bill neither creates new forms of criminality nor does it change current sentencing requirements when a perpetrator is found guilty. Rather, it expands the authority of the US Department of Justice to collaborate with local authorities to prosecute such crimes or, where local authorities are resistant, to investigate and prosecute those crimes on its own. The law also provides major increases in funding for the Department of Justice and local law enforcement to use in prosecuting these crimes, lest local officials use budgetary tactics and constraints to turn a blind eye to hate violence. And it offers special additional resources for the prosecution of youth for hate crimes. In other words, the bill produces and enables inegalitarian conditions within the very practices (such as making and enforcing the law) that constitute its identity and function as an apparatus of equality.

Yet, even as the Shepard-Byrd Act corrects what it takes to be the fulcrum of the inegalitarian conditions that threaten the justice of equality —namely, socially biased law enforcement—the egalitarian perspective championed by its reformist advocates is contradicted by the very National Defense Appropriations Act of 2010 with which the hate-crimes bill was passed. The NDAA funds a military institution that at that time had an official policy allowing for the violent policing and summary eviction of perceived homosexuality within its membership. This policy, which was repealed by President Obama on December 22, 2010, was called "don't ask, don't tell." Created as a compromise between military institutional interests (within which the rights of domination are contractually established as individuals enter the military) and the liberal right of privacy, the policy effectively banned not homosexuality per se, but only those people whose speech and conduct triggered a military perception of homosexuality within its jurisdiction. This emphasis on the military's perception of sexual orientation was uncannily coincident with the outlawing of hate crimes based on the perceived sexual orientation or gender identity of a victim. The rules organizing the military institutions make ambiguous who can perpetrate assaults that will be framed as arbitrary hate violence, as well as what constitutes for the state an assault against someone's perceived sexual orientation and gender identity, as stipulated by the hate-crimes law passed with the NDAA of 2010.[13]

Moreover, coming in the wake of the disclosure that since at least 2004—when the "private" photographs of military personnel stationed at the US-occupied Abu Ghraib prison were circulated in the media— military personnel have made repeated use of sexual violence (both homophobic, Orientalist, heteronormative, and nationalistic) in military jails and interrogation centers, the NDAA also makes ambiguous the legal and military distinction between private life or activity and perceived social and sexual identities. As the Abu Ghraib photographs reveal, military personnel playing sodomy for the jailer's or interrogator's camera appear to be within the purview of acceptable military identity, even if the behavior is considered distasteful or odious in certain contexts, especially in relation to so-called traditional societies.[14] However, playing sodomy in instances when and where the military camera is not present —that is, where direct institutional perception is absent and barred, and where those who play do not do so under the military's eye—appears to constitute the military's perception of homosexual identity.

Ironically, for a member of the military to be perceived as an offending homosexual under the "don't ask, don't tell" policy, he or she must in fact not visibly enact homosexual practices when in front of peers or superiors, but must enact them unseen by the military. This was what the military perceived as offending homosexuality. There was, in other words, a vicious tautology involved, in which the policy produced homosexuality as always already guilty, even and especially when that homosexuality was conforming to the very terms elaborated by military policy. It was, counterintuitively, precisely not showing and not telling one's homosexuality that confirmed the military perception of a homosexuality that affronted and disregarded military policy, actively and perversely going unseen, enacting and flaunting its unseeable homosexuality right in front of an always perceiving military eye.[15] All the while the policy did not perceive as excludable—that is, as offending homosexual identity— homosexual acts the military directly and immediately perceived, especially when it participated as a voyeuristic party to the acts it was watching, as in the case of homophobic and Orientalist acts of sodomy that were apparently a regular aspect of enemy interrogation. That is, the military's perception of homosexuality was finally a profoundly self-structured, though disavowed, perception and rage about those identities that it interrupted and limited, while it constructed its own fantasy about its capacity for total perception.

"Don't ask, don't tell" was a policy that tried to combine the military's rights of domination—which, with the exclusion of acts of malicious destruction or violation, are nearly infinite if they can be proved to have a rational basis—with an individual's right of privacy, that zone of unreason and freedom that needs no justification, and that is restricted only by the principle of not harming others. For the military, homosexuality falls into the right of privacy and thus the caesura within the space organized by rights of domination. Perhaps it is for this reason that the military is fixated on homosexuality and expends so much unnecessary energy on publicly shaming and expelling homosexuals, even to the point of undermining its own functional abilities—as when it used "don't ask, don't tell" to expel desperately needed translators with Arabic, Farsi, and other non-Western language capabilities throughout the 1990s. It is not because homosexuality restricts the military's rights of domination or resists its power that the military pursues this imaginary threat beyond all rationality. Rather, it does so as the only way to prove to itself that those bodies that travel as the right of privacy within military space are precisely what mark its limits of perceiving and knowing. These legal limits become the target of the institution's seemingly paranoid violence, turning the subject of privacy into what lies beyond the military's jurisdiction. That is, the military relies on and is tied to the concept of jurisdiction in order to address, touch, control, and destroy the "beyond" of that jurisdiction.

In a manner that is thoroughly racialized, the military actively pursues homosexuality to prove that the right of privacy, or freedom as the rights of unreason, produces less a limit to its scope than a shift in its tactics, one in which subjects of privacy or free unreason are less a limit on its powers than the basis by which it cultivates a new strategy and way of seeing to capture the figural beyond-its-jurisdiction. "Don't ask, don't tell" finally was a policy that upheld the fantasy of an omnipotent and omniscient institutional military power, one that operates not through the eradication of its own limits but precisely through their ongoing but injured manifestation. For a time so thoroughly a part of a military institution that has fought racial wars for two centuries, the policy produced an offending homosexuality that, in relation to the "otherness" of the racial enemy, is not an opacity that military power can see into and through, but precisely that which is and remains the nontransparent within the transparent vision produced by military rationality and instrumentality.

MODERN RACE WAR

As scholars such as Paul Kramer, John Dower, Lydia Liu, Mahmood Mamdani, and Anthony Anghie have shown, modern race wars perhaps best define the uniqueness of modern military violence used by the nation-state.[16] Modern militaries are entirely conditioned by the nation-state. They draw up, invent, and renew their instruments of force from the productive forces uniquely available to nation-states. Militaries have access through national governments to unparalleled wealth generated by the collection of taxes, the distribution of bonds, and other resources. They have access either through conscription or the labor market to a consistent supply of human resources.[17] Equally important, they are able to maximize the use of that force in specified geographical zones, against a recognized opponent or set of opponents, and within certain contested territorial boundaries. Only through their dependence on the universal political society established by the nation-state—which includes diplomatic efforts, international law in general, laws of war and combat in particular, treaties, and parastatal regulatory bodies—do military actions and their violence have the character and appearance of discreetness, so that they do not provoke neutral parties that would otherwise find the military slaughter of populations, for example, a breach of civilization, a forfeiture of national sovereignty, and the irrational behavior of an untamed power.[18]

By citing the rules of political society before conducting a specific military action, national militaries are able to unleash disproportionate force without being perceived as threats to other parties possessing force. That is, by operating within the terms established by political society and international law, militaries can unleash a high level of technological and instrumental fury and might on the battlefield, without concern that their neighbors and friends might find such displays a threat to them or to the international order. By keeping other states neutral, military power appears to be and actually is stronger, more concentrated, and more awesome than if its actions produced reactions that challenged its power, divided its forces, and dissipated its strength. Indeed, just as the United States was declared in 1989 to be the sole remaining superpower—with the size, scale, and resources of a military befitting that title—the unilateralism of the neoconservatives since the beginning of the twenty-first century have left the country in a condition of imperial overextension. The US military, although no smaller and possibly larger than it was in 1989, is now engaged in multiple wars, which makes it substantively weaker. Both materially and legally, sovereign nation-states are the conditions of possibility of modern Western militaries and of the force they are capable of producing. Western militaries become ever more rational and rationalized, for the express reason that—as a rational apparatus of violence for the nation-state—they are able to produce and use a more awesome quantity and quality of force. This has been most acutely true in the use of national sovereignty by Western militaries to produce wars against non-Western peoples, from indigenous tribes to civilizations with long histories.[19]

Western national sovereignty has historically produced non-Western societies, geographies, and resources as outside political society and has enabled the military production of race wars, or the strategic use of disproportionate force unique to modern rational institutional capabilities, against those societies. Without the rules of sovereignty organizing Western nation-states, modern Western military violence could and would not have discovered the means for making distinct race wars, for they were produced in spaces and against peoples whose identities were determined by the nation-state and the Westphalian system. And since the nation-state is the condition of possibility of modern militaries, further producing military violence based on structures of rationality and rationalization, race also figures as a unique target for military violence. Race is the "other" of the nation-state, the limit of sovereignty, and hence also outside the boundaries of the rational. Thus the racial enemy is a unique problem for the military. On the one hand, the kind of disproportionate force that the military uses is predicated on and justified by the position that the racial enemy is outside the terms of sovereignty, the nation-state, civility, rationality, and political society. Yet on the other hand, this disproportionate force remains a rational force, constrained by its production through the nation-state, and so uniquely vulnerable to an irrational and nonrational violence and to race itself, in ways that merely growing or expanding its existing means of rational violence cannot address. In this perspective of military violence as a rational violence, if it is to be an effective counterviolence to race— and race is exactly that which demands a counterviolence—it must produce a supplemental violence that is in excess of rational or modern sovereign violence, a violence that might best be called cruelty or extreme violence.[20]

For a military whose condition of possibility is the nation-state, and for a nation-state whose sovereignty was forged through taking turns in making and observing race wars between Western sovereign states and nonsovereign peoples, race is both effect and cause of the development of national sovereignty. As such, race is the limit of that sovereignty, the nonrational remainder in a modern world that has discovered the possibility of rational social relations. For the forces that supplicate sovereign power, race is precisely that which calls forth the constant use and demonstration of an extreme violence or cruelty alongside and within the practices of the military's supposed rational violence—if the military does not in a flash commit itself to such cruelty, it has not in fact demonstrated itself to be an effective counterviolence to those barbaric "others" whose racialization is both cause and effect of modern sovereignty—that is, national sovereignty.

Like the view that concludes, in soberness and sadness, that it is because there still remain people who lack humanity and thus respond only to the violence represented by torture that there are rational torturers— and not vice versa—Western military violence figures race as the cause of the military's recourse to cruelty and extreme violence. If race was constitutive of the development and consolidation of national sovereignty in the West, as well as the powerful rational militaries that developed through the nation-state form, it is also the mark of a certain limit posited by those self-same institutions of the state, such as the military. Race reveals the national conditions of possibilities of Western militaries—that the modern Western nations and the institutions they developed were determined by empire—and so also figures as a very specific material threat for national institutions. Race is the threat that all national institutions of the West have historically specific and structured limits, their conditions of possibility that are constitutive to their development, growth, and persistence. Yet for this reason, race figures metaleptically as the outside to those very limits upon which modern rational formations depend.

Especially in the case of the global hegemon or superpower (but which Western nation is not this, in relation to its colonial regions and racial populations?), the Western military's raison d'être is to establish through the nation-state a rational mimesis of omnipotent power. So, unsurprisingly, for Western military power, race is not only a threat, but exactly that kind of threat it most relishes, because the presence of race demands and calls forth the development of a military counterviolence that is entirely different in quality and kind from rational violence. This other violence is a violence whose appearance must contain an element that is specifically irrational—appearing variously as acts of private sadism, institutional cruelty, or extreme violence—and that is beyond any calculus of functionality or rational expenditure. Race figures for the military as the opportunity to exceed its own rationalized conditions of possibility, developed in the interest of a rational mimesis of pure omnipotence. In producing race as the cause of a distinct mode of institutional counterviolence, military power develops an expression of violence or force that, in exceeding its rational conditions of possibility, in fact fulfills their purpose. Racial violence—callous, cruel, and extreme but always exceptional—is the supplement that gives the appearance of a rational military power that has achieved a perfect mimesis of an omnipotence, which by definition is beyond or, more properly, is also its own limits and conditions.

It is for this reason that I believe cruel, callous, or irrational violence is neither an aberration of the Western rational military formation, nor an interruption to the acts of an otherwise committed rational mind. Rather, this exceptional violence is generated by the production of an immanent limit that is and must be repeatedly crossed if the military is to be a specifically rational violence that also fulfills the promise of a fantastical sovereignty. Precisely because race is the exception without precedent—always contingent, never the same; geographical and religious one moment, then biological, then cultural, then socioreligious, and so forth—it cannot ever be fully rationalized by military power. Indeed, its very mercurialness within rational frames, its surplus one moment and its spectrality the next, is evidence of its violence. In producing an effective counterviolence to race, it is crucial that training the human elements of a national military to cross the limits of rational violence—to know how and when to spontaneously enact cruelty or extreme violence—happens in an equally supplemental and almost mystical way. This eruption of racial counterviolence is not something that rational or official training could ever perfectly render in a manual, as a method, or through a structured lecture (though the occasional spontaneous joke that fits so felicitously within a structured lecture, and whose racial or sexual appropriateness and sensitivity is sure to be dissected later by a panel of censors, is a good way to do it).

Extreme violence is not a military violence that will appear with a steady rhythm and punctuality of application; this is not its temporality. It is not a violence that can be jurisdictionally located, even if all we were talking about were some quasi-jurisdiction called "out there." Nor, finally, is this violence the exclusive effect of an official but top-secret chain of command—for all of those methods would finally undermine, by transforming it, this supplemental violence, cruelty devised exclusively as a counterviolence to the unreason of race, to a rational structure of violence where it is no longer fully effective, since race is what exceeds rational conditions and cannot be addressed only rationally. Rather, this violence and its training must remain at the level of immaterial relations, a culture of racial cruelty that lives as an ethos and disarticulated possibilities in the gaps of rational practices. Although rational structures can easily be appropriated for racist purposes, as in the case of official or state-based white supremacy, they also seek a supplemental violence that is precisely the counterviolence to race, that is specifically outside the bounds of rational practice but without which rational practice, as a mimesis of omnipotence, would be without meaning or real purpose. Hence, well after the end of the racist purposing of rational structures— marked, for example, by the racial integration of the military or the banning of racial language and ideologies to describe the war area or enemy —race persists within military power, necessitating a vigilant counterviolence, an extreme violence, wherever and whenever rational force is deployed by the sovereign nation-state.

DON'T ASK, DON'T SEE

This is most clearly expressed in a published defense of "don't ask, don't tell" that sought to explain the military's need for and use of the policy for a rather outlandish, public, and strangely vigorous pursuit of homosexuals within its ranks. Written by Merrill A. McPeak, a retired general who as Air Force chief of staff from 1990 to 1994 had helped shape the policy, this New York Times piece defended the policy and institutionalized homophobic violence in general as an important ingredient in making successful and "cohesive" warriors. The general reminds his audience that "sometimes [armies] win or lose because of material factors, because one side has the greater numbers or better equipment. But armies are sure to lose if they pay no attention to the ideas that succeed in battle. Unit cohesion is one such idea."[21] When sovereign armies fight one another, the side with greater numbers or better equipment usually wins. Yet McPeak implies that when sovereign armies such as that of the United States lose to nonsovereign combatants—as in the Vietnam War, the disavowed specter that haunts his writing—the factors of equipment and numbers are irrelevant in understanding that loss, since rational civilization is marked in part by its hugely superior supplies of both. It is only in the one-sided race wars between sovereign nations and uncivilized peoples that the true variables between success and failure can be found. Like the fictional Marlow of Conrad's Heart of Darkness, for McPeak it is ultimately ideas—of racial and masculine unity and difference—that determine military victory, especially when fighting nonsovereign enemies. Sounding more like a nineteenth-century US military officer defending the tactic of playing Indian before fighting Indians, McPeak writes:

> We know, or ought to, that warriors are inspired by male bonding, by comradeship, by the knowledge that they survive only through relying on each other. To undermine cohesion is to endanger everyone.
>
> I know some will see these ingredients of the military lifestyle as a sort of absurd, tough-guy game played by overgrown boys. But to prepare warriors for a life of hardship, the military must remain a kind of adventure, apart from the civilian world and full of strange customs. To be a fighter pilot or a paratrooper or a submariner is to join a self-contained, resolutely idealistic society, largely unnoticed and surprisingly uncorrupted by the world at large.
>
> I do not see how permitting open homosexuality in these communities enhances their prospects of success in battle. Indeed, I believe repealing "don't ask, don't tell" will weaken the warrior culture at a time when we have a fight on our hands.[22]

As McPeak claims, making American warriors requires something more than and other than making them equivalent expressions of rational activity. The process also involves infusing the military institution with that more mystical aspect called "warrior culture," where "adventure," "strange customs," and racial cruelty abound. Thus at any moment, when the arbitrariness and unreason of race suddenly reappears, such as now "when we have a fight on our hands"—the institution will be represented by soldiers who possess not only the rationality of the "civilian world" but also the more important, intangible, "idealistic," and "uncorrupted" capacities for the only kind of violence, pure and cohesive counterviolence, that wins one-sided sovereign wars. It is also for this reason that I believe we ought to see the military fixation on and pursuit of homosexuals in the era of "don't ask, don't tell" through a genealogy of race.

Homosexuality figures for the twenty-first-century military as another limit produced by the military's ever-changing national conditions of possibility—in this instance, signified by the rationalization of its perception through the dual legal code of rights of privacy and the contracted rights of domination possessed by the institution. Going beyond this limit, through practices that might appear both arbitrary and cruel to the "civilian world," enables the fulfillment—not the abandonment—of the drive to rationally achieve a mimesis of omnipotent power. When defenders of the military speak of the rational purpose and necessity of its targeting, shaming, and expelling homosexuals from its ranks after the imposition of "don't ask, don't tell"—although all scientific studies have revealed that when a member of a military unit discloses his or her homosexuality, this does not effect in any measurable way group cohesion, desertion rates, rates of HIV infection, or anything else—what they are referring to, I believe, is the necessity of protecting extreme violence or a right of irrationality and cruelty that can and will be used when needed, because it is needed at the very core of the military institution constituted through the nation-state. The defenders of the homosexual witch hunts during the era of "don't ask, don't tell" seek to protect that most important Western military asset, the intangible racialized freedom to act with a discretionary and arbitrary cruelty so necessary in a world in which rational violence, organized and constrained by national sovereignty, must do battle with unreason and the irrational itself—that is, with race. To that end, it is only after the policy was imposed that homosexuality could figure as part of this genealogy of racial cruelty, and not, for example, as part of the genealogy of national masculinity that many have argued was constitutive of the military in the Cold War. This is also why women have been overrepresented targets. Moreover, this constitutive determination by racial cruelty occurred only after the passage of "don't ask, don't tell" because it was only through the policy that a certain kind of homosexuality figured as that offending limit that revealed the military's national conditions of possibility. Perhaps for the same reason, there was an aggressive use of the policy to eject homosexuals during the so-called war on terror in Iraq and Afghanistan. To be clear, it is not that homosexual military personnel have been made into a race, or made analogous to blacks and Latinos, or to Asian and Middle Eastern enemies. Rather, homosexuality within the military gains its meaning and identity only through an active racial matrix that is as central to the production of actual force and its continued disregard for civilian casualties and collateral damage is it is to the fantasy of omnipotence that is definitional to the military of a Western nation-state and that codes its own terror as civilization.

Both the war on terror and the logic of preemptive defense that organized the use of national sovereignty and military force to invade and occupy Iraq and Afghanistan not only repeat the genealogy of race wars, but they also reproduce the destabilizing and contradictory centrality of race to every Western assertion of national sovereignty. It is at the very moment that the nation form once again enables the US military to unleash an unmatchable rational violence through the use of international law, producing Iraq and Afghanistan as nonsovereign regions claimed by American sovereignty (or as regions formally but not substantively sovereign), that we see a resurgence of military practices—from homosexual witch hunts after the implementation of "don't ask, don't tell" to torture; the reopening of the former US prison for Haitian migrants, Guantánamo; and playing sodomy in military prisons—that confirm just how acutely the military perceives these wars as the return of the unreason of race for which rational violence and force are never wholly sufficient, and that explain the drawing up of torture memos, enemy combatant statutes, international policing treatises, and so forth. We have been returned to that moment—though we never really left it—when the military's rational perception must extend as well to what it cannot perceive, such as the unreason of race, and the race warrior it must do battle with. It is entirely possible that many in the military relish the prospect of battle with this racial warrior and the kind of violence it brings because, despite how badly the war might be going when judged in political terms or even as a measure of military strategy and capacity, it is entirely a success when measured in terms of the military's ability to daily produce and see over and over again its effects on what it accepts as beyond rational perception.

Hence, we should interpret the spate of functionally irrational expulsions of homosexuals under "don't ask, don't tell"—during a period in which the military was grievously understaffed and strategically lacking in precisely the resources possessed by many of those violently expelled, such as Arabic, Indonesian, or Farsi language skills—as neither accidental nor wholly self-destructive. The resources of those who were homophobically expelled are finally rational assets, important assets for those who are members of political society. But the military's protection of arbitrary homophobic violence in the era of "don't ask, don't tell" also had a specific fantasized military value, a very important one during wars with race—that is, wars with nonsovereign regions and networks. For it is during these race wars in particular that the military must claim to itself and to the national sovereignty it serves that is has the power and ability to be both a system of violence founded on national sovereignty and rational (legal and scientific) practice as well as an omnipotent violence that succeeds by becoming its constitutive or determining conditions— the only effective counterviolence to the arbitrary violence of race. In its implementation of "don't ask, don't tell," the military operated through the rational perception that it received from the sovereign nation, a founding condition that shaped the very possibility of using its forces and modes of weaponry in Afghanistan, Iraq, Pakistan, and other countries of the global south. And it did so while also, in a fantasy of omnipotence, demonstrating through expelling offending homosexuals, that it was capable of seeing or engaging what was by its own logic and definition out of sight.

Every conviction of homosexuality under "don't ask, don't tell" proved homosexuality to be a racial offense. As the vanishing point of legalized military perception, homosexuality flaunted itself, most especially when it was obeying the letter of the policy, as that which is outside or beyond the rational omniscience of military perception. Hence, military homophobic violence is an unstable supplement to the rational perception through which the military claims and gruesomely enacts on nonnational others its execution of the nation's sovereign violence. Finding, shaming, and legally expelling homosexuals serves the fantasy of a rational force that, in becoming a counterviolence to the rationally invisible spectrality of race, becomes a perfect mimesis of omnipotence. Legally expelling homosexuals under "don't ask, don't tell" was the military's proof to itself of the achievement of that wishful fantasy that seeks to exceed its own felicitous conditions of reality, for it showed the military's capacity through an act of counterviolence to see what is by rational and legal definition not present at all.

Therefore, the military repeated this seemingly arbitrary and violently phobic practice over and over again, despite internal and governmental protest, for each instance provisionally affirmed that as an institution produced through defining and conditioned rational capacities—in the case of "don't ask, don't tell," capacities of legal and rational perception—it remained omnipotent within itself. These phobic practices sought to avoid the simple truth that legal and rational capacities are by their very definition limited; there is no perception that is not conditioned by and dependent on its relations, not only to a set of embodied rules but also to a specific limiting horizon, a set of objects, a source of light, and so forth. Unable to repeal the perceptual capacities out of which it emerges and on which it is structured, homophobic violence enables the fantasy that, through its own more vigorous activity, it will not be limited by its own capacity—that from its vigor, it could also perceive in the form of marking, touching, and injuring in counterviolence that which was persistently unperceivable by rational perception. Institutionally cultivated homophobic violence, whether targeted at homosexual military personnel or racialized enemies—the Arab and Muslim prisoners of Abu Ghraib, Bagram Airbase, and elsewhere—tries to prove and manifest in social reality a thoroughly racial military fantasy of pure sovereignty (what I have been calling the rational mimesis of pure omnipotence), in which, magically, the conditions that make US military power and perception possible (including the rule of law, or constitutional state apparatus, that both funds it at levels higher than any other military in the world and that now imposes the right of privacy upon it) in no way limit that conditionally generated power and perception. Like humans, God and the military perceive, and so have conditions of perception; yet unlike humans, God and the military are that which are also those very conditions of perception of what is beyond perception itself, the unperceived that is also a condition of perception.

The use of homophobic violence to mark racial and sexual "otherness" within the military's horizon of perception and rational activity proves its fantasy that this is a military force and power that is entirely based on rational, instrumental, legal, and technological—in sum, modern—conditions of possibility, and at the same time is capable of demonstrating, as a counterviolence to race, that it is also beyond its own conditions of possibility. Thus we return to the not-visible conditions of possibility discussed in the introduction. Whereas the Shepard-Byrd Act seeks to eliminate state institutional conditions that foster arbitrary and immediate violence, the National Defense Appropriations

Act funds a military (or apparatus of state violence) that uses institutional violence to eliminate (only to recruit and eliminate again) what it perceives as the imperceptible threat that defies its legitimate capacities for universal perception. And furthermore, in relation to the US war in Iraq, since the NDAA funds a war whose legitimacy—when measured by the international norms governing state violence in contexts of self-defense—is increasingly suspect, the egalitarian principle grounding the view of the hate-crimes legislation as evidence of the nation as a source of social progress is even further troubled. We can appreciate now the degree to which it is the specific work of liberal nationalism to interpret the passage of hate-crimes law as ideally separable from the larger context of its passage, a stunningly dramatic instance in which the domestic is figured as coherently separable from the foreign policies within which it is embedded and under which it thrives.

Indeed, when read together, these acts appear to confirm John Stuart Mill's observations about the—today we would add "Western"—nation-state. Surveying England's actions during its so-called civilizing mission 150 years ago, Mill wrote the seemingly logical phrase "a democrat at home and a despot abroad." This combination appears to remain, though now through different international bodies, normative to Western liberalism. That is, the abstract categories of "domestic" and "foreign," "home" and "abroad" seem foundational to liberalism's capacity for self-assessment. This is so much the case that even in this instance, in which a domestic hate-crimes law was passed with a military appropriations bill, the abstract categories of the domestic and the foreign seem so constitutive of the reformist view that at the exact moment in which those categories would appear to contradict the immediate reality of the hate-crimes bill's passage, they appear most powerfully constitutive. The domestic nation is defined by a shared commitment to the values of equal human dignity, freedom, the rule of law, and accountable, representative government, while foreign space is ultimately, under the nation's sovereign powers, presumably illegitimate within the US domestic sphere but necessary for the development of nations and their populations elsewhere.[23]

We can see how these abstractions organizing the reformist vision and understanding are crucial to their position that the US state has achieved, or at least strives for, egalitarian wholeness. For reformists, these abstractions—the domestic and foreign, police and military, democratic rule of law and sovereignty, hate violence and legitimate violence—are crucial for staving off the ambiguities that otherwise threaten to crowd out the apparent clarity by which they approach and promote the state. The liberal principle of egalitarianism that organizes political modernity demands that a search for logical noncontradiction be pursued in circumstances of contradiction, lest the ambiguity of current practices of state become more socially pervasive. In this instance, the problem is that the affirmation that protections from anti-GLBTQ violence prove the state is an egalitarian apparatus is at once contradicted by the larger context in which that affirmation is advanced.

It is for this reason that some of the reformist organizations that pursued the egalitarian principle constituting their perspectives on the passage of the hate-crimes bill spoke of it as only one of the building blocks to full equality, the others being equal treatment in employment, marriage, and the military. Indeed, even gay and lesbian organizations and civil rights organizations that have been against the war have found it impossible to speak of the use of "don't ask, don't tell" as anything other than an exclusionary practice that is anti-egalitarian, culturally homophobic, and so forth—as if homophobia were a consistent meaning and practice in all social and historical instances, merely codified by law and now brought to national attention because of the war's activation of this previously dormant institution. Even the most critical of these reformist organizations have made statements against the military's use of torture, against the breaking of international law, against indefinite detention, and simultaneously for the unimpeded military inclusion and incorporation of homosexuals, figuring that incorporation as definitively antihomophobic, a step toward the real acceptance of sexual differences. These paradoxes of social politics appear necessary from egalitarian standpoints, lest the critiques of that perspective undermine the possibility of taking a robust stand on homophobia, and vice versa. Yet if homophobia after the end of "don't ask, don't tell" is seen through a late modern genealogy of race, perhaps so-called antihomophobic emancipatory politics would have a different coherence, one that could construe the critique of military homophobia as coinciding with the critique of national sovereignty—a sovereignty for which race is its condition of possibility and that therefore continues to cultivate, out of its own logic, the counterviolence of cruelty as its unstable, though persistent and necessary, supplement.

Indeed, recall when US torture photos were disseminated publicly, and government officials responded uniformly with expressions of shock and disgust. One question always operated as the frame within which the long history of US racial globalism that is American sovereignty could be presented as the story of American exceptionalism in global modernity. Executive commissions, congressional hearings, internal investigations—all were established to ask the same question: "How could this have happened?" The International Gay and Lesbian Human Rights Committee offered an answer repeated by many GLBTQ groups, arguing that the rampant torture was in part a consequence of rampant and state-sanctioned homophobia within the military. Some gays and lesbians testified to the shame they shared with the tortured in the pictures. Yet when we remove the racializing prop of American exceptionalism and state egalitarianism, we can better see the metalepsis at work here, how sexuality mediates the violent racial and material conditions that the nation amends and conserves within itself. We are extricated from the frames that would locate the repeal of homophobia as conducive to ending homophobic or sexual torture, that would find an equivalence between the effect and experiences of the military's pursuit and legal prosecution of homosexuals and its pursuit and destruction of the racialized subjects, communities, and life worlds that—through the universal rule of law that governs the Western nation-states—are transformed into lives devoid of value. When we see the links between Western sovereignty and racial warfare, we will no longer be exercised by the exceptionalist question, "How is this possible?" Released from its grip, we might be able to ask instead: What are our responsibilities? What formations of struggle and knowledge must we build when our sexuality mediates the global and racial violence that is part of the nation's constitutive conditions of possibility? If we fail to ask these questions, it will be our sexuality that now threatens oblivion for the past and present shadows traced across this book. And the fragmented alternatives that such shadows demand and hold will be transformed through our unquestioned national conditions of possibility into mere difference, humiliated and captured on photographs that provide their own exceptionalist captions.

1 See "Obama Signs Hate Crimes Bill into Law," *Washington Times*, October 29, 2009.

2 See Christopher Drew, "Victory for Obama over Military Lobby," *New York Times*, October 29, 2009.

3 The 2010 NDAA is the largest single appropriation to the Department of Defense. However, when measured as a percentage of the gross domestic product (GDP), the amount is lower than appropriations for defense spending during the Reagan administration (1980–88). Additionally, the total amount of defense spending annually in the George W. Bush administration (2000–2008) exceeded this amount because of the accounting techniques and supplemental appropriations used by that administration. Nonetheless, the contents of the 2010 NDAA support the claim that its passage was a victory for the Democratic Party over the military-industrial oligarchy that supports the Republican Party. Yet neither party seemed to notice the social and political meanings of "disclosure," "procedure," and "transparency," and the information that those terms relate when used to characterize the single largest defense appropriations bill signed by a US president—and signed during a period in which the United States is actively committed to regional wars as crucial to its national security. In the interest of national security, the United States has engaged in practices that disrespect other regions' sovereignty as well as international laws against

enemy torture and rules of engagement that are supposed to prevent excessive civilian casualties. See Barack Obama, "Remarks by the President at the Signing of the National Defense Authorization Act for Fiscal Year 2010" (press conference, the White House, Washington, October 28, 2009), http://www .whitehouse.gov/the-press-office/remarks-president-signing-national-defense -authorization-act-fiscal-year-2010.

4 Barack Obama, "Remarks by the President at the Acceptance of the Nobel Peace Prize" (speech, Oslo City Hall, Norway, December 10, 2009), http:// www.whitehouse.gov/the-press-office/remarks-president-acceptance-nobel-peace-prize.

5 "Obama Signs Hate Crimes Bill into Law," CNN.com, October 28, 2009, http://www.cnn.com/2009/POLITICS/10/28/hate.crimes/index.html/.

6 Obama, "Remarks by the President at the Signing of the National Defense Authorization Act."

7 Rea Carey, "Signing of Hate Crimes Measure Is Historic," National Gay and Lesbian Task Force, October 28, 2009, http://www.thetaskforce.org/press/ releases/pr_102809.

8 "President Signs Hate Crimes Bill into Law: 31 Advocacy Groups Hail Historic Event," Lambda Legal Defense and Education Fund, October 28, 2009, http:// www.lambdalegal.org/news/pr/xny_20091028_president-signs-hate-crimes . html. The joint statement, titled "History in the Making," also appears on the websites of the other signing organizations.

9 See Ilene Rose Fineman, *Citizenship Rites: Feminist Soldiers and Feminist Antimilitarists* (New York: New York University Press, 2000), 89–94; and Rogers M. Smith, *Civic Ideals: Conflicting Visions of Citizenship In U.S. History* (New Haven: Yale University Press, 1997).

10 In his classic account of nationalism, Benedict Anderson reminds us that the inescapable question for any study of nationalism is not so much how modern nations condition one to kill for the nation-state, but rather why it is that one is willing to die for the nation-state. To the degree that, following Anderson, we can understand the national community as promising seemingly "horizontal" affiliation, we can read the egalitarian principle of national horizontality between members of the national community psychoanalytically. In a psychoanalytic reading, this apparent horizontality that inspires the citizen to offer his life for the nation is in fact mediated by an exclusive and prior vertical bond between citizen and state that conditions the possible kinds of group sociality —or "horizontal relations," as Anderson calls them—that modern citizens achieve in collective actions such as pursuing state reform, defending personal rights, or going to war. See Benedict Anderson, *Imagined Communities: Reflections on the Origin and Spread of Nationalism* (New York: Verso, 1996), 7. As Freud notes, modern mass formations—whether the urban crowd, the sports mob, or female students at a boarding school—achieve the kinds of horizon-

tal affiliations that make spontaneous mass action and violence possible not through a rupture of the vertical relation of subject and authority, but rather through an unconscious and bodily drive for a pure coincidence and substitution between a member of the crowd and the prized subject of authority's interests. In contrast to his contemporaries who argued that mobs, masses, and crowds were the degenerate limits of mass civilization, Freud gave a Nietzschean account of Western modernity. In this view, the forms of horizontality in Western mass societies figured by instances of spontaneous mass violence, crowd actions, or the inhuman acts of carnage committed by soldiers in European wars are not the "other" of the law of civilization, but in fact just one of its manifestations and cruel possibilities. For Freud, the apparent horizontality exhibited in spontaneous violence stems from an internecine hostility among members of closed groups, a wholesome and wholesale identification with one's peers that is driven by the fear that the peer possesses the attention of the superego's desires and by an aggression to substitute for, or at least equitably share in, the status of being the object of a shared superego's desire. For Freud, then, it is the primacy of the vertical bond (central to the ethical claims of modern citizenship) that conditions the apparently egoless horizontality and unethical violence of the mob, the military unit, or, for that matter, the democratic masses. Freud's work thus anticipates and supplements important historical and sociological arguments about the links between European mass democracies and fascism. Whereas those accounts tend to focus on the institutional, legal, and bureaucratic structures developed by the mass democratic German state before its takeover by the Nazis and without which Nazism's spectacular rate of expansion would not have been possible, Freud's account stresses that it is liberal citizenship as the modern sociality that institutes universally the vertical bond between citizen and state—which conditions all forms of community within the European nation-state—that is both responsible for, and persists as the ongoing necessary condition for, fascism. Like Anderson, Freud reminds us that we need to distinguish between the so-called horizontality conditioned by citizenship that might at ·first appear contrary to the ethical individualist values of citizenship, such as US white supremacist violence ranging from lynching to urban mob actions, and those forms of horizontality and collectivity that are produced and cemented by their "otherness" to political modernity. See Sigmund Freud, *Group Psychology and the Analysis of the Ego*, trans. James Strachey (New York: Liveright, 1951). For a stunning and rigorous psychoanalytic understanding of subjectivity as an effect of the nation-state formation that violently polices and defines, through communication and the social bond, the valued and disposable lives within diasporas constituted by contemporary US wars, see Grace Cho, *Haunting the Korean Diaspora: Shame, Secrecy and the Forgotten War* (Minneapolis: University of Minnesota Press, 2008). On race as the "other" of citizen sociality, see David Eng, *Racial Cas-*

tration: Managing Masculinity in Asian America (Durham: Duke University Press, 2001).

11 The liberal political philosophical tradition on which this perspective relies is discussed in Ronald Dworkin, *Sovereign Virtue: The Theory and Practice of Equality* (Cambridge: Harvard University Press, 2002).

12 See the press statement by the NAACP released October 29, 2009, at http://www.naacp.org/press/entry/naacp-applauds-us-senate-passage-of-the-matthew-shepard-and-james-byrd/.

13 See Wendy Brown, *Politics out of History* (Princeton: Princeton University Press, 2001).

14 See David Lloyd and Lisa Lowe, eds., *The Politics of Culture in the Shadow of Capital* (Durham: Duke University Press, 1997); Saskia Sassen, *Globalization and Its Discontents: Essays on the New Mobility of People and Money* (New York: New Press, 1999); Inderpal Grewal and Caren Kaplan, ed., *Scattered Hegemonies: Postmodernity and Transnational Feminist Practices* (Minneapolis: University of Minnesota Press, 1994). See also Gayatri Chakravorty Spivak, "Diasporas Old and New: Women in the Transnational World," *Textual Practice* 10, no. 2 (1996): 245–269.

15 See Saidiya Hartman, *Scenes of Subjection: Terror, Slavery and Self-Making in Nineteenth Century America* (New York: Oxford University Press, 1997).

16 See Ruth Wilson Gilmore, *Golden Gulag: Prisons, Surplus, Crisis and Opposition in Globalizing California* (Berkeley: University of California Press, 2007), 85–86.

17 Mary Dudziak, *Cold War Civil Rights: Race and the Image of American Democracy* (Princeton: Princeton University Press, 2000). See also Penny M. Von Eschen, *Race against Empire: Black Americans and Anti-Colonialism, 1937–1957* (Ithaca: Cornell University Press, 1997).

18 David Ciepley, *Liberalism in the Shadow of Totalitarianism* (Cambridge: Harvard University Press, 2006), 231–314.

19 See Brenda Gayle Plummer, *Rising Wind: Black Americans and U.S. Foreign Affairs, 1935–1960* (Chapel Hill: University of North Carolina Press, 1996); Kimberlé Crenshaw, "Race, Reform, and Retrenchment: Transformation and Legitimation in Anti-Discrimination Law," *Harvard Law Review* 101, no. 7 (May 1988), 1331–87; Jacquelyn Dowd Hall, "The Long Civil Rights Movement and the Political Uses of the Past," *Journal of American History* 91, no. 4 (March 2005): 1233–63; George Lipsitz, "Frantic to Join . . . the Japanese Army: The Asia Pacific War in the Lives of African American Soldiers and Civilians," in *The Politics of Culture in the Shadow of Capital*, ed. David Lloyd and Lisa Lowe, 324–52 (Durham: Duke University Press, 1997); Nikhil Pal Singh, *Black Is a Country: Race and the Unfinished Struggle for Democracy* (Cambridge: Harvard University Press, 2004).

20 Singh, *Black Is a Country*, 44. See also Brent Hayes Edwards's argument in *The*

Practice of Diaspora: Literature, Translation, and the Rise of Black Internationalism (Cambridge: Harvard University Press, 2003) that diaspora figures as the productive reopening of a "blackness" prematurely closed or "settled" through the false prop of the monolingual nation form and the American exceptionalist account of twentieth-century modernity.

21 See Richard Ohmann, *The Politics of Letters* (Middletown, Conn.: Wesleyan University Press, 1987), 80, and see also 68–91.

22 Glenn Omatsu, "The Four Prisons and the Movements of Liberation: Asian American Activism from the 1960s to the 1990s," in *The State of Asian America: Activism and Resistance in the 1990s*, ed. Karin Aquilar-San Juan (New York: South End Press, 1994), 20–21.

23 See Grace Kyungwong Hong and Roderick A. Ferguson, *Strange Affinities: The Gender and Sexual Politics of Comparative Racialization* (Durham: Duke University Press, 2011).

24 Cathy Cohen has forcefully argued in *The Boundaries of Blackness: AIDS and the Breakdown of Black Politics* (Chicago: University of Chicago Press, 1999) that this process has intensified and that it constituted an important dimension of late-twentieth-century black politics that examined and contested the means by which intragroup marginalization or disposability was produced through the very institutions that secured emancipation in the state for middle-class and heterosexual and patriarchal blacks. For Cohen, "linked-fate" politics emerged in this complex terrain of late-twentieth-century black political life.

25 Kimberlé Crenshaw, "Demarginalizing the Intersection: A Black Feminist Critique of Anti-Discrimination Doctrine, Feminist Theory, and Anti-Racist Politics," *University of Chicago Forum*, 1989, 148–49.

26 See ibid., 139–67. For a related and linked critique of standpoint theory in this same period, see Judith Butler's influential essays on feminism and identity subversion, especially *Gender Trouble: Feminism and the Subversion of Identity* (New York: Routledge, 1990). For Butler, the modern positivism that reinforces the binary gendering of heterosexual hegemony and that produces gender as an interpretation of a factual sex in US political culture and academic social science is to this self-same state form that in the 1980s is also realized through a medico-juridical discursive field. Both Crenshaw and Butler, through diverse concerns, interrogate political practices that internalize and fortify juridical conceptions of power through a reliance on positivist accounts of social difference.

27 Roderick Ferguson, *Aberrations in Black: Toward a Queer of Color Critique* (Minneapolis: University of Minnesota Press, 2003): 110–37.

28 Evelynn Hammonds, "Black (W)holes and the Geometry of Black Female Sexuality," *differences* 6, no. 2–3 (1994): 130.

29 Michel Foucault, "Governmentality," in *The Foucault Effect: Studies in Governmentality*, ed. Graham Burchell, Colin Gordon, and Peter Miller, 87–104 (Chi-

cago: University of Chicago Press, 1991); Timothy Mitchell, "Society, Economy and the State Effect," in *State/Culture: State Formation after the Cultural Turn*, ed. George Steinmetz, 76–97 (Ithaca: Cornell University Press: 1999).

30 See Judith Butler, "Conditions of Possibility for Politics—and Then Some," in *Contingency, Hegemony and Universality: Contemporary Dialogues on the Left*, ed. Judith Butler, Ernesto Laclau, and Slavoj Žižek, 159–79 (London: Verso, 2000); and Lisa Lowe, *Immigrant Acts: On Asian American Cultural Politics* (Durham: Duke University Press, 1996), 8–10, 90–92, 97–127.

31 Walter Benjamin offers one of the richest immanent critiques of scientific or Western Marxism. For Benjamin, capitalist modernity is constituted in a dialectic of destruction and sociality, in which social life unfolds as a heterogeneous tableau of material fragments. Thus modernity cultivates and demands new allegorical modes of perception and experience that are braided with and yet operate athwart modern practices of knowledge, practices that displace or seek to integrate the materially and forcibly recirculated fragments of modernity—as well as the accumulation of fragments that is modernity—within philosophic, scientific, and aesthetic epistemic registers that affirm the totality's wholeness. See Benjamin, *The Arcades Project*, trans. Howard Eiland and Kevin McLaughlin (Cambridge: Harvard University Press, 1999). On modern allegory as a critique of the sovereign representational regimes of the symbol, see Benjamin, *The Origin of German Tragic Drama*, trans. John Osborne (London: Verso, 1998).

32 My emphasis. Ferguson, *Aberrations in Black*, 4–10. On post-1960s political subjects as gesturing toward the complex and transnationally linked social formations out of which they are produced, see 143. Ferguson writes: "Making the queer of color and woman of color subjects the basis of critical inquiry means that we must imbue theme with *gestural* rather than emulative functions" (143; emphasis added). For a critique of Western Marxism and a thorough rethinking of historical materialism, see Walter Benjamin, "On the Concept of History," in *Walter Benjamin: Selected Writings, 1938–1940*, ed. Howard Eiland and Michael W. Jennings, trans. Edmund Jephcott (Cambridge: Harvard University Press, 2003), 401–24.

33 This latter mode of interpretation can be found in Michael Hardt and Antonio Negri's presentation of postmodern globalization, in *Multitude: War and Democracy in the Age of Empire* (New York: Penguin, 2004). For these scholars, the US war on drugs and war on terror are exemplary of a postnational and postmodern reorientation of the relation between politics and war. In global postmodernity (sometimes called "real capitalism"), war—manifested as the ongoing practice of security—disrespects national boundaries, the divisions between the domestic and the foreign, and the separation of violence from morality, gaining instead a primary ontological status to which the institutions of the classical modern nation-state are finally subordinate and supplicant.

Hardt and Negri write: "What is specific to our era, as we claimed earlier, is that war has passed from the final element of the sequences of power—lethal force as a last resort—to the first and primary element, the foundation of politics itself" (21).

34 In Weber's early-twentieth-century ruminations on the structure of domination that characterizes social relations within the industrial nation-state, we have a definition of the state as that form of political community that successfully lays claim to the monopoly of legitimate physical violence within a bounded territory. See Max Weber, "Politics as a Vocation," in Max Weber, *The Vocation Lectures*, ed. David Owen and Tracy B. Strong and trans. Rodney Livingstone, 32–93 (Indianapolis: Hackett, 2004).

35 Weber famously thought of twentieth-century modernity as producing either an instrumental rationality defined by goal-oriented social practices, or a value rationality that can serve as a norm for social practices. For Weber, the dangers of instrumental rationality were to be found in the realization of an advanced bureaucratic social formation, for which instrumentality led to a political subject of pure sensuousness without substantive characteristics or values. Members of the Frankfurt school argued that this was the ultimately comic (and teleological) dialectic of the European scientific enlightenment. See Max Weber, *The Protestant Ethic and the Spirit of Capitalism and Other Writings*, trans. Peter Baehr and Gordon C. Wells (New York: Penguin, 2002); and Max Horkheimer and Theodor W. Adorno, *Dialectic of Enlightenment: Philosophical Fragments*, ed. Gunzelin Schmid Noerr and trans. Edmund Jephcott (Stanford: Stanford University Press, 2002).

36 See Louis Althusser, "Ideology and Ideological State Apparatuses: Notes Towards an Investigation," in *Lenin and Philosophy and Other Essays,* trans. Ben Brewster (New York: Monthly Review Press, 1971): 127–88.

37 See Ferguson, *Aberrations in Black*, on the development of modern sociology through the production of racialized nonheteronormativity. For an account of the development of the professional disciplines and the modern research university in the United States as regulatively tied to social theories of racial degeneracy in urban capitalism, see Louis Menand, *The Metaphysical Club: A Story of Ideas in America* (London: Flamingo, 2001), 235–334. For a discussion of the racist origins of the legal movement for academic freedom, championed by the American Association of University Professors and key to the development of self-regulating and accrediting disciplinary bodies, see ibid., 409–33. On the development of modern statistics within the era of racial exclusion, see Mae Ngai, *Impossible Subjects: Illegal Aliens and the Making of Modern America* (Princeton: Princeton University Press, 2005), 21–55. On the development of modern institutional geography through the production of American colonial and racial practices, see Neil Smith, *American Empire: Roosevelt's Geographer and the Prelude to Globalization* (Berkeley: University of California Press,

2003). On the development of professional anthropology in the United States, see Lee Barker, *From Savage to Negro: Anthropology and the Construction of Race, 1896–1954* (Berkeley: University of California Press, 1998). On the development of American social sciences within the research university generally, see Dorothy Ross, *The Origins of American Social Science* (Cambridge: Cambridge University Press, 1991); and Mary Furner, *A Crisis in the Professionalization of American Social Sciences, 1865–1905* (Lexington: University of Kentucky Press, 1975).

38 Giorgio Agamben understands this process of originary exclusion as the archaic root of sovereign violence, arguing that in current times this violence operates in and through the forms of governmental power that have as their target the social welfare of populations for the political state, a form of power that Michel Foucault calls biopower. Agamben seeks to use the term "sovereign violence" only for this form of violence braided together with political modernity. I have elected to use the term "legitimate violence" in part to mark the specific twentieth-century character of the development of this formation of violence and, Weber's ambivalence notwithstanding, the specific positivist and proceduralist structures conditioning this violence. See Giorgio Agamben, *Homo Sacer: Sovereign Power and Bare Life,* trans. Daniel Heller-Roazen (Stanford: Stanford University Press, 1998). See also Foucault, *The History of Sexuality: An Introduction,* 1st ed., vol. 1, trans. Robert Hurley (New York: Vintage, 1990).

39 These latter elements are part of the new military arsenal. Their invention and use directly ties specific military needs for weaponry with state needs for legitimate violence, producing new formations, apparatuses, and institutions of legitimate violence that cross classically modern boundaries between (normatively speaking) the state's rational and instrumental capacities for sovereign violence, signified by its military force, and its ability to use legitimate violence to enforce specific precepts of civil reason. Each of the three forms of armament mentioned in the text allegedly possesses precision design, akin to the surgical practice of arthroscopy that excises or eradicates local targets. Not coincidentally, the strongest critiques of the use of these armaments have not been that they are used by the US military in ways that disrespect the ideal that universal national sovereignty governs state actions. Rather, the most effective critiques have been that the armaments have failed to be precise, failed to localize the harm they targeted, and have excised the wrong part of the population in a particular area, for example. Indeed, the critique of sovereign invasion has often been a secondary and corollary critique of this first and primary critique of failed instrumental forms of legitimate violence. In Edward W. Said and David Barsamian, *Culture and Resistance: Conversations with Edward W. Said* (Cambridge, Mass.: South End, 2003), Said's final writings on the strategic and social failure of US and UK sanctions and the blockade against Iraq

after the first Gulf War—in which smart bombs were used extensively, with horrendous imprecision and collateral damage—Said clearly articulates this transformation of US sovereign or military violence (figured as the enforcement of international laws and agreements) by practices of legitimate violence (historically targeted at domestic populations). As Said reminds us, though the technologies and institutional formations are new, this is a persistent feature of US and Western colonial and racial wars, producing ongoing forms of opposition. That is, the current technological conditions enabling the production of armaments that combine sovereign and legitimate violence (figured in smart bombs as the weapon and the camera each bomb contains), as the US state seeks to reconcile its advocacy of the liberal nation form with its overt drive to hegemonically structure asymmetrical global social relations, have themselves generated new forms and sites of anti-imperialist and antiracist critique and practice. Said writes: "As a result, we have Colin Powell, traveling throughout the Middle East, in February [of 2001], advocating something called 'smart sanctions' which struck me as a complete misnomer and again a fantasy to suggest that the United States can in fact cause people to go against their own interests to line up with the United States" (92).

40 Marc H. Morial, "Matthew Shepard and James Byrd, Jr. Hate Crimes Prevention Act Signed into Law" (National Urban League, November 11, 2009), http://www.nul.org/content/tbe45-matthew-shepard-and-james-byrd-jr-hate-crimes-prevention-act-signed-law.

41 Martin Luther King Jr., "Remarks Delivered at Africa Freedom Dinner at Atlanta University," in *The Papers of Martin Luther King, Jr.: Threshold of a New Decade, January 1959–December 1960*, ed. Clayborne Carson (Berkeley: University of California Press, 2005), 5:203.

42 Ibid., 5:204.

43 Ibid., 5:203, 204.

44 See Tom Shachtman, *Airlift to America: How Barack Obama, Sr., John F. Kennedy, Tom Mboya, and 800 East African Students Changed Their World and Ours* (New York: St. Martin's, 2009), especially the chapter titled "American Labor and the Rise of Tom Mboya" and the foreword by Harry Belafonte.

45 See Avery Gordon, *Ghostly Matters: Haunting and the Sociological Imagination* (Minneapolis: University of Minnesota Press, 1997).

46 In her unpublished manuscript "The Revolution Starts at Home," Morgan Bassichis describes the collaboration between the Audre Lorde Project, a New York–based queer of color organizing and community center, and the Community United against Violence, a San Francisco–based organization working against antitransgender violence. The organizations convened a meeting to contest the 2010 NDAA, dissenting from "the idea that more policing, imprisonment, and prosecution will solve the devastating rates of murder and violence in our communities."

47 Jasbir Puar, *Terrorist Assemblages: Homonationalism in Queer Times* (Durham: Duke University Press, 2007), xi.

48 Karl Marx and Frederick Engels, *The Communist Manifesto*, ed. Gareth Stedman Jones, trans. Samuel Moore (New York: Penguin, 2002), 223.

49 See Edward Said, *Beginnings: Intention and Method* (New York: Basic Books, 1975).

One | FREEDOM AND VIOLENCE

1 It also came in the decades during which the United States systematically installed through federalization its sovereign control over Native Americans, while extending its civilizing mission to include the wholesale possession of entire societies in the Caribbean, Asia, the Philippines, and the Pacific islands.

2 This is the perspective offered by Rogers M. Smith in *Civic Ideals: Conflicting Visions of Citizenship in U.S. History* (New Haven: Yale University Press, 1999), 410–69. See also K. Anthony Appiah, "The Uncompleted Argument: Du Bois and the Illusion of Race," in *"Race," Writing and Difference*, ed. Henry Louis Gates Jr. (Chicago: University of Chicago Press, 1986), 21–37.

3 Adolph Reed Jr., *W. E. B. Du Bois and American Political Thought: Fabianism and the Color Line* (New York: Oxford University Press, 1997), 116.

4 Ibid., 123–24.

5 See, for example, Joy James, *Transcending the Talented Tenth: Black Leaders and American Intellectuals* (New York: Routledge, 1997); and Hazel Carby, *Race Men: The W. E. B. Du Bois Lectures* (Cambridge: Harvard University Press, 2000).

6 See, for example, Susan Gilman and Alys Eve Weinbaum, eds., *Next to the Color Line: Gender, Sexuality, and W. E. B. Du Bois* (Minneapolis: University of Minnesota Press, 2007).

7 W. E. B. Du Bois, *The Souls of Black Folk* (Chicago: A. C. McClurg, 1903; with introduction by Donald B. Gibson and notes by Monica M. Elbert, New York: Penguin, 1989), 126.

8 Dorothy Ross offers a rich portrait of Turner as a liberal positivist who was nonetheless avidly committed to American exceptionalism. Yet curiously, she avoids the implication that for Turner, US exceptionalism had reached a logical aporia. To the degree that the exceptional nation required expansion, exceptionalism threatened to transform the US state into a variant of the European imperial state. See Ross, "From Historico-Politics to Political Science," in *The Origins of American Social Science* (Cambridge: Cambridge University Press, 1991), 257–302.

9 Etienne Balibar argues that the nation form is a historically produced and determined social form. In contrast to Western historicist logic that posits that the nation form is the exclusive and ideal political and social form of modern capitalism, he argues for a more complex understanding of how and why the

nation form came into existence in the West, and how it continued to spread globally. He suggests that before we historicize the nation form as a consequence of modern capitalism, we must specify and historicize modern capitalism itself. Modern capitalism, Balibar proposes, emerged within a world economy. It required the formation of cores and peripheries; that is, it produced the context for the nation form and for the colony form in the same instance. The nation form became hegemonic only in the context of the system of constraints within which the world economy operated. Balibar's reorientation of the study of nations within the context of modern colonial capitalism is provocative in several regards. First, it questions Western Marxism's determinism about the origins and rise of the nation form as an organic product of Western capitalism. Instead, both the nation form and Western capitalism are situated within the contradictions of global colonial capitalism. Second, Balibar's situating of the nation form within the system of constraints of the modern world economy further dramatizes the multiplicity of contradictions—beyond the primary contradiction of capital and labor, coded as working-class antagonism in the metropole—that are formative sites of irresolution and disturbance in the reproduction of the nation form. In this book, following the work of Lisa Lowe, I argue for understanding race as a contradictory formation within racialized capitalism in the United States, which always contributes to the overdetermination of capitalist contradictions. If the racialization of social groups in the United States was essential for national economic and political formation from the late eighteenth century to the middle of the twentieth, it also exacerbated the contradictions by which the nation form was partially and momentarily undone. It is for this reason that I argue for seeing particular racialized spaces during this broad time span as social forms of antinationalism—that is, as counterhegemonic forms and practices that inscribe themselves within the hegemony of the nation form. See Etienne Balibar, "The Nation Form: History and Ideology," in *Race, Nation, Class: Ambiguous Identities*, by Etienne Balibar (translated by Chris Turner) and Immanuel Wallerstein, 89–90 (London: Verso, 1991); and Lisa Lowe, *Immigrant Acts: On Asian American Cultural Politics* (Durham: Duke University Press, 1996), 1–36. See also Lisa Lowe and David Lloyd, Introduction, in *The Politics of Culture in the Shadow of Capital*, ed. David Lloyd and Lisa Lowe (Durham: Duke University Press, 1997), 1–32.

10 Akhil Gupta and James Ferguson, "Beyond 'Culture': Space, Identity and the Politics of Difference," *Cultural Anthropology* 7, no. 1 (February 1992): 6–22.

11 See Frantz Fanon, *The Wretched of the Earth*, trans. Constance Farrington (New York: Grove, 1968); and Ranajit Guha, *A Rule of Property for Bengal: An Essay on the Idea of Permanent Settlement* (Paris: Mouton, 1963; reprint, Durham: Duke University Press, 1996).

12 For a useful overview of Turner's context, see the introduction by John Mack Faragher in *Reading Frederick Jackson Turner: "The Significance of the Frontier in*

American History" and Other Essays, ed. John Mack Faragher (New Haven: Yale University Press, 1996), 1–10.

13 Frederick Jackson Turner, *History, Frontier, and Section: Three Essays*, with introduction by Martin Ridge (Albuquerque: University of New Mexico Press, 1993), 12, 60.

14 Ibid., 61.

15 R. Smith, *Civic Ideals*, 392–96.

16 The term "anti-social" and its particular usage in this context are Turner's. He writes: "Complex society is precipitated by the wilderness into a kind of primitive organization based on the family. The tendency is anti-social. It produces antipathy to control, and particularly to any direct control" (82). As his usage indicates, the "social" was a term that by the end of the nineteenth century had come to designate practices and relations within civil society that could be used for and rationalized by state governance. See Faragher, Introduction. For more on the forms of meaning associated with the "social" and the emergence of those meanings within the context of twentieth-century governmentality, see Barbara Cruikshank, *The Will to Empower: Democratic Citizens and Other Subjects* (Ithaca: Cornell University Press, 1999).

17 Contemporary Chicano criticism has provided us with the theoretical model of the "borderlands" as an alternative way of understanding what Turner calls "frontier space." The borderlands concept is an alternative to the nation form as an ideology and social space. Within the borderlands, Chicano critics assert, we see the multiple processes and national formations that produce the particularity of hybridized space that cannot be assimilated to any single national space. Borderlands recover the materiality of social spaces on the edge of national formations, and the forms of subjectivity that these spaces create. It is precisely because the borderlands are unique spaces of material production and social creation that they cannot be assimilated to the core/periphery or center/margin logic that governs Turner's frontier concept. See José David Saldívar, *Border Matters: Remapping American Cultural Studies* (Berkeley: University of California Press, 1997), xii–xiii. For an excellent overview of the concept of the borderlands in Chicano studies, see Carl Gutiérrez-Jones, "Desiring (B)orders," *Diacritics* 25, no. 1 (Spring 1995): 99–112.

18 David W. Noble, "The Anglo-Protestant Monopolization of "America" in *José Marti's "Our America": From National to Hemispheric Cultural Studies*, ed. Jeffery Belnap and Raul Fernandez (Durham: Duke University Press, 1998), 262, 255. See also Bruce Greenfield, "The Problems of the Discoverer's Authority in Lewis and Clark's History," in *Macropolitics of Nineteenth Century Literature*, ed. Jonathan Arac and Harriet Ritvo (Philadelphia: University of Pennsylvania Press, 1991), 12–36.

19 This of course is the logic behind two crucial pieces of US imperialist policy: the ideology of manifest destiny and the Monroe Doctrine.

20 Michael Walzer, *Spheres of Justice: A Defense of Pluralism and Equality* (New York: Basic Books, 1983), 44. He also writes: "Countries are territorial states" (42). Walzer's theory of territoriality as fundamental to the rights of the liberal citizen is based upon his reading of Hobbes. Among the natural rights of man that are retained when the social contract is signed, Hobbes argued, is first the right to self-defense and then "the use of fire, water, free air, *and place to live in, and . . .* all things necessary for life" (quoted in Walzer, *Spheres of Justice,* 43). See Thomas Hobbes, *The Elements of Law, Natural, and Politic,* ed. Ferdinand Tönnies (Cambridge: Cambridge University Press, 1928). See also Hobbes, *Leviathan,* ed. Richard Tuck (Cambridge: Cambridge University Press, 1996).

21 Bourgeois nationalists slyly translated the early Enlightenment claims of the individual's natural right to place as the natural right of the citizen to land. In this way, American bourgeois nationalists posited land as the basis both for legitimating the white settler's right to foreign territory, stolen from indigenous tribes, and for citizens' right of self-governance—that is, for territorial rather than imperial state rule. Walzer points out: "The right is not indeed to a particular place, but it is enforceable against the state, which exists to protect it; the state's claim to territorial jurisdiction derives ultimately from this individual right to place" (Walzer, *Spheres of Justice,* 43). A characteristic liberal theorist, Walzer can neither acknowledge, account for, nor theorize about the racialized foundations of the American nation-state. As I have been arguing, it is the racialized trope of land that brings liberal and racialist theories of the nation-state into alignment. The bourgeois nationalist claim to land enabled the European settler to appropriate the territory of the indigenous peoples, to claim both sovereignty from England and exclusive territoriality, and to disenfranchise nonpropertied subjects, especially African and African American slaves (Walzer, *Spheres of Justice*).

22 For an analysis of Du Bois's modern black political theory in the context of dominant strains of European romantic nationalism generally, and of German nationalist thought in particular, see Paul Gilroy, *The Black Atlantic: Modernity and Double Consciousness* (Cambridge: Harvard University Press, 1993), 112–33.

23 See Michael Omi and Howard Winant, *Racial Formation: From the 1960s to the 1990s,* 2nd ed. (New York: Routledge, 1994), 53–76.

24 For a brilliant study of the inextricability of cultural hybridity and racial intersubjectivity for the constitution of and for constituting American whiteness, see Eric Lott, *Love and Theft: Blackface Minstrelsy and the American Working Class* (New York: Oxford University Press, 1993).

25 Michael Rogin writes: "Whereas the political *Declaration of Independence* made an anticolonial revolution in the name of the equality of all men, the declaration of cultural independence emerged not to free oppressed folk but to constitute national identity out of their subjection. White supremacy, white over black and red, was the content of this national culture; its form was black

and red over white, blacking up and Indianization" ("The Two Declarations of American Independence," in *Race and Representation: Affirmative Action*, ed. Robert Post and Michael Rogin [New York: Zone, 1998], 73).

26 In "Is There a Neo-Racism?" (in *Race, Nation, Class: Ambiguous Identities*, by Etienne Balibar [translated by Chris Turner] and Immanuel Wallerstein [London: Verso, 1991], 17–28), Etienne Balibar distinguishes between the formation of a racist community "among whom there exists a bond of 'imitation' over a distance" and "individuals and collectivities that are prey to racism . . . [that] find themselves constrained to see themselves as a community" (18). By stressing the difference between the form of collectivity that is established in the interest of racial supremacy and the form of community erected through and against that supremacy, Balibar points to important contradictions in the latter form that prevent its simple reproduction. In the case of the community, the interiorization of the racial identity would also be the moment of a parallel awareness of the internalization of both the force and power relations that such an interiorization performs. The rearticulation of the ascribed identity or name by the community is also the moment at which racialized subjects can become aware of the denial of their own right to form a community and practice naming as they see fit. Finally, the contradictory nature of the latter "form of community" persistently threatens to highlight the degree to which material social violence grounds discursive identities. Extending Balibar's theory of minority identities as contradictory and only complexly reproduced, we can counter contemporary leftist arguments that perceive the assertion of racial identity as mere identity politics. First, we must distinguish between the forms of identity politics (rarely understood as such, though often used as the basis of evaluation) that collect a community of racists to deny the social redistribution of resources due to the complex achievement of identity in a previously disunified class. Second, attending to the specificity of minoritized groups, we must understand that the reproduction of minority categories such as black and Latino is always dependent on material circumstances that reassert their centrality. Precisely because the articulation of a minority identity is necessarily unstable and held together only through the force of circumstance, we ought to interrogate the leftist claim that identity politics is a form of permanent false consciousness. Instead, the rearticulation of ascriptive identities by aggrieved social subjects is logically the basis for a trajectory of social struggle that exceeds the "instance or moment of its rearticulation." Lisa Lowe (*Immigrant Acts*, 60–83) has argued in relation to Asian American formations that a politics of difference ought to structure the next phase of antiracist political struggle and contest. Such a politics begins by emphasizing Asian American differences—of gender, sexuality, class, and national origin—as sites that open up alternative terrains of struggle and instances of counterhegemonic engagement. For an account of the way in which blackness must always already imply

the trajectory of its unraveling, even at those moments when it seems most concrete, see Stuart Hall, "New Ethnicities," in *Stuart Hall: Critical Dialogues in Cultural Studies*, ed. David Morley and Kuan-Hsing Chen (London: Routledge 1996), 441–49. For more on the specificity of identity politics among the community of racists and its mode of reproduction, see George Lipsitz, *The Possessive Investment in Whiteness: How Whites Profit through Identity Politics* (Philadelphia: Temple University Press, 1997).

27   As this brief anecdote suggests, racialization is always a gendered process. The figure of the white female child as recurring trope in narratives of racialization can be appreciated if we pause to consider the frequency of its representation in many diasporic and nationalist black male writings, by authors from Frantz Fanon to Richard Wright and from Frederick Douglass to James Baldwin. The allegory of the loss of identity through racist interdiction is captured within a heterosexual matrix, in which gender identity assumes a prior fixity. In fact, it is the prior stabilization of gendered subjectivity and the binary construction of heterosexual genders that reinforces racial binarism, structuring critiques of that racism as a perversion of gender and sexual normativity. Indeed, the few instances in the narrative of *The Souls* where Du Bois stages a reconciliation between "White and Black striving" and racial discord are not constructed through figurations of citizenship but through the symbolization of equal manhood. In the post-Reconstruction period during which *The Souls* was written and published, the entitlements of citizenship such as the franchise were restricted to men—both white and nonwhite—while moral discourse operated as an effective alternative for the continued denial or selective in-clusion of previously disenfranchised subjects into representation in the state. The combination—indeed, the overdetermination—of racial, gendered, and sexual discourses destabilized the binary operation and representation of each discursive formation, opening unexpected sites of crisis and vulnerability within the racial social order. In this manner, new social subjects have a central place in Du Bois's text, if they are rather separate from the narrative of racial striving. The black female prostitute as a figure for subaltern differences recurs repeatedly in *The Souls* and suggests an important investigative locus for any project fundamentally concerned with the displacement of the reigning social order, and the multiplicity of linked and nonequivalent social ideologies by which that social order is reproduced.

Additionally, if we can conceive of manhood as a terrain or space of recon-ciliation of the black subject with the racial state—in that it marks the state's function both to recognize the preexisting masculinity of black men and to extend its resources and powers to produce that masculinity among black men—then we can understand differently Du Bois's attempt to stage the ori-gins of black culture (as irreconcilable to the nation form) within black wom-en's spaces. For example, many critics have argued that Du Bois proposes the sorrow songs as the ur-form of black culture, but few critics have pursued the implication of Du Bois's placement of the origin of this form for himself, for example, in the black female body, that of his grandfather's grandmother. Although at first we might discount such a move as enforcing the modern spatialization of cultural tradition within the private feminine sphere, that would be to discount the way in which modern capitalist slavery operated through the child's maternal line. Instead, we might extend Du Bois's attempt to locate black culture within the gendered spaces of the slave system, working through the protocols of his text to suggest that it is the doubleness of black women's spaces that makes them a centrally located emblem of black cultural production. On the one hand, black women's spaces constitute a central platform for the reproduction—in both its sexual and social connotations—of the racial social order. On the other hand, black women's spaces are generative sites of resistance culture, where resistance is often coded in the language and appearance of nurturance and alternative social sites such as the home. Furthermore, we can break with the protocols of Du Bois's text, thinking against the heterosexual matrix, and place—in contingent relation to such women's spaces—the spaces of the gendered sexual subaltern figured as prostitute space to destabilize heterosexual gendering within a black social formation. In other words, in examining the social histories of the gendered sexual subaltern—which for Du Bois, the sociologist, are figured mostly as statistics of incidence of prostitution in black and nonblack communities in the postbellum period—we can disrupt the way in which women's space and maternal space are conflated in the interest of the racial social order, in the process breaking and fragmenting the involution of sexual with social reproduction. For more on the contradictory formation of black women within the modern racial slave mode of production, see the brilliant and foundational essay by Angela Y. Davis, "Reflections on the Black Woman's Role in the Community of Slaves," in Angela Y. Davis, *The Angela Y. Davis Reader*, ed. Joy James (Malden, Mass.: Blackwell, 1998), 111–29. In that essay, Davis argues that the slaves' living quarters were a privileged space or "realm which was furthermost removed from the immediate arena of domination" (115). Within this space, the black woman performed the chores and duties of "domestic work." Yet within the context of the slave household, organized not through blood, kinship, or paternity or maternity but by the slave owner's capital, slave women's domestic work—however much reinforced by patriarchal ideologies—was ultimately a part of the social labor of slavery and not an instance of "women's unpaid work in the household" or an instance of "female slavery" within a feudal mode of production. Moreover, Davis subtly argues, slave women performed the "only labor of the slave community which could not be directly and immediately claimed by the oppressor" (116). Davis's focus on the slave woman's position in modern capitalism—as one that destabilizes the capitalist mode of production

through the slave woman's nonequivalence to the subject of the national proletariat posited by Marxism, the subject of woman posited by liberal feminism,
and the subject of manhood posited by antiracist nationalism—is deepened by
her attention to slave women's spaces as sites of alternative and resistance
culture within, rather than outside of, the dominant social formation.

28 For a critique of the construction of the "talented tenth" within black political
discourse and its effects on black political mobilization, institution building,
and community practices, see James, *Transcending the Talented Tenth*. See also
Kevin Gaines, *Uplifting the Race* (Chapel Hill: University of North Carolina
Press, 1997).

29 For example, in "Worlds of Color: The Negro Mind Reaches Out" (in *The New
Negro: An Interpretation*, ed. Alain Locke [New York: A. and C. Boni, 1925;
reprint, with a new preface by Allan H. Spear, New York: Johnson Reprint,
1968], 385–414), Du Bois defines pan-Africanism as a movement whose symbolic meanings and positioning is far more important than its material instantiation, for which the conditions for its existence as a social movement on
the ground did not exist at that moment. The form of black cosmopolitanism
that pan-Africanism represents, then, should not be faulted for its lack of
material realization, or discounted simply because it was a primarily discursive
formation. The real effects of pan-Africanism as a discursive and symbolic
formation on black political consciousness and the black war of position ought
not to be discounted. For a review of pan-Africanism as a movement and as a
genealogy for contemporary black diasporic politics and critical theories, see
Sidney J. Lemelle and Robin D. G. Kelley, eds., *Imagining Home: Class, Culture,
and Nationalism in the African Diaspora* (New York: Verso, 1994). See also
Brenda Gayle Plummer, *Rising Wind: Black Americans and U.S. Foreign Affairs,
1935–1960* (Chapel Hill: University of North Carolina Press, 1996), 9–36.

30 Contemporary scholars such as Sterling Stuckey (*Slave Culture: Nationalist
Theory and the Foundations of Black America* [New York: Oxford University
Press, 1987]) have put much effort into documenting the existence of African
cultural practices and forms of consciousness among African and black slaves
in the United States. Building on that work, the literary scholar Eric Sundquist
has suggested that Du Bois similarly proposed that African social forms persisted in the United States among emancipated blacks. For Sundquist, double
consciousness is an example of Du Bois's commitment to find evidence of the
existence of African culture among US blacks: "The doubling at issue is not
simply that of 'Negro' and 'American'—that is Black American versus a universalized, colorless American—but rather African versus American . . . 'Negro' is
thus not equivalent to 'black American' but is already a term of the diaspora for
Du Bois, pointing to a 'nation' . . . whose double consciousness is grounded in
the soil of slavery but may ultimately be traced to an African home" (*To Wake
the Nations: Race in the Making of American Literature* [Cambridge: Harvard

University Press, 1993], 487–88). My reading has emphasized the philosophical and epistemological dimensions of Du Bois's concept of double consciousness, which I believe is not about the retrieval of African pasts in the present but is focused on the ways in which black racialization has been understood within a binary formulation that projects blackness as a simulacrum, an inauthentic copy used to naturalize whiteness and connect it to a postgenocide, continental white territory. No amount of information retrieval will automatically displace the self-evidence of this binary, and information can paradoxically reinforce it (see the next note). For this reason I believe that we ought to distinguish between double consciousness, which is Du Bois's recognition of prevailing epistemic constructions of blackness as imitations and simulacra, and the sorrow song, which is for Du Bois a site at which the past—comprised of a variety of languages and tribal groupings in Africa and the survival cultures produced on the slave ships—is inserted into the present. David Lloyd has eloquently characterized colonial racialization as the process by which the non-Western subject is cut off from the contemporaneity of the colonial social formation and reconstituted as Western simulacrum and derivative. See David Lloyd, "Race under Representation," Oxford Literary Review 13 (Spring 1991): 62–94; and "Nationalisms against the State," in The Politics of Culture in the Shadow of Capital, ed. David Lloyd and Lisa Lowe (Durham: Duke University Press, 1997), 173–98. Lisa Lowe [Critical Terrains: French and British Orientalisms (Ithaca: Cornell University Press, 1991]) has suggested that binary discursive formulations produce monolithic representations—such as the West and the Orient, or America and Africa—of social referents that are, in fact, internally heterogeneous and stratified by class, and as well as being overdetermined by intersecting discursive formations of race, gender, and sexuality. Judith Butler ("Imitation and Gender Insubordination," in Inside/Out: Lesbian Theories, Gay Theories, ed. Diana Fuss [New York: Routledge, 1991], 17–31) has argued that the naturalization of heterosexuality as authentic and original is effected by the prior installation and discursive construction of homosexuality as copy and imitation. Gayatri Chakravorty Spivak ("Can the Subaltern Speak?," in Marxism and the Interpretation of Culture, ed. Lawrence Grossberg and Carey Nelson [Urbana: University of Illinois Press, 1988], 271–313) argues that we must rigorously submit our own systems of knowing and strategies of political engagement to a persistent and deconstructive critique, if the postcolonial feminist is to speak to and hear the speech act of the gendered subaltern of the Global South. I would argue that double consciousness is the beginning of such a persistent critique.

31 Du Bois's idea of double consciousness can be fruitfully connected to Frantz Fanon's Black Skin/White Masks (translated by Charles Lam Markman [London: Pluto, 1986]). Although both authors are interested in theories of race and consciousness, Du Bois chooses metaphors that emphasize the mind and

spirit—black essence—while Fanon chooses a metaphor that emphasizes the epidermis and the exterior body. However, in both theories—one developed in the context of industrializing racial capitalism in the United States and the other in the context of colonial capitalism in Martinique and North Africa—race or blackness is precisely not an original substance, such as a latent African-ness. Instead, to feel one's "twoness,—an American, a Negro" (*Souls*, 5) is to experience the mode by which racialized discourse inaugurates the splitting of the subject into white and black, or original and simulacrum. Blackness is not one part of the doubleness; it is the entire experience of doubleness. Blackness, as the "seventh son," is a prime integer indivisible into prior terms and forms. For Du Bois, double consciousness is a critique of the positing of the racialized subject as simulacrum. Additionally, Du Bois's theorization of the subject of consciousness through an interrogation of blackness concurs with aspects of Freudian psychoanalysis—namely, the emergence of consciousness (or the ego) through the process of splitting, foreclosure, and repression. Fanon would deepen this critique and elaborate on a theory of the epidermis, rejecting mind/body and surface/depth dualities in favor of a theory of consciousness that is at once a theory of embodiment and one of skin. Fanon also extends Du Bois's critique of double consciousness by explicitly connecting language to the processes of splitting and bodily constitution, through his investigation of the colonized subject's entrance into the imperialist language systems. In this way, the work of Fanon and Du Bois remains critical for any theory that posits the subject's entrance into language and the symbolic as a form of splitting and differentiation. In addition to recognizing the splitting and differentiation of the subject through the axis of sexual difference, we must also recognize the formation of the ego through the axis of racial difference. For more on how consciousness and the body are simultaneously constructed through discursive structures, see Judith Butler, *Bodies That Matter: On the Discursive Limits of "Sex"* (New York: Routledge, 1993). For a revision of Butler's theory of performativity and the speech act, which takes into account the body as a component of the speech act through a rearticulation of Pierre Bourdieu's concept of habitus, see Judith Butler, *Excitable Speech: A Politics of the Performative* (New York: Routledge, 1997), 141–63.

32 Robert B. Stepto, *From behind the Veil: A Study of Afro-American Narrative* (Urbana: University of Illinois Press, 1979), 66.

33 Ibid., 59.

34 Ibid., 67.

35 Ibid., 71.

36 Ibid., 70, 76.

37 Ibid., 76.

38 Ibid., 77.

39 See Roderick Ferguson, *Aberrations in Black: Toward a Queer of Culture Cri-*

tique (Minneapolis: University of Minnesota Press, 2004). For a social history of the meanings of "dirt" within the United States, see Phyllis Palmer, *Domesticity and Dirt* (Philadelphia: Temple University Press, 1989). Palmer writes: "Dirtiness appears always in a constellation of the suspect qualities that, along with sexuality, immorality, laziness, and ignorance, justify social rankings of race, class, and gender." Examining representations that connected southern rural black people with dirtiness, Du Bois exposed the connection between aesthetic criteria—such as the beautiful and the ugly—and social discourses of management. The conjoining of dirtiness with ugliness is a bonding of aesthetic and social critique. For Du Bois, modern aestheticism was deeply implicated in and interwoven with other modern forms, such as the democratic political state, alienating the bodies and modes of living of black people from both the cultural and political terrains of the nation-state. See ibid., 137–51.

40 Stepto, *From behind the Veil*, 73.

41 Lost, destroyed, or mangled furniture is often a metonym for the web of racist and invidious social practices that remain unaddressed by the state and racist social polity. In Toni Morrison's *The Bluest Eye* (New York: Holt, Rinehart and Winston, 1970; reprint, New York: Alfred Knopf, 1993), we are introduced to the pervasiveness of social power in the lives of the racialized poor by an account of the Breedloves' household. Looming large in that space is a piece of new furniture that is delivered with marks and slashes in the upholstery; the Breedloves are forced to live with it because the store owner refuses to follow the usual policy of exchange. With no possible recourse to the law, the Breedloves must accommodate this transgression that lodges itself in the center of their domestic and private life. The best they can do is repel identification, coded as ownership, with the object and what it signifies, constituting it as furniture without memories. In Morrison, as in Du Bois, the affective and economic dimensions of racism are collapsed within a single trope, denying the division of social space into public and private domains. The domestic space is violated by racialization, whose markings pervade and disorganize poor black life. In addition, keeping in mind that objects as commodities are "congealed" social labor, expressing the social relations between individuals, the furniture as racialized commodity recasts or extends the Marxist critique of the commodity form. The furniture without memories exposes the degree to which racialization operates within all levels of the fundamental class process, including production, appropriation, and distribution. Moreover, the furniture that does not hold memories beautifully allegorizes the ways in which, within the context of racialized industrial capitalism, narratives that predict the rise of commodity culture and the erosion and eclipsing of traditional cultures— suggesting that the process is uniform and homogenizing—need to be greatly qualified. Instead, racialized capitalism produces recalcitrant cultural sites, formed in part by the inability of indigent and racialized workers and social

groups to partake in the market of commodities they work to produce. When furniture goes without memories, the social history of these recalcitrant communities is inscribed upon other objects and within a different set of social practices, which must be excavated if we are to reconstruct the social consciousness of folks within those communities. The intertextuality between Du Bois's chapters on the Black Belt and Morrison's creative writing is rarely commented upon. Besides Morrison's reference to furniture, which is most surely a resignification of the furniture in Du Bois's Black Belt chapter, Morrison's third novel, *The Song of Solomon* (New York: Knopf, 1977), shares its title with the opening epigraph or sorrow song that Du Bois uses to begin his "Of the Black Belt" chapter. In many ways, Morrison is heir to Du Bois in her attempt to construct and interpret the meaning of racialized life within black social spaces. In *The Song of Solomon* as in *Souls*, these are spaces that are complexly woven into the larger social structure and always mediated by the social relations within that structure. Yet unlike Du Bois, Morrison pries open these spaces for the reader with the use of a heroic female narrator, exploring more explicitly the connections between gender, race, and sexuality in the constitution of social space.

42 The relationship of white womanhood to citizenship during this period is complex and profoundly ambivalent. On the one hand, women were denied many of the most important rights of citizenship, such as the franchise. On the other hand, as Du Bois's account indicates—though it does not elaborate upon this point—white women, particularly of the bourgeois class, often found both strategic alignment with and formal representation through the state by aligning themselves with the racist imperatives of the state, which represented the racist civil polity. For example, many of the first states to grant women the right to inherit property during the first half of the nineteenth century were the southern slave states, in part to resolve the complex question of the social status of slaves after the death of their master. Furthermore, as historians of the suffrage movement have documented, middle-class and elite women leaders of the suffrage movement routinely advanced proposals for female suffrage by stressing the enfranchisement of women (coded as white) as a way to dilute the effectiveness of the black vote and to support white interests. Although it is important to distinguish between the positioning of women by the patriarchal state that bases women's mode of political participation on their autonomous agency and that can contain important critiques of citizenship, that positioning did more to divide women—according to race—than it did to unify them as a class. It is for this reason that I would argue for seeing white womanhood as a category whose critique of citizenship must be distinguished from the critique of citizenship that is formed through an examination of the history of racialized women and men in the United States. "White womanhood," as I use the term here, is not an essential category but a socially constituted and legally codified

subject position, which required white female solidarity with white supremacy while simultaneously constituting white women's social identities and roles through the regulative practices of male patriarchy, particularly in the slave households of the South. For example, during the exclusion era, all women— even whites—who married racial aliens lost their American citizenship, a policy that denied white women their whiteness. Thus, white womanhood is both regulated by the patriarchy and formative of white supremacy. See Elizabeth Fox-Genovese, "Placing Women's History in History," *New Left Review* 133 (May–June 1982): 5–29; and *Within the Plantation Household: Black and White Women of the Old South* (Chapel Hill: University of North Carolina Press, 1988).

Two | LEGAL FREEDOM AS VIOLENCE

1 Nella Larsen, *Quicksand* (New York: Penguin, 2002), 12 (emphasis added).
2 Jennifer D. Brody, *Punctuation: Art, Politics, and Play* (Durham: Duke University Press, 2008), 112.
3 See Mieke Bal, *Quoting Caravaggio: Contemporary Art, Preposterous History* (Chicago: University of Chicago Press, 1999), 8.
4 On the transatlantic system of states, see Brinley Thomas, *The Industrial Revolution and the Atlantic Economy: Selected Essays* (London: Routledge, 1993), especially, 144–81.
5 See Paul Gilroy, *The Black Atlantic: Modernity and Double Consciousness* (Cambridge: Harvard University Press, 1993).
6 See Andreas Fahrmeir, Olivier Faron, and Patrick Weil, eds., *Migration Control in the North Atlantic World: The Evolution of State Practices in Europe and the United States from the French Revolution to the Inter-War Period* (New York: Berghahn, 2003).
7 On the *jus publicum Europaeum* and the Pax Britannica, see Carl Schmitt, *The Nomos of the Earth in the International Law of the Jus Publicum Europaeum*, ed. and trans. G. L. Ulmen (New York: Telos, 2003).
8 W. E. B. Du Bois, *The Souls of Black Folk* (Chicago: A. C. McClurg, 1903; with introduction by Donald B. Gibson and notes by Monica M. Elbert, New York: Penguin, 1989), 149.
9 See Robert Boyce, *The Great Interwar Crisis and the Collapse of Globalization* (New York: Palgrave, 2009).
10 See George Lipsitz, "Frantic to Join . . . the Japanese Army: The Asia Pacific War in the Lives of African American Soldiers and Civilians," in *The Politics of Culture in the Shadow of Capital*, ed. David Lloyd and Lisa Lowe (Durham: Duke University Press, 1997): 324–52.
11 On the distinction between the US political economies in the Atlantic and the Pacific, see Bruce Cumings, *Dominion from Sea to Sea: Pacific Ascendancy and American Power* (New Haven: Yale University Press, 2009).

12 Cherene Sherrard-Johnson, *Portraits of the New Negro Woman: Visual and Literary Culture in the Harlem Renaissance* (New Brunswick, N.J.: Rutgers University Press, 2007), 3.

13 See Gerald Horne, *The White Pacific: U.S. Imperialism and Black Slavery in the South Seas* (Honolulu: University of Hawaii Press, 2007), 129–45.

14 The most prominent example is George Hutchinson, *In Search of Nella Larsen: A Biography of the Color Line* (Cambridge: Belknap Press of Harvard University Press, 2006).

15 See, for example, Michael Denning, *The Cultural Front: The Laboring of American Culture in the Twentieth Century* (New York: Verso, 1996).

16 See Brent Hayes Edwards, *The Practice of Diaspora: Literature, Translation, and the Rise of Black Internationalism* (Cambridge.: Harvard University Press, 2003).

17 On the postwar communist and Wilsonian discourses of self-determination, see Erez Manela, *The Wilsonian Moment: Self-Determination and the International Origins of Anticolonial Nationalism* (New York: Oxford University Press, 2007).

18 Edward Said, *Culture and Imperialism*, 1st ed. (New York: Knopf, 1993), 95.

19 See Alys Eve Weinbaum, "Interracial Romance and Black Internationalism," and Brent Hayes Edwards, "Late Romance," in *Next to the Color Line: Gender, Sexuality, and W. E. B. Du Bois*, ed. Alys Eve Weinbaum and Susan Gilman (Minneapolis: University of Minnesota Press, 2007): 96–123 and 124–149, respectively.

20 Mae Ngai, *Impossible Subjects: Illegal Aliens and the Making of Modern America* (Princeton: Princeton University Press, 2005).

21 See Dorothy Ross, *The Origins of American Social Science* (Cambridge: Cambridge University Press, 1991), 219–55.

22 Quoted in Mae Ngai, *Impossible Subjects*, 25 (emphasis added).

23 See Irma Watkin-Owen, *Blood Relations: Caribbean Immigrants and the Harlem Community, 1900–1930* (Bloomington: Indiana University Press, 1996).

24 Nancy F. Cott, "Marriage and Women's Citizenship in the United States, 1830–1934," *American Historical Review* 103, no. 5 (December 1998): 1460.

25 I do not mean to suggest that local and state officials and bodies did not use their powers to help make and sustain the forms of racial terror most brutally dramatized in lynching. I simply mean to indicate that the infliction of that terror and violence, in the case of lynching, was rarely the result of a judicial or state decree executed by a state bureaucracy or agent. Rather, the source and authority of lynching's violence was nonstatist. See Steven Hahn, *A Nation under Our Feet: Black Political Struggles in the Rural South, from Slavery to the Great Migration* (Cambridge: Belknap Press of Harvard University Press, 2003); and Jacqueline Goldsby, *A Spectacular Secret: Lynching in American Life and Literature* (Chicago: University of Chicago Press, 2005).

26 See Farah Jasmine Griffin, *Who Sets You Flowin': The African American Migration Narrative* (New York: Oxford University Press, 1995).

27 On music as alternative aesthetic of the narration of history and subjectivity in racial capitalism, see Fred Moten, *In the Break: The Aesthetics of the Black Radical Tradition* (Minneapolis: University of Minnesota Press, 2003); and, Brent Hayes Edwards, "Introduction: The Genres of Postcolonialism," *Social Text* 22, no. 1 (2004): 1–15.

28 See Michelle Ann Stephens, *Black Empire: The Masculine Global Imaginary of Caribbean Intellectuals in the United States, 1914–1962* (Durham: Duke University Press, 2005).

29 See Hazel Carby, *Reconstructing Womanhood: The Emergence of the Afro-American Woman Novelist* (New York: Oxford University Press, 1987), especially 62–94.

30 See Patricia Hill Collins, *Black Feminist Thought: Knowledge, Consciousness, and the Politics of Empowerment* (New York: Routledge, 2000); Jacqueline Goldsby, *A Spectacular Secret*; and M. Jacqui Alexander, *Pedagogies of Crossing: Meditations on Feminism, Sexual Politics, Memory, and the Sacred* (Durham: Duke University Press, 2005).

31 See Evelyn Brooks Higginbotham, "Rethinking Vernacular Culture: Black Religion and Race Records in the 1920s and 1930s," in *The House That Race Built: Black Americans, U.S. Terrain*, ed. Wahneema Lubiano (New York: Pantheon, 1997), 157–76.

32 Cheryl A. Wall, *Women of the Harlem Renaissance* (Bloomington; Indiana University Press, 1995), 89.

33 See Deborah McDowell, *The Changing Same: Black Women's Literature, Criticism and Theory* (Bloomington: Indiana University Press, 1995): 78–100.

34 Hazel Carby, *Reconstructing Womanhood: The Emergence of the Afro-American Woman Novelist* (New York: Oxford University Press, 1987), 164.

35 See Evelyn Brooks Higginbotham, *Righteous Discontent: The Women's Movement in the Black Baptist Church, 1880–1920* (Cambridge: Harvard University Press, 1993).

36 Alain Locke, *The New Negro* (New York: Touchstone, 1997), 7.

37 See Joseph R. Roach, *Cities of the Dead: Circum-Atlantic Performance* (New York: Columbia University Press, 1996), 6.

38 See Raymond Williams, *Marxism and Literature* (New York: Oxford University Press, 1977).

39 Thadious M. Davis, introduction to *Quicksand*, by Nella Larsen (New York: Penguin Classics, 2002), xi.

40 Daphne A. Brooks, *Bodies in Dissent: Spectacular Performances of Race and Freedom, 1850–1910* (Durham: Duke University Press, 2006), 5.

41 Alys Eve Weinbaum, "Racial Masquerade: Consumption and Contestation of American Modernity," in *The Modern Girl around the World: Consumption, Modernity, and Globalization*, by Alys Eve Weinbaum, L. M. Thomas, P. Rama-

murthy, U. G. Poiger, M. Y. Dong, and T. E. Barlow, 120–46 (Durham: Duke University Press, 2008), 128.

42 See Henry Yu, *Thinking Orientals: Migration, Contact, and Exoticism in Modern America* (New York: Oxford University Press, 2001), 42–46. See also Robert Ezra Park, *Race and Culture* (Glenco: Free Press, 1950).

43 Davis's introduction to *Quicksand*; Sherrard-Johnson's *Portraits*.

44 Cherene Sherrard-Johnson, "'A Plea For Color': Nella Larsen's Iconography of the Mulatta," *American Literature* 76, no. 4 (2004): 835.

45 Ibid., 836.

46 Ibid., 842.

47 See Chris Friday, *Organizing Asian American Labor: The Pacific Coast Canned-Salmon Industry, 1870–1942* (Philadelphia: Temple University Press, 1994).

48 See Park, *Race and Culture*.

49 See, for example, Larsen, *Quicksand*, 23, 88, 107, 114, and 129.

50 Walter Benjamin, *The Arcades Project*, translated by Howard Eiland and Kevin McLaughlin (Cambridge: Harvard University Press, 1999).

51 It's worth remembering that Helga's petty attempts at uplift are interpreted by the women of the town as at best cosmopolitan and snobbish, and at worst a bid for dominance through the imposition of a new regime of cultural and aesthetic values. Though Helga shows contempt for what she perceives as a lack of aesthetic sensibility among the women of the town, we should remember that she also shows contempt for the urban "race women" and the new Negro movement in Harlem, as well as for the racism of the modernist movement in cosmopolitan Copenhagen. The uniformity of her affective contempt toward all cultural systems is what contributes to the reader's sense of her unreliability and her identity as figure. See ibid.

52 Quoted in Wall, *Women of the Harlem Renaissance*, 93.

Interlude

1 See Mae Ngai, *Impossible Subjects: Illegal Aliens and the Making of Modern America* (Princeton: Princeton University Press, 2005); and Jonathan Xavier Inda, *Targeting Immigrants: Government, Technology, and Ethics* (Malden, Mass.: Blackwell, 2006).

2 See Angela Y. Davis, *Abolition Democracy: Beyond Empire, Prisons, and Torture* (New York: Seven Stories Press, 2005); and Michelle Alexander, *The New Jim Crow: Mass Incarceration in the Age of Colorblindness* (New York: New Press, 2010).

Three | RIGHTS-BASED FREEDOM

1 Rahman made his remarks at a symposium called Shifting Grounds for Asylum: Female Genital Surgery and Sexual Orientation, held at the New York University School of Law on October 16, 1997. The proceedings were tran-

scribed, edited, and published as Timothy Wei and Margaret Satterthwaite, "Shifting Grounds for Asylum: Female Genital Surgery and Sexual Orientation," *Columbia Human Rights Law Review* 29, no. 2 (1998): 467–531.

2 On ideological state apparatuses, see Louis Althusser, "Ideology and Ideological State Apparatuses (Notes toward an Investigation)," In *Lenin and Philosophy and Other Essays*, trans. Ben Brewster (New York: Monthly Review Press, 1971).

3 See Lisa Lowe, "Angela Davis: Reflections on Race, Class, and Gender in the USA," in *The Politics of Culture in the Shadow of Capital*, ed. Lisa Lowe and David Lloyd (Durham: Duke University Press, 1997), 304–23; and Lisa Lowe, *Immigrant Acts: On Asian American Cultural Politics* (Durham: Duke University Press, 1996), 29–30.

4 Jodi Melamed, "The Spirit of Neoliberalism: From Racial liberalism to Neo-Liberal Multiculturalism," *Social Text* 24, no. 4 (Winter 2006): 16.

5 By a "history of sexuality," I mean to reference Foucault's argument that modern social power constitutes the very object—sex—that it then seeks to regulate. A historicist inspection of the repression of sexuality and its gradual emergence from repressive law, Foucault argues, naturalizes and makes invisible the diverse processes that affix sex within the body as a unitary ideal. See Michel Foucault, *The History of Sexuality: An Introduction*, vol. 1, trans. Robert Hurley (New York: Vintage, 1990).

6 On the Chinese prostitute and the Chinese bachelor as racialized and sexualized figures constituted by US law and its apparatuses, see Nayan Shah, *Contagious Divides: Epidemics and Race in San Francisco's Chinatown* (Berkeley: University of California Press, 2001). See also Lisa Lowe, *Immigrant Acts: On Asian American Cultural Politics* (Durham: Duke University Press, 1996), 1–36.

7 The Immigration and Naturalization Service (INS) ceased to exist on March 1, 2003. After George W. Bush signed the Homeland Security Act of 2002, the functions of the INS were transferred to the Department of Homeland Security.

8 See Saskia Sassen, *Losing Control?: Sovereignty in an Age of Globalization* (New York: Columbia University Press, 1996), 33–62.

9 See David Eng, "Transnational Adoption and Queer Diasporas," *Social Text* 21, no. 3 (Fall 2003): 1–37.

10 Gayatri Chakravorty Spivak, "Diasporas Old and New: Women in the Transnational World," *Textual Practice* 10, no. 2 (1996): 248.

11 Ibid., 249.

12 For a discussion of the differences between postcolonial and postimperial (or Global Southern and Global Northern) state formations under neoliberalism, see M. Jacqui Alexander, "Erotic Autonomy," in *Feminist Genealogies and Democratic Futures*, ed. M. Jacqui Alexander and Chandra Talpade Mohanty (New York: Routledge, 1999), 63–100. On the splitting of nation and state, see Spivak, "Diasporas Old and New," 249, 255–63. On the possibilities of postcolonial resignification of citizenship, and more generally on the catechresis of West-

ern regulative governmental terms in postcolonial space, see Spivak, "Post-structuralism, Marginality, Post-coloniality and Value," in *Literary Theory Today*, ed. Peter Collier and Helga Geyer-Ryan (Cambridge, UK: Polity Press, 1992), 219–41.

13 See Ruth Wilson Gilmore, "Globalization and US Prison Growth: From Military Keynesianism to Post-Keynesian Militarism," *Race and Class* 40, nos. 2–3 (1998–99): 171–87.

14 On the racialization of the terrorist, the organization of the state through the discourse of security, and the rise of new racial formations, see Leti Volpp, "The Citizen and the Terrorist," UCLA *Law Review* 49 (2002): 1575–1600. Also see Muneer Ahmed, "Homeland Insecurities: Racial Violence the Day after September 11," *Social Text* 20, no. 3 (Fall 2002): 101–15. On the racialized sexualization of the figure of the terrorist, see Jasbir Puar and Amit Rai, "Monster, Terrorist, Fag: The War on Terrorism and the Production of Docile Patriots," *Social Text* 20, no. 3 (Fall 2002): 117–48.

15 For example, in "The Nation Form: History and Ideology" (in *Race, Nation, Class: Ambiguous Identities*, by Etienne Balibar [translated by Chris Turner] and Immanuel Wallerstein [London: Verso, 1991], 96–100), Etienne Balibar pursues the allegorical reading of psychoanalysis in his theory of the nation-state and the citizen subject. Balibar disaggregates the nation and the state as naming different processes and, hence, different components of the subject's interpellation. While the nation figures as an ideal nation and is responsible for the subject's patriotism, ensuring the collective promise to face death for the nation, the state, as a mythicized abstraction, prefigures the unity between individuals and between individual and the collectivity, cementing individuality to the model of citizenship. Balibar calls this latter feature "fictive ethnicity" and defines it as critical in fusing the individual with the national community. Recasting the notion of identification, Balibar argues that individuals are interpellated through the structures of language and race into citizens who share an ethnicity. Although whiteness has historically operated as the form of racialization that has secured the fictive ethnicity of the US citizen, in the contemporary period it is multiculturalism that secures that citizen's fictive ethnicity as multicultural citizen. The multicultural subject is the racial formation of the national citizen, prefiguring the citizen's ability to claim universality, for which the state figures as a synecdoche of the universal. This is nowhere more powerfully articulated than in our current social formation, in which the US citizen of Arab descent or of Muslim faith is promoted as a figure of multiculturalism, while the Arab citizen of an Arab state or a Muslim citizen of an Arab or Muslim state is promoted as a figure of a monstrous monoculturalism that threatens the universality represented by the US multicultural state and that must be repudiated, expelled, violated, or preemptively destroyed. The racialization of the Arab and Muslim US citizen subject as a US multicultural subject (who has available the possibility of membership in universal

culture) is constitutively linked to the negative racialization of the Arab or Muslim immigrant, nonimmigrant resident, and non-US national as a social anachrony whose very presence invites violence and violation, a violation coded as violent humanization. Rewriting the formula created in seventeenth-century England, "the king is dead, long live the king"—which distinguished between the crown and the king's body, killing the body when it did not conform to the sovereign subject of the crown—we can argue that as the multicultural citizen subject is now installed as the sovereign, it would be possible for an American president to say, "The Arabs and Muslims are dead; long live our [US multicultural] Arab and Muslim brothers and sisters." On the sovereign's two bodies, see Ernst H. Kantorowicz, *The King's Two Bodies* (Princeton: Princeton University Press, 1997). See also David Lloyd, "Ethnic Cultures, Minority Discourse and the State," in *Colonial Discourse/Postcolonial Theory*, ed. Francis Barker, Peter Hulme, and Margaret Iversen (Manchester, England: University of Manchester Press, 1996), 221–38.

16 Karl Marx, "The Eighteenth Brumaire of Louis Bonaparte," in Karl Marx, *Surveys from Exile*, ed. David Ferbach, trans. Ben Fowkes (New York: Penguin, 1992), 2:184.

17 Ibid., 2:240.

18 Nicholas Ricccarei, "Same-Sex Marriages Often a Family Affair," *Los Angeles Times*, February 16, 2004.

19 Foucault, *The History of Sexuality*, 1:106.

20 Judith Butler, characteristically prescient and perceptive, argued that the idea of gay marriage always already invokes the idea of kinship in the United States, France, and elsewhere. Family is the space of their intersection. See Judith Butler, "Is Kinship Always Already Heterosexual," *differences* 13, no. 1 (2002): 14–44.

21 Ibid., 17–23.

22 See Roderick Ferguson, *Aberrations in Black: Toward a Queer of Color Critique* (Minneapolis: University of Minnesota Press, 2004), 1–29, 135–48.

23 See Chandan Reddy and Natalie Bennett, "Communities at a Crossroads: U.S. Right Wing Policies and Lesbian, Gay, Bisexual, Two Spirit and Transgender Immigrants of Color in New York City" (New York: Audre Lorde Project, 2004).

24 See Paul Wickham Schmidt, ed., *Understanding the Immigration Act of 1990: AILA's New Law Handbook* (Washington: American Immigration Lawyers Association, 1991), 5–9. See also Harry Gee Jr., "Family Sponsored Immigration (The Numbers Game)," and Lenni B. Benson, "Overview of Employment-Based Immigration—The First Three Preferences," both in ibid., 38–44 and 15, respectively. On the expansion of the labor market for low-end services and unskilled labor, see Saskia Sassen, *Globalization and Its Discontents: Essays on the New Mobility of People and Money* (New York: Free Press, 1998), and *The Global City* (Princeton: Princeton University Press, 1991).

25 The Immigration Act of 1990 stipulates that petitioning families must agree to shoulder the possible social cost of admitted immigrants. See Schmidt, *Understanding the Immigration Act of 1990*.

26 Moreover, this was effected by ideologically centering the Immigration Act of 1990 on a middle-class subject of migration.

27 See the interviews with GLBTQ immigrants of color collected for this study, all archived at the Audre Lorde Project. See also Reddy and Bennett, "Communities at a Crossroads."

28 In pursuing this reading of the issues, I have been aided by Wendy Brown, *States of Injury: Power and Freedom in Late Modernity* (Princeton: Princeton University Press, 1995), 135–65.

29 This has also been true of the figure of the "DL" or "the down low." as it's currently used by the Centers for Disease Control and Prevention and the media for naming certain African American nonheteronormative formations that cannot become homosexual.

30 For a review of this literature, see Brown, *States of Injury*, 3–29.

31 Roderick Ferguson, *Aberrations in Black* (Minneapolis: University of Minnesota Press, 2004), 16.

32 Ibid., 17.

33 Ibid.

34 Ibid., 39, 56, 9.

35 Ibid., 17.

36 Spivak, "Diasporas Old and New," 245–69. For a description of the post-state class system as part of the concept of "empire," see Michael Hardt and Antonio Negri, *Empire* (Cambridge: Harvard University Press, 2000). In Introduction, in *The Ethics of Kinship: Ethnographic Inquiries*, ed. James D. Faubion (Lanham, Md.: Rowman and Littlefield, 2001), Faubion writes of the supplement in relation to contemporary theories of kinship: "If the older anthropology of kinship is thus still with us, it has also had to endure the perturbations of an ever more unruly 'supplement' (a term I use in the Derridian sense, to denote the necessary and perhaps antithetical resolution of a primary, a hegemonic, an intellectually comfortable category)" (1). See also John Borneman, "Caring and Being Cared For: Displacing Marriage, Kinship, Gender and Sexuality," in ibid., 29–46. As a supplement, the gay Pakistani immigrant must be distinguished from the Chinese prostitute and Chinese bachelor of the nineteenth century and the early twentieth, as both those earlier figures were produced both materially and discursively in the United States as constitutive exclusions and hence as constitutively excluded.

37 See Ethne Luibheid, *Entry Denied: Controlling Sexuality at the Border* (Minneapolis: University of Minnesota Press, 2002).

38 This is, in fact, how the Human Rights Campaign has addressed queer immigrant formations and politics, in its lobbying for the Permanent Partners Immigration Act of 2003, which never became law. The act would have ex-

tended to gays and lesbians the same legal rights that heterosexual citizens possess in immigration matters. See David Crary, "U.S. Immigration Law Not Friendly to Gay Couples," *Seattle Times*, November 24, 2003. See also, Human Rights Campaign, "Permanent Partners Immigration Act," http://www.hrc.org.

39 Michel Foucault, *The Archaeology of Knowledge*, trans. A. M. Sheridan Smith (New York: Pantheon, 1972), 129.

40 Judith Butler, *Frames of War: When Is Life Grievable?* (London: Verso, 2009).

41 Judith Butler, *Bodies That Matter: On the Discursive Limits of "Sex"* (New York: Routledge, 1993), v.

42 See, for example, Tim Dean, *Beyond Sexuality* (Chicago: University of Chicago Press, 2000); Lee Edelman, *No Future: Queer Theory and the Death Drive* (Durham: Duke University Press, 2004); Heather Love, *Feeling Backward: Loss and the Politics of Queer History* (Cambridge: Harvard University Press, 2007); and Antonio Viego, *Dead Subjects: Toward a Politics of Loss in Latino Studies* (Durham: Duke University Press, 2007).

43 Edelman, *No Future*, 8.

44 Louis Althusser and Étienne Balibar, *Reading Capital* (London: Verso, 1997), 209–24.

Four | BEYOND A FREEDOM WITH VIOLENCE

1 See Melissa Victoria Harris-Lacewell, *Barbershops, Bibles, and BET: Everyday Talk and Black Political Thought* (Princeton: Princeton University Press, 2004), 3–11.

2 *Loving v. Virginia*, 388 U.S. 1 (1967).

3 *McLaughlin v. Florida*, 379 U.S. 184 (1964).

4 It may have been no accident that the Supreme Court of Massachusetts delivered its decision affirming gay marriage, in *Goodridge v. Department of Public Health*, on May 17, 2004, fifty years to the date after the US Supreme Court's decision in *Brown v. Board of Education* 347 U.S. 483 (1954), often seen as the precedent-setting modern civil rights case.

5 Janet Halley, "Like Race," in *What's Left of Theory? New Work on the Politics of Literary Theory*, ed. Judith Butler, John Guillory, and Kendall Thomas (New York: Routledge, 2000), 40–75.

6 Siobhan B. Somerville, "Queer Loving," *GLQ* 11, no. 3 (2005): 337.

7 Ibid., 345–46. See also Darren Lenard Hutchinson, "Out Yet Unseen: A Racial Critique of Gay and Lesbian Legal Theory and Political Discourse," *Connecticut Law Review* 29, no. 2 (Winter, 1997): 561–646; and Mary Eaton, "Homosexual Unmodified: Speculation on Law's Discourse, Race, and the Construction of Sexual Identity," in *Legal Inversions: Lesbians, Gay Men, and the Politics of Law*, ed. Herman Didi and Carl F. Stychin (Philadelphia: Temple University Press, 1995), 46–73.

8 On the extension of normalization to African Americans and its creation of

nonheteronormative differences of race, see also Roderick Ferguson, *Aberrations in Black: Toward a Queer of Color Critique* (Minneapolis, University of Minnesota Press, 2004).

9 Somerville, "Queer Loving," 357.

10 Jasmyne Cannick, "Gays First, Then Illegals," *Advocate*, April 4, 2006, http://www.advocate.com/article.aspx?id=43754.

11 On the worldliness of the civil rights movement appropriated as American exceptionalist drama, see Nikhil Pal Singh, *Black Is a Country: Race and the Unfinished Struggle for Democracy* (Cambridge: Harvard University Press, 2004), 1–57.

12 Henry Campbell Black and Joseph R. Nolan, *Black's Law Dictionary: Definitions of the Terms and Phrases of American and English Jurisprudence, Ancient and Modern*, 6th ed. (St. Paul, Minn.: West, 1990), 84.

13 Ibid.

14 Lisa Duggan, *The Twilight of Equality? Neoliberalism, Cultural Politics, and the Attack on Democracy* (Boston: Beacon Press, 2003), 65. See also Jasbir Puar, *Terrorist Assemblages: Homonationalism in Queer Times* (Durham: Duke University Press, 2007).

15 *Naim v. Naim*, 197 Va. 80.

16 *Loving v. Virginia*, 7.

17 Howard Winant, *The World Is a Ghetto: Race and Democracy Since World War II* (New York: Basic, 2001), 133–36. See also Jodi Melamed, "The Spirit of Neoliberalism: From Racial Liberalism to Neoliberal Multiculturalism," *Social Text* 24, no. 4 (Winter 2006): 1–25.

18 See Kimberlé Crenshaw, "Race, Reform, and Retrenchment: Transformation and Legitimation in Anti-Discrimination Law," in *Critical Race Theory: The Key Writings That Formed the Movement*, ed. Kimberlé Crenshaw (New York: New Press, 1995), 110–15. See also Singh, *Black Is a Country*.

19 Patricia J. Williams (*The Alchemy of Race and Rights* [Cambridge: Harvard University Press, 1991], 216–38) and Crenshaw ("Race, Reform, and Retrenchment") have argued a similar point, in different contexts—that of property law and antidiscrimination law. Both, as practitioners of critical race theory, suggest that it is not enough to simply unmask the ideology of the law as a guarantor of capitalist social relations and capitalist hegemony, as critical legal theory seeks to do; rather, we must also address the legal sphere as actively producing, constraining, and shaping racial identities and meanings as well as being shaped by those meanings. The state is not just a site that sits above or separate from racial struggle; it is a central terrain of conflict over racial meanings. Both scholars stress that formal equality—the legal remedy for racism within US racial capitalism from the 1970s onward—is limited to what Crenshaw calls "symbolic oppression," which she says fails to address "material oppression" ("Race, Reform, and Retrenchment," 114). Yet neither suggests that

formal equality is the only way in which race can be adjudicated in the law. Rather, current law and legal norms concerned with racial remedy have rarely championed the racial meanings promoted by race-based social movements or intellectuals of those movements, such as critical race theorists.

20 William N. Eskridge, "Equality Practice: Liberal Reflections on the Jurisprudence of Civil Unions: The 2000 Edward C. Sobota Lecture," *Albany Law Review* 64 (2001): 855–56.

21 That is, Eskridge circumvents any account of the history of slavery, continental genocide, and racialized immigration as the primary conditions of determination of the state regulation of marriage. Rather, marriage regulation by the state, and the practices of racial marking and ascription of which it is a part, is presented in Eskridge's normative account as, instead, the unequal state recognition of its subjects via marriage regulation. For an account that reveals the centrality of these conditions of determination for the writing of marriage laws and jurisprudence in Virginia, see Peter Wallenstein, "Race, Marriage, and the Law of Freedom: Alabama and Virginia, 1860s–1960s," *Chicago-Kent Law Review* 70, no. 2 (1994–95): 371–438.

22 Randall Kennedy, "Marriage and the Struggle for Gay, Lesbian, and Black Liberation," *Utah Law Review* no. 3 (2005): 787–88.

23 George Chauncey, *Why Marriage? The History Shaping Today's Debate over Gay Equality* (New York: Basic, 2004), 161.

24 Kennedy, "Marriage and the Struggle for Gay, Lesbian, and Black Liberation," 781.

25 Ibid., 801.

26 Ibid., 797–98.

27 *Lawrence v. Texas*, 539 U.S. 558 (2003).

28 *Loving v. Virginia*, 13.

29 See George Chauncey, *Gay New York: Gender, Urban Culture, and the Makings of the Gay Male World, 1890–1940* (New York: Basic, 1994).

30 Foucault uses the term "discontinuities" to discuss ruptures, transformations, or changed arrangements within a modern social formation. See Michel Foucault, *The Archaeology of Knowledge*, trans. A. M. Sheridan Smith (New York: Pantheon, 1972).

31 Of course, this is the logic and mode of relation that undergirds the white liberal institutional desire for Black History Month, or any other month or week dedicated to the public recognition of groups historically marginalized by the inheriting institution's—coded as our—modernity.

32 Quoted in Kennedy, "Marriage and the Struggle for Gay, Lesbian, and Black Liberation," 788.

33 Walter Benjamin, "Theses on the Philosophy of History," in *Illuminations*, ed. Hannah Arendt, trans. Harry Zohn (New York: Harcourt, Brace and World, 1968), 256.

34 Ibid., 255.

35 By unrecognizable intimacies, I mean that they are forms of intimacy that are undesirable to us as intimacies. See Katherine Franke, "Becoming a Citizen: Post-Bellum Regulation of African American Marriage," *Yale Journal of Law and Humanities* 11 (1999): 251.

36 *Loving v. Virginia*, 1.

37 *Korematsu v. United States*, 323 U.S. 214 (1944).

38 *Loving v. Virginia*, 6–7.

39 Ibid., 12. It is worth asking if the Supreme Court would have ratified *Loving* in the way that it did had the plaintiff in the case been a black man or a black woman. That is, in adjudicating the case of a black man's or black woman's right to marry, would the justices have placed the same emphasis on the plaintiff's fundamental right for the orderly pursuit of happiness? Though the term is of general reference in the period, if we take seriously the "man" in this statement, we see that *Loving* overturns white supremacy only by affirming the liberal theory of the male prerogative for private life as the precondition for formal equality in the public sphere. One wonders what would happen to that right in the hands of a black woman or a black man.

40 In fact, what's especially interesting about the majority opinion is that the justices are not working with a white-black or white-nonwhite dichotomy so characteristic of most of the Court's civil rights decisions in this period. Rather, in *Loving* the justices refute the reason for banning interracial intimacy by pointing out that the law only prohibited black-white interracial marriage, and not marriage between members of these groups and of other racial groups.

41 See George Lipsitz, *Rainbow at Midnight: Labor and Culture in the 1940s* (Urbana: University of Illinois Press, 1994), 157–204.

42 Duggan, *The Twilight of Equality?*, 43–66.

43 See Ruth Wilson Gilmore, *Golden Gulag: Prisons, Surplus, Crisis and Opposition in Globalizing California* (Berkeley: University of California Press, 2007).

44 Ibid., 245.

45 See Michel Foucault, *The History of Sexuality: An Introduction*, 1st ed., vol. 1, trans. Robert Hurley (New York: Vintage, 1990).

Conclusion

1 Representative texts include Gary Gerstle, *American Crucible: Race and Nation in the Twentieth Century* (Princeton: Princeton University Press, 2001); George Chauncey, *Gay New York: Gender, Urban Culture, and the Makings of the Gay Male World, 1890–1940* (New York: Basic, 1994); Judith N. Shklar, *American Citizenship: The Quest for Inclusion* (Cambridge: Harvard University Press, 1991); and Nancy F. Cott, *The Grounding of Modern Feminism* (New Haven: Yale University Press, 1987).

2 See Elizabeth Fox-Genovese and Eugene D. Genovese, *Fruits of Merchant*

Capital: Slavery and Bourgeois Property in the Rise and Expansion of Capitalism (New York: Oxford University Press, 1983); Daniel T. Rodgers, *Atlantic Crossings: Social Politics in a Progressive Age* (Cambridge: Belknap Press of Harvard University Press, 1998); and Anthony Molho and Gordon S. Wood, *Imagined Histories: American Historians Interpret the Past* (Princeton: Princeton University Press, 1998).

3 Julian P. Boyd, Charles T. Cullen, John Catanzariti, Barbara B. Oberg et al., eds., *The Papers of Thomas Jefferson* (Princeton: Princeton University Press, 1950), 4:237–38.

4 See Ira Katznelson, *When Affirmative Action Was White: An Untold History of Racial Inequality in Twentieth-Century America* (New York: W. W. Norton, 2005); Ellen Fitzpatrick, *History's Memory: Writing America's Past, 1880–1980* (Cambridge: Harvard University Press, 2002); and David Hollinger, *Postethnic America: Beyond Multiculturalism* (New York: Basic, 1995).

5 See Rogers M. Smith, *Civic Ideals: Conflicting Visions of Citizenship in U.S. History* (New Haven: Yale University Press, 1997).

6 See Frantz Fanon, *The Wretched of the Earth*, trans. Richard Philcox (New York: Grove, 2004), 1–62.

7 See Ruth Wilson Gilmore, "Globalization and US Prison Growth: From Military Keynesianism to Post-Keynesian Militarism," *Race and Class* 40, nos. 2–3 (1998–99): 171–87.

8 See Walter Benjamin, "Critique of Violence," in *Walter Benjamin: Selected Writings, 1913–1926*, ed. Marcus Paul Bullock, Michael William Jennings, Howard Eiland, and Gary Smith, trans. Edmund Jephcott (Cambridge: Harvard University Press, 1996), 1:236–52.

9 See Robert Cover, "Violence and the Word," *Yale Law Journal* 95 (1986): 1601–29. See also Jacques Derrida, "Force of Law: The 'Mystical Foundation of Authority,'" trans. Mary Quaintance, *Cardozo Law Review* 11 (1990): 919–1045.

10 Obviously the production of law is not the only product of the state that should be understood as an organized division of labor. There is also, for example, the production of governance, security, knowledge and so forth, each of which has its own division of labor. A single institution, such as the modern university, can be part of multiple divisions of labor corresponding to distinct state needs.

11 See, for example, Timothy Lynch, "Testimony of Tim Lynch, Director, Project on Criminal Justice, Cato Institute, before the Subcommittee on Crime, Terrorism, and Homeland Security, Committee on the Judiciary, United States House of Representations: The Hate Crimes Prevention Act of 2007" (testimony, the Cato Institute, April 17, 2007), http://www.cato.org/testimony/ct-tl04172007.html. Lynch testified that prosecuting hate crimes is the state's euphemism for prosecuting "thought crimes."

12 Nat Hentoff, a senior fellow at the Cato Institute, writes that throughout "the Bush-Cheney creation of a society under surveillance and unprecedented gov-

ernment secrecy, I have often praised Sen. Patrick Leahy, D-Vt., for resisting that administration's penchant for degrading the Constitution." Yet Leahy became part of that same ideology when he helped pass the Shepard-Byrd Act. For Hentoff, Sen. John McCain got it right when he said on the Senate floor: "Our legal system is based on identifying, capturing and punishing criminals, and not on using the power of government to try to divine biases." See Nat Hentoff, "Hate Crime Bill Goes against Constitution," *Pasadena Star News*, July 30, 2009.

13 For a liberal critique of "don't ask, don't tell," see Kenji Yoshino, "Assimilationist Bias in Equal Protection: The Visibility Presumption and the Case of 'Don't Ask, Don't Tell,' " *Yale Law Journal* 108, no. 3 (December 1998), 485–571.

14 See Jasbir Puar, *Terrorist Assemblages: Homonationalism in Queer Times* (Durham: Duke University Press, 2007), 82–113.

15 Most US military prosecutions of homosexuality in the "don't ask, don't tell" era relied heavily on private e-mail messages, private conversations, and off-duty activities to prove the homosexuality of the offending enlisted person as well as to prove that he or she refused to abide by the policy. It seems an irrelevant contradiction to the military process that most of the evidence came from deliberatively private zones of activity.

16 See Paul Kramer, *The Blood of Government: Race, Empire, the United States and the Philippines* (Chapel Hill: University of North Carolina Press, 2006); John Dower, *War without Mercy: Race and Power in the Pacific War* (New York: Pantheon, 1986); Lydia Liu, *The Clash of Empires: The Invention of China in Modern World Making* (Cambridge: Harvard University Press, 2004); Mahmood Mamdani, *Good Muslim, Bad Muslim: America, the Cold War, and the Roots of Terror* (New York: Pantheon, 2004); and Antony Anghie, *Imperialism, Sovereignty, and the Making of International Law*, 1st paperback ed. (Cambridge: Cambridge University Press, 2007).

17 See Charles Tilly, *Coercion, Capital, and European States, AD 990–1992*, rev. paperback ed. (Cambridge, Mass.: Blackwell, 1992).

18 See Anghie, *Imperialism, Sovereignty, and the Making of International Law.*

19 See Erez Manela, *The Wilsonian Moment: Self-Determination and the International Origins of Anticolonial Nationalism* (New York: Oxford University Press, 2007).

20 See Etienne Balibar, *Politics and the Other Scene*, trans. Christine Jones, James Swenson, and Chris Turner (New York: Verso, 1998), and "Violence and Civility: On the Limits of Political Anthropology," *differences* 20, nos. 2–3 (2009): 9–35.

21 Merrill A. McPeak, "Don't Ask, Don't Tell, Don't Change," *New York Times*, March 4, 2010.

22 Ibid.

23 See Victor Bascara, *Model-Minority Imperialism* (Minneapolis: University of Minnesota Press, 2006); and Amy Kaplan, *The Anarchy of Empire in the Making of U.S. Culture* (Cambridge: Harvard University Press, 2005), 1–22.

BIBLIOGRAPHY   Court Cases

Bolling v. Sharpe, 347 U.S. 497 (1954).
Bowers v. Hardwick, 478 U.S. 186 (1986).
Brown v. Board of Education, 347 U.S. 483 (1954).
Korematsu v. United States, 323 U.S. 214 (1944).
Lawrence v. Texas, 539 U.S. 558 (2003).
Loving v. Virginia, 388 U.S. 1 (1967).
McLaughlin v. Florida, 379 U.S. 184 (1964).
Naim v. Naim, 197 Va. 80 (1955).
Plessy v. Ferguson, 163 U.S. 537 (1896).
Romer v. Evans, 517 U.S. 620 (1996).

Books and Articles

Agamben, Giorgio. *Homo Sacer: Sovereign Power and Bare Life*. Translated by Daniel Heller-Roazen. Stanford: Stanford University Press, 1998.
Ahmed, Muneer. "Homeland Insecurities: Racial Violence the Day after September 11." *Social Text* 20, no. 3 (Fall 2002): 101–15.
Alexander, M. Jacqui. "Erotic Autonomy as a Politics of Decolonization: An Anatomy of Feminist and State Practice in the Bahamas Tourist Economy." In *Feminist Genealogies and Democratic Futures*, edited by M. Jacqui Alexander and Chandra Talpade Mohanty, 63–100. New York: Routledge, 1999.
——. *Pedagogies of Crossing: Meditations on Feminism, Sexual Politics, Memory, and the Sacred*. Durham: Duke University Press, 2005.
Alexander, Michelle. *The New Jim Crow: Mass Incarceration in the Age of Colorblindness*. New York: New Press, 2010.

Althusser, Louis. "Ideology and Ideological State Apparatuses (Notes toward an Investigation)." In *Lenin and Philosophy and Other Essays*. Translated by Ben Brewster. New York: Monthly Review Press, 1971.

Althusser, Louis, and Etienne Balibar. *Reading Capital*. Translated by Ben Brewster. London: Verso, 1997.

Anderson, Benedict. *Imagined Communities: Reflections on the Origin and Spread of Nationalism*. New York: Verso, 1996.

Anghie, Antony. *Imperialism, Sovereignty, and the Making of International Law*. 1st paperback ed. Cambridge: Cambridge University Press, 2007.

Appiah, K. Anthony. "The Uncompleted Argument: Du Bois and the Illusion of Race." In *"Race," Writing and Difference*, edited by Henry Louis Gates Jr., 21–37. Chicago: University of Chicago Press, 1986.

Bal, Mieke. *Quoting Caravaggio: Contemporary Art, Preposterous History*. Chicago: University of Chicago Press, 1999.

Balibar, Etienne. "Is There a Neo-Racism?" In Etienne Balibar (translated by Chris Turner) and Immanuel Wallerstein, *Race, Nation, Class: Ambiguous Identities*, 17–28. London: Verso, 1991.

———. "The Nation Form: History and Ideology." In Etienne Balibar (translated by Chris Turner) and Immanuel Wallerstein, *Race, Nation, Class: Ambiguous Identities*, 86–106. London: Verso, 1991.

———. *Politics and the Other Scene*. Translated by Christine Jones, James Swenson, and Chris Turner, New York: Verso, 1998.

———. "Some Questions on Politics and Violence." *Assemblage*, no. 20 (April 1993): 12–13.

———. "Violence and Civility: On the Limits of Political Anthropology." *differences* 20, nos. 2–3 (2009): 9–35.

Barker, Lee. *From Savage to Negro: Anthropology and the Construction of Race, 1896–1954*. Berkeley: University of California Press, 1998.

Bascara, Victor. *Model-Minority Imperialism*. Minneapolis: University of Minnesota Press, 2006.

Bassichis, Morgan. "The Revolution Starts at Home." Unpublished manuscript.

Benjamin, Walter. *The Arcades Project*. Translated by Howard Eiland and Kevin McLaughlin. Cambridge: Harvard University Press, 1999.

———. "Critique of Violence." In *Walter Benjamin: Selected Writings, 1913–1926*, edited by Marcus Paul Bullock, Michael William Jennings, Howard Eiland, and Gary Smith, and translated by Edmund Jephcott, 1:236–52. Cambridge: Harvard University Press, 1996.

———. "On the Concept of History." In *Walter Benjamin: Selected Writings, 1938–1940*, edited by Howard Eiland and Michael W. Jennings, and translated by Edmund Jephcott, 4:401–24. Cambridge: Harvard University Press, 2003.

———. *The Origin of German Tragic Drama*. Translated by John Osborne. London: Verso, 1998.

——. "Theses on the Philosophy of History." In Walter Benjamin, *Illuminations*, edited by Hannah Arendt and translated by Harry Zohn, 253–64, New York: Harcourt, Brace and World, 1968.

Benson, Lenni B. "Overview of Employment-Based Immigration—The First Three Preferences." In *Understanding the Immigration Act of 1990: AILA's New Law Handbook*, edited by Paul Wickham Schmidt, 1–15. Washington: American Immigration Lawyers Association, 1991.

Black, Henry Campbell, and Joseph R. Nolan. *Black's Law Dictionary: Definitions of the Terms and Phrases of American and English Jurisprudence, Ancient and Modern*. 6th ed. St. Paul, Minn.: West, 1990.

Borneman, John. "Caring and Being Cared For: Displacing Marriage, Kinship, Gender and Sexuality." In *The Ethics of Kinship: Ethnographic Inquiries*, edited by James D. Faubion, 29–46. Lanham, Md.: Rowman and Littlefield, 2001.

Boyce, Robert. *The Great Interwar Crisis and the Collapse of Globalization*. New York: Palgrave, 2009.

Brody, Jennifer D. *Punctuation: Art, Politics, and Play*. Durham: Duke University Press, 2008.

Brooks, Daphne A. *Bodies in Dissent: Spectacular Performances of Race and Freedom, 1850–1910*. Durham: Duke University Press, 2006.

Brown, Wendy. *Politics out of History*. Princeton: Princeton University Press, 2001.

——. *States of Injury: Power and Freedom in Late Modernity*. Princeton: Princeton University Press, 1995.

Butler, Judith. *Bodies That Matter: On the Discursive Limits of "Sex."* New York: Routledge, 1993.

——. "Conditions of Possibility for Politics—and Then Some." In *Contingency, Hegemony and Universality: Contemporary Dialogues on the Left*, edited by Judith Butler, Ernesto Laclau, and Slavoj Žižek, 159–79. London: Verso, 2000.

——. *Excitable Speech: A Politics of the Performative*. New York: Routledge, 1997.

——. *Frames of War: When Is Life Grievable?* London: Verso, 2009.

——. *Gender Trouble: Feminism and the Subversion of Identity*. New York: Routledge, 1990.

——. "Imitation and Gender Insubordination." In *Inside/Out: Lesbian Theories, Gay Theories*, edited by Diana Fuss, 17–31. New York: Routledge, 1991.

——. "Is Kinship Always Already Heterosexual?" *differences* 13, no. 1 (2002): 14–44.

Carby, Hazel. *Race Men: The W. E. B. Du Bois Lectures*. Cambridge: Harvard University Press, 2000.

——. *Reconstructing Womanhood: The Emergence of the Afro-American Woman Novelist*. New York: Oxford University Press, 1987.

Chandler, Nahum. "Originary Displacement." *boundary 2* 27, no. 3 (2000): 249–86.

Chauncey, George. *Gay New York: Gender, Urban Culture, and the Makings of the Gay Male World, 1890–1940*. New York: Basic, 1994.

——. *Why Marriage? The History Shaping Today's Debate over Gay Equality.* New York: Basic, 2004.

Cho, Grace. *Haunting the Korean Diaspora: Shame, Secrecy and the Forgotten War.* Minneapolis: University of Minnesota Press, 2008.

Ciepley, David. *Liberalism in the Shadow of Totalitarianism.* Cambridge: Harvard University Press, 2006.

Cohen, Cathy. *The Boundaries of Blackness: AIDS and the Breakdown of Black Politics.* Chicago: University of Chicago Press, 1999.

Cott, Nancy F. *The Grounding of Modern Feminism.* New Haven: Yale University Press, 1987.

——. "Marriage and Women's Citizenship in the United States, 1830–1934." *American Historical Review* 103, no. 5 (December 1998): 1440–74.

Cover, Robert. "Violence and the Word." *Yale Law Journal* 95 (1986): 1601–29.

Crenshaw, Kimberlé. "Demarginalizing the Intersection: A Black Feminist Critique of Anti-Discrimination Doctrine, Feminist Theory, and Anti-Racist Politics." *University of Chicago Legal Forum* (1989): 139–67.

——. "Race, Reform, and Retrenchment: Transformation and Legitimation in Anti-Discrimination Law." *Harvard Law Review* 101, no. 7 (May 1988): 1331–87.

——. "Race, Reform, and Retrenchment: Transformation and Legitimation in Anti-Discrimination Law." In *Critical Race Theory: The Key Writings That Formed the Movement,* edited by Kimberlé Crenshaw, 103–27. New York: New Press, 1995.

Cruikshank, Barbara. *The Will to Empower: Democratic Citizens and Other Subjects.* Ithaca: Cornell University Press, 1999.

Cumings, Bruce. *Dominion from Sea to Sea: Pacific Ascendency and American Power.* New Haven: Yale University Press, 2009.

Davis, Angela Y. *Abolition Democracy: Beyond Empire, Prisons, and Torture.* New York: Seven Stories Press, 2005.

——. "Reflections on the Black Woman's Role in the Community of Slaves." In Angela Y. Davis, *The Angela Y. Davis Reader,* edited by Joy James, 111–29. Malden, Mass.: Blackwell, 1998.

Davis, Thadious M. Introduction. In Nella Larsen, *Quicksand,* vii–xxxiv. New York: Penguin Classics, 2002.

Dawson, Michael C. *Black Visions: The Roots of Contemporary African-American Political Ideologies.* Chicago: University of Chicago Press, 2001.

Dean, Tim. *Beyond Sexuality.* Chicago: University of Chicago Press, 2000.

Denning, Michael. *The Cultural Front: The Laboring of American Culture in the Twentieth Century.* New York: Verso, 1996.

Derrida, Jacques. "Force of Law: The 'Mystical Foundation of Authority.' " Translated by Mary Quaintance. *Cardozo Law Review* 11 (1990): 919–1045.

Dower, John. *War without Mercy: Race and Power in the Pacific War.* New York: Pantheon, 1986.

Du Bois, W. E. B. *The Philadelphia Negro: A Social Study.* Philadelphia: University of Pennsylvania Press, 1996.

———. "Returning Soldiers." *The Crisis* 18 (May 1919): 13.

———. *The Souls of Black Folk.* Chicago: A. C. McClurg, 1903. With introduction by Donald B. Gibson and notes by Monica M. Elbert, New York: Penguin, 1989.

———. "Worlds of Color: The Negro Mind Reaches Out." In *The New Negro: An Interpretation,* edited by Alain Locke, 385–414. New York: A. and C. Boni, 1925. Reprint, with a new preface by Allan H. Spear, New York: Johnson Reprint, 1968.

Dudziak, Mary. *Cold War Civil Rights: Race and the Image of American Democracy.* Princeton: Princeton University Press, 2000.

Duggan, Lisa. *The Twilight of Equality? Neoliberalism, Cultural Politics, and the Attack on Democracy.* Boston: Beacon, 2003.

Dworkin, Ronald. *Sovereign Virtue: The Theory and Practice of Equality.* Cambridge: Harvard University Press, 2002.

Eaton, Mary. "Homosexual Unmodified: Speculation on Law's Discourse, Race, and the Construction of Sexual Identity." In *Legal Inversions: Lesbians, Gay Men, and the Politics of Law,* edited by Herman Didi and Carl F. Stychin, 46–73. Philadelphia: Temple University Press, 1995.

Edelman, Lee. *No Future: Queer Theory and the Death Drive.* Durham: Duke University Press, 2004.

Edwards, Brent Hayes. "Introduction: The Genres of Postcolonialism." *Social Text* 22, no. 1 (2004): 1–15.

———. "Late Romance." In *Next to the Color Line: Gender, Sexuality, and W. E. B. Du Bois,* edited by Alys Eve Weinbaum and Susan Gilman, 124–49. Minneapolis: University of Minnesota Press, 2007.

———. *The Practice of Diaspora: Literature, Translation, and the Rise of Black Internationalism.* Cambridge: Harvard University Press, 2003.

Eng, David. *Racial Castration: Managing Masculinity in Asian America.* Durham: Duke University Press, 2001.

———. "Transnational Adoption and Queer Diasporas." *Social Text* 21, no. 3 (Fall 2003): 1–37.

Eskridge, William N. "Equality Practice: Liberal Reflections on the Jurisprudence of Civil Unions; The 2000 Edward C. Sobota Lecture." *Albany Law Review* 64 (2001): 853–84.

Fahrmeir, Andreas, Olivier Faron, and Patrick Weil, eds. *Migration Control in the North Atlantic World: The Evolution of State Practices in Europe and the United States from the French Revolution to the Inter-War Period.* New York: Berghahn, 2003.

Fanon, Frantz. *Black Skin/White Masks.* Translated by Charles Lam Markman. London: Pluto, 1986.

———. *The Wretched of the Earth.* Translated by Richard Philcox. New York: Grove, 2004.

Faragher, John Mack. Introduction. In *Reading Frederick Jackson Turner: "The Significance of the Frontier in American History" and Other Essays*, edited by John Mack Faragher, 1–10. New Haven: Yale University Press, 1996.

Faubion, James D. Introduction. In *The Ethics of Kinship: Ethnographic Inquiries*, edited by James D. Faubion, 1–28. Lanham, Md.: Rowman and Littlefield, 2001.

Ferguson, Roderick. *Aberrations in Black: Towards a Queer of Color Critique*. Minneapolis: University of Minnesota Press, 2004.

Fineman, Ilene Rose. *Citizenship Rites: Feminist Soldiers and Feminist Antimilitarists*. New York: New York University Press, 2000.

Fitzpatrick, Ellen F. *History's Memory: Writing America's Past, 1880–1980*. Cambridge: Harvard University Press, 2002.

Foucault, Michel. *The Archaeology of Knowledge*. Translated by A. M. Sheridan Smith. New York: Pantheon, 1972.

———. "Governmentality." In *The Foucault Effect: Studies in Governmentality*, edited by Graham Burchell, Colin Gordon, and Peter Miller, 87–104. Chicago: University of Chicago Press, 1991.

———. *The History of Sexuality: An Introduction*. Vol. 1, 1st ed. Translated by Robert Hurley. New York: Vintage, 1990.

Fox-Genovese, Elizabeth. "Placing Women's History in History." *New Left Review* 133 (May–June 1982): 5–29.

———. *Within the Plantation Household: Black and White Women of the Old South*. Chapel Hill: University of North Carolina Press, 1988.

Fox-Genovese, Elizabeth, and Eugene D. Genovese. *Fruits of Merchant Capital: Slavery and Bourgeois Property in the Rise and Expansion of Capitalism*. New York: Oxford University Press, 1983.

Franke, Katherine. "Becoming a Citizen: Post-Bellum Regulation of African American Marriage." *Yale Journal of Law and Humanities* 11 (1999): 251–311.

Freud, Sigmund. *Group Psychology and the Analysis of the Ego*. Translated by James Strachey. New York: Liveright, 1951.

Friday, Chris. *Organizing Asian American Labor: The Pacific Coast Canned-Salmon Industry, 1870–1942*. Philadelphia: Temple University Press, 1994.

Furner, Mary. *A Crisis in the Professionalization of American Social Sciences, 1865–1905*. Lexington: University of Kentucky Press, 1975.

Gaines, Kevin. *Uplifting the Race*. Chapel Hill: University of North Carolina Press, 1997.

Gee, Harry, Jr. "Family Sponsored Immigration (The Numbers Game)." In *Understanding the Immigration Act of 1990: AILA's New Law Handbook*, edited by Paul Wickham Schmidt, 38–44. Washington: American Immigration Lawyers Association, 1991.

Gerstle, Gary. *American Crucible: Race and Nation in the Twentieth Century*. Princeton: Princeton University Press, 2001.

Gilman, Susan, and Alys Eve Weinbaum, eds. *Next to the Color Line: Gender, Sexuality, and W. E. B. Du Bois.* Minneapolis: University of Minnesota Press, 2007.

Gilmore, Ruth Wilson. *Golden Gulag: Prisons, Surplus, Crisis and Opposition in Globalizing California.* Berkeley: University of California Press, 2007.

——. "Globalization and US Prison Growth: From Military Keynesianism to Post-Keynesian Militarism." *Race and Class* 40, nos. 2–3 (1998–99): 171–87.

Gilroy, Paul. *The Black Atlantic: Modernity and Double Consciousness.* Cambridge: Harvard University Press, 1993.

Goldsby, Jacqueline. *A Spectacular Secret: Lynching in American Life and Literature.* Chicago: University of Chicago Press, 2005.

Gordon, Avery. *Ghostly Matters: Haunting and the Sociological Imagination.* Minneapolis: University of Minnesota Press, 1997.

Greenfield, Bruce. "The Problems of the Discoverer's Authority in Lewis and Clark's History." In *Macropolitics of Nineteenth Century Literature,* edited by Jonathan Arac and Harriet Ritvo, 12–36. Philadelphia: University of Pennsylvania Press, 1991.

Grewal, Inderpal, and Caren Kaplan, eds. *Scattered Hegemonies: Postmodernity and Transnational Feminist Practices.* Minneapolis: University of Minnesota Press, 1994.

Griffin, Farah Jasmine. *Who Sets You Flowin': The African American Migration Narrative.* New York: Oxford University Press, 1995.

Guha, Ranajit. *A Rule of Property for Bengal: An Essay on the Idea of Permanent Settlement.* Paris: Mouton, 1963. Reprint, Durham: Duke University Press, 1996.

Gupta, Akhil, and James Ferguson. "Beyond 'Culture': Space, Identity and the Politics of Difference." *Cultural Anthropology* 7, no. 1 (February 1992): 6–22.

Gutiérrez-Jones, Carl. "Desiring (B)orders." *Diacritics* 25, no. 1 (Spring 1995): 99–112.

Hahn, Steven. *A Nation under Our Feet: Black Political Struggles in the Rural South, from Slavery to the Great Migration.* Cambridge: Belknap Press of Harvard University Press, 2003.

Halley, Janet. "Like Race." In *What's Left of Theory? New Work on the Politics of Literary Theory,* edited by Judith Butler, John Guillory, and Kendall Thomas, 40–75. New York: Routledge, 2000.

Hall, Jacquelyn Dowd. "The Long Civil Rights Movement and the Political Uses of the Past." *Journal of American History* 91, no. 4 (March 2005): 1233–63.

Hall, Stuart. "New Ethnicities." In *Stuart Hall: Critical Dialogues in Cultural Studies,* edited by David Morley and Kuan-Hsing Chen, 441–49. London: Routledge, 1996.

Hammonds, Evelynn. "Black (W)holes and the Geometry of Black Female Sexuality." *differences* 6, nos. 2–3 (1994): 126–45.

Hardt, Michael, and Antonio Negri. *Empire.* Cambridge: Harvard University Press, 2000.

———. *Multitude: War and Democracy in the Age of Empire*. New York: Penguin, 2004.

Harris-Lacewell, Melissa Victoria. *Barbershops, Bibles, and BET: Everyday Talk and Black Political Thought*. Princeton: Princeton University Press, 2004.

Hartman, Saidiya. *Scenes of Subjection: Terror, Slavery, and Self-Making in Nineteenth Century America*. New York: Oxford University Press, 1997.

Herman, Didi, and Carl F. Stychin. *Legal Inversions: Lesbians, Gay Men, and the Politics of Law*. Philadelphia: Temple University Press, 1995.

Higginbotham, Evelyn Brooks. "Rethinking Vernacular Culture: Black Religion and Race Records in the 1920s and 1930s." In *The House That Race Built: Black Americans, U.S. Terrain*, edited by Wahneema Lubiano, 157–76. New York: Pantheon, 1997.

———. *Righteous Discontent: The Women's Movement in the Black Baptist Church, 1880–1920*. Cambridge: Harvard University Press, 1993.

Hill Collins, Patricia. *Black Feminist Thought: Knowledge, Consciousness, and the Politics of Empowerment*. New York: Routledge, 2000.

Hobbes, Thomas. *The Elements of Law, Natural, and Politic*, edited, with a preface and notes, by Ferdinand Tönnies. Cambridge: Cambridge University Press, 1928.

———. *Leviathan*, edited by Richard Tuck. Cambridge: Cambridge University Press, 1996.

Hollinger, David A. *Postethnic America: Beyond Multiculturalism*. New York: Basic, 1995.

Hong, Grace Kyungwong, and Roderick A. Ferguson. *Strange Affinities: The Gender and Sexual Politics of Comparative Racialization*. Durham: Duke University Press, 2011.

Horkheimer, Max, and Theodor W. Adorno. *Dialectic of Enlightenment: Philosophical Fragments*, edited by Gunzelin Schmid Noerr and translated by Edmund Jephcott. Stanford: Stanford University Press, 2002.

Horne, Gerald. *The White Pacific: U.S. Imperialism and Black Slavery in the South Seas*. Honolulu: University of Hawaii Press, 2007.

Hutchinson, Darren Lenard. "Out Yet Unseen: A Racial Critique of Gay and Lesbian Legal Theory and Political Discourse." *Connecticut Law Review* 29, no. 2 (Winter 1997): 561–646.

Hutchinson, George. *In Search of Nella Larsen: A Biography of the Color Line*. Cambridge: Belknap Press of Harvard University Press, 2006.

Inda, Jonathan Xavier. *Targeting Immigrants: Government, Technology, and Ethics*. Malden, Mass.: Blackwell, 2006.

James, Joy. *Transcending the Talented Tenth: Black Leaders and American Intellectuals*. New York: Routledge, 1997.

Kantorowicz, Ernst H. *The King's Two Bodies*. Princeton: Princeton University Press, 1997.

Kaplan, Amy. *The Anarchy of Empire in the Making of U.S. Culture*. Cambridge: Harvard University Press, 2005.

Katznelson, Ira. *When Affirmative Action Was White: An Untold History of Racial Inequality in Twentieth-Century America*. New York: W. W. Norton, 2005.

Kennedy, Randall. "Marriage and the Struggle for Gay, Lesbian, and Black Liberation." *Utah Law Review* no. 3 (2005): 781–802.

King, Martin Luther, Jr. "Remarks Delivered at Africa Freedom Dinner at Atlanta University." In *The Papers of Martin Luther King, Jr.: Threshold of a New Decade, January 1959–December 1960*, edited by Clayborne Carson, 5:203–4. Berkeley: University of California Press, 2005.

Kramer, Paul. *The Blood of Government: Race, Empire, the United States and the Philippines*. Chapel Hill: University of North Carolina Press, 2006.

Larsen, Nella. *Quicksand*. With introduction by Thadious M. Davis. New York: Penguin Classics, 2002.

———. *Quicksand; and, Passing*. Edited by Deborah E. McDowell. New Brunswick, N.J.: Rutgers University Press, 1986.

Lemelle, Sidney J., and Robin D. G. Kelley, eds. *Imagining Home: Class, Culture, and Nationalism in the African Diaspora*. New York: Verso, 1994.

Lipsitz, George. "Frantic to Join . . . the Japanese Army: The Asia Pacific War in the Lives of African American Soldiers and Civilians." In *The Politics of Culture in the Shadow of Capital*, edited by David Lloyd and Lisa Lowe, 324–52. Durham: Duke University Press, 1997.

———. *The Possessive Investment in Whiteness: How Whites Profit through Identity Politics*. Philadelphia: Temple University Press, 1997.

———. *Rainbow at Midnight: Labor and Culture in the 1940s*. Urbana: University of Illinois Press, 1994.

Liu, Lydia. *The Clash of Empires: The Invention of China in Modern World Making*. Cambridge: Harvard University Press, 2004.

Lloyd, David. "Ethnic Cultures, Minority Discourse and the State." In *Colonial Discourse/Postcolonial Theory*, edited by Francis Barker, Peter Hulme, and Margaret Iversen, 221–38. Manchester, England: University of Manchester Press, 1996.

———. "Nationalisms against the State." In *The Politics of Culture in the Shadow of Capital*, edited by David Lloyd and Lisa Lowe, 173–98. Durham: Duke University Press, 1997.

———. "Race under Representation." *Oxford Literary Review* 13 (Spring 1991): 62–94.

Lloyd, David, and Lisa Lowe, eds. *The Politics of Culture in the Shadow of Capital*. Durham: Duke University Press, 1997.

Locke, Alain. *The New Negro*. New York: Touchstone, 1997.

Lott, Eric. *Love and Theft: Blackface Minstrelsy and the American Working Class*. New York: Oxford University Press, 1993.

Love, Heather. *Feeling Backward: Loss and the Politics of Queer History*. Cambridge: Harvard University Press, 2007.

Lowe, Lisa. *Critical Terrains: French and British Orientalisms*. Ithaca: Cornell University Press, 1991.

——. *Immigrant Acts: On Asian American Cultural Politics*. Durham: Duke University Press, 1996.

Lowe, Lisa, and David Lloyd. Introduction. In *The Politics of Culture in the Shadow of Capital*, edited by David Lloyd and Lisa Lowe, 1–32. Durham: Duke University Press, 1997.

Luibhéid, Ethne. *Entry Denied: Controlling Sexuality at the Border*. Minneapolis: University of Minnesota Press, 2002.

Lynch, Timothy. "Testimony of Tim Lynch, Director, Project on Criminal Justice, Cato Institute, before the Subcommittee on Crime, Terrorism, and Homeland Security, Committee on the Judiciary, United States House of Representations: The Hate Crimes Prevention Act of 2007" (testimony, the Cato Institute, April 17, 2007). http://www.cato.org/testimony/ct-tl04172007.html.

Mamdani, Mahmood. *Good Muslim, Bad Muslim: America, the Cold War, and the Roots of Terror*. New York: Pantheon, 2004.

Manela, Erez. *The Wilsonian Moment: Self-Determination and the International Origins of Anticolonial Nationalism*. New York: Oxford University Press, 2007.

Marx, Karl. "The Eighteenth Brumaire of Louis Bonaparte." In Karl Marx, *Surveys from Exile*, edited by David Ferbach and translated by Ben Fowkes, 2:143–249. New York: Penguin, 1992.

Marx, Karl, and Friedrich Engels. *The Communist Manifesto*, edited by Gareth Stedman Jones and translated by Samuel Moore. New York: Penguin, 2002.

McDowell, Deborah. *The Changing Same: Black Women's Literature, Criticism and Theory*. Bloomington: Indiana University Press, 1995.

Melamed, Jodi. "The Spirit of Neoliberalism: From Racial Liberalism to Neoliberal Multiculturalism." *Social Text* 24, no. 4 (Winter 2006): 1–25.

Menand, Louis. *The Metaphysical Club: A Story of Ideas in America*. London: Flamingo, 2001.

Mitchell, Timothy. "Society, Economy and the State Effect." In *State/Culture: State Formation after the Cultural Turn*, edited by George Steinmetz, 76–97. Ithaca: Cornell University Press, 1999.

Molho, Anthony, and Gordon S. Wood. *Imagined Histories: American Historians Interpret the Past*. Princeton: Princeton University Press, 1998.

Morial, Marc H. "Matthew Shepard and James Byrd, Jr. Hate Crimes Prevention Act Signed into Law" (National Urban League, November 11, 2009). http://www.nul.org/content/tbe45-matthew-shepard-and-james-byrd-jr-hate-crimes-prevention-act-signed-law.

Morrison, Toni. *The Bluest Eye*. New York: Holt, Rinehart and Winston, 1970. Reprint, New York: Alfred Knopf, 1993.

——. *The Song of Solomon*. New York: Knopf, 1977.

Moten, Fred. *In the Break: The Aesthetics of the Black Radical Tradition*. Minneapolis: University of Minnesota Press, 2003.

Newfield, Christopher. *Ivory and Industry: Business and the Making of the American University, 1880–1980*. Durham: Duke University Press, 2003.

Ngai, Mae. *Impossible Subjects: Illegal Aliens and the Making of Modern America*. Princeton: Princeton University Press, 2005.

Noble, David W. "The Anglo-Protestant Monopolization of 'America.'" In *José Martí's "Our America": From National to Hemispheric Cultural Studies*, edited by Jeffery Belnap and Raul Fernandez, 253–74. Durham: Duke University Press, 1998.

Obama, Barack. "Remarks by the President at the Acceptance of the Nobel Peace Prize" (speech, Oslo City Hall, Norway, December 10, 2009). http://www .whitehouse.gov/the-press-office/remarks-president-acceptance-nobel-peace-prize.

——. "Remarks by the President at the Signing of the National Defense Authorization Act for Fiscal Year 2010" (press conference, the White House, Washington, October 28, 2009). http://www.whitehouse.gov/the-press-office/remarks-president-signing-national-defense-authorization-act-fiscal-year-2010.

Ohmann, Richard. *The Politics of Letters*. Middletown, Conn.: Wesleyan University Press, 1987.

Omatsu, Glenn. "The Four Prisons and the Movements of Liberation: Asian American Activism from the 1960s to the 1990s." In *The State of Asian America: Activism and Resistance in the 1990s*, edited by Karin Aquilar-San Juan, 20–21. New York: South End Press, 1994.

Omi, Michael, and Howard Winant. *Racial Formation: From the 1960s to the 1990s*. 2nd ed. New York: Routledge, 1994.

Palmer, Phyllis. *Domesticity and Dirt*. Philadelphia: Temple University Press, 1989.

Park, Robert Ezra. *Race and Culture*. Glencoe: Free Press, 1950.

Plummer, Brenda Gayle. *Rising Wind: Black Americans and U.S. Foreign Affairs, 1935–1960*. Chapel Hill: University of North Carolina Press, 1996.

Puar, Jasbir. *Terrorist Assemblages: Homonationalism in Queer Times*. Durham: Duke University Press, 2007.

Puar, Jasbir, and Amit Rai. "Monster, Terrorist, Fag: The War on Terrorism and the Production of Docile Patriots." *Social Text* 20, no. 3 (Fall 2002): 117–48.

Reddy, Chandan, and Natalie Bennett. *Communities at a Crossroads: U.S. Right Wing Policies and Lesbian, Gay, Bisexual, Two Spirit and Transgender Immigrants of Color in New York City*. A Report by the Audre Lorde Project for the Nathan Cummings Trust, New York, 2004.

Reed, Adolph, Jr. *W. E. B. Du Bois and American Political Thought: Fabianism and the Color Line*. New York: Oxford University Press, 1997.

Roach, Joseph R. *Cities of the Dead: Circum-Atlantic Performance*. New York: Columbia University Press, 1996.

Rodgers, Daniel T. *Atlantic Crossings: Social Politics in a Progressive Age*. Cambridge: Belknap Press of Harvard University Press, 1998.

Rogin, Michael. "The Two Declarations of American Independence." In *Race and*

Representation: Affirmative Action, edited by Robert Post and Michael Rogin, 73–96. New York: Zone, 1998.

Ross, Dorothy. *The Origins of American Social Science*. Cambridge: Cambridge University Press, 1991.

Said, Edward. *Beginnings: Intention and Method*. New York: Basic Books, 1975.

———. *Culture and Imperialism*. 1st ed. New York: Knopf, 1993.

Said, Edward W., and David Barsamian. *Culture and Resistance: Conversations with Edward W. Said*. Cambridge, Mass.: South End, 2003.

Saldívar, José David. *Border Matters: Remapping American Cultural Studies*. Berkeley: University of California Press, 1997.

Sassen, Saskia. *Globalization and Its Discontents: Essays on the New Mobility of People and Money*. New York: New Press, 1998.

———. *The Global City*. Princeton: Princeton University Press, 1991.

———. *Losing Control? Sovereignty in an Age of Globalization*. New York: Columbia University Press, 1996.

Schmidt, Paul Wickham. "Overview of the Immigration Act of 1990." In *Understanding the Immigration Act of 1990: AILA's New Law Handbook*, edited by Paul Wickham Schmidt, 1–29. Washington: American Immigration Lawyers Association, 1991.

———, ed. *Understanding the Immigration Act of 1990: AILA's New Law Handbook*. Washington: American Immigration Lawyers Association, 1991.

Schmitt, Carl. *The Nomos of the Earth in the International Law of the Jus Publicum Europaeum*, edited and translated by G. L. Ulmen. New York: Telos, 2003.

Shachtman, Tom. *Airlift to America: How Barack Obama, Sr., John F. Kennedy, Tom Mboya, and 800 East African Students Changed Their World and Ours*. New York: St. Martin's, 2009.

Shah, Nayan. *Contagious Divides: Epidemics and Race in San Francisco's Chinatown*. Berkeley: University of California Press, 2001.

Sherrard-Johnson, Cherene. *Portraits of the New Negro Woman: Visual and Literary Culture in the Harlem Renaissance*. New Brunswick, N.J.: Rutgers University Press, 2007.

Shklar, Judith N. *American Citizenship: The Quest for Inclusion*. Cambridge: Harvard University Press, 1991.

Singh, Nikhil Pal. *Black Is a Country: Race and the Unfinished Struggle for Democracy*. Cambridge: Harvard University Press, 2004.

Smith, Neil. *American Empire: Roosevelt's Geographer and the Prelude to Globalization*. Berkeley: University of California Press, 2003.

Smith, Rogers M. *Civic Ideals: Conflicting Visions of Citizenship in U.S. History*. New Haven: Yale University Press, 1997.

Soja, Edward W. *Postmodern Geographies: The Reassertion of Space in Critical Social Theory*. London: Verso, 1989.

Somerville, Siobhan B. "Queer Loving." *GLQ* 11, no. 3 (2005): 335–70.

Spivak, Gayatri Chakravorty. "Can the Subaltern Speak?" In *Marxism and the Interpretation of Culture*, edited by Lawrence Grossberg and Carey Nelson, 271–313. Urbana: University of Illinois Press, 1988.

——. "Diasporas Old and New: Women in the Transnational World." *Textual Practice* 10, no. 2 (1996): 245–69.

——. *Outside in the Teaching Machine*. New York: Routledge, 1993.

——. "Poststructuralism, Marginality, Post-coloniality and Value." In *Literary Theory Today*, edited by Peter Collier and Helga Geyer-Ryan, 219–41. Cambridge, UK: Polity Press, 1992.

Stephens, Michelle Ann. *Black Empire: The Masculine Global Imaginary of Caribbean Intellectuals in the United States, 1914–1962*. Durham: Duke University Press, 2005.

Stepto, Robert B. *From behind the Veil: A Study of Afro-American Narrative*. Urbana: University of Illinois Press, 1979.

Stuckey, Sterling. *Slave Culture: Nationalist Theory and the Foundations of Black America*. New York: Oxford University Press, 1987.

Sundquist, Eric. *To Wake the Nations: Race in the Making of American Literature*. Cambridge: Harvard University Press, 1993.

Thomas, Brinley. *The Industrial Revolution and the Atlantic Economy: Selected Essays*. London: Routledge, 1993.

Tilly, Charles. *Coercion, Capital, and European States, AD 990–1992*. Rev. paperback ed. Cambridge, Mass.: Blackwell, 1992.

Turner, Frederick Jackson. *History, Frontier, and Section: Three Essays*. With introduction by Martin Ridge. Albuquerque: University of New Mexico Press, 1993.

Viego, Antonio. *Dead Subjects: Toward a Politics of Loss in Latino Studies*. Durham: Duke University Press, 2007.

Volpp, Leti. "The Citizen and the Terrorist." UCLA *Law Review* 49 (2002): 1575–1600.

Von Eschen, Penny M. *Race against Empire: Black Americans and Anti-Colonialism, 1937–1957*. Ithaca: Cornell University Press, 1997.

Wall, Cheryl A. *Women of the Harlem Renaissance*. Bloomington: Indiana University Press, 1995.

Wallenstein, Peter. "Race, Marriage, and the Law of Freedom: Alabama and Virginia, 1860s–1960s." *Chicago-Kent Law Review* 70, no. 2 (1994–95): 371–438.

Walzer, Michael. *Spheres of Justice: A Defense of Pluralism and Equality*. New York: Basic, 1983.

Watkin-Owen, Irma. *Blood Relations: Caribbean Immigrants and the Harlem Community, 1900–1930*. Bloomington: Indiana University Press, 1996.

Weber, Max. "Politics as a Vocation." In Max Weber, *The Vocation Lectures*, edited by David Owen and Tracy B. Strong and translated by Rodney Livingstone, 32–93. Indianapolis: Hackett, 2004.

———. *The Protestant Ethic and the Spirit of Capitalism and Other Writings.* Translated by Peter Baehr and Gordon C. Wells. New York: Penguin, 2002.

Wei, Timothy, and Margaret Satterthwaite. "Shifting Grounds for Asylum: Female Genital Surgery and Sexual Orientation." *Columbia Human Rights Law Review* 29, no. 2 (1998): 467–531.

Weinbaum, Alys Eve. "Interracial Romance and Black Internationalism." In *Next to the Color Line: Gender, Sexuality, and W. E. B. Du Bois,* edited by Alys Eve Weinbaum and Susan Gilman, 96–123. Minneapolis: University of Minnesota Press, 2007.

———. "Racial Masquerade: Consumption and Contestation of American Modernity." In *The Modern Girl around the World: Consumption, Modernity, and Globalization,* by Alys Eve Weinbaum, L. M. Thomas, P. Ramamurthy, U. G. Poiger, M. Y. Dong, and T. E. Barlow, 120–46. Durham: Duke University Press, 2008.

Williams, Patricia J. *The Alchemy of Race and Rights.* Cambridge: Harvard University Press, 1991.

Williams, Raymond. *Marxism and Literature.* New York: Oxford University Press, 1977.

Winant, Howard. *The World Is a Ghetto: Race and Democracy Since World War II.* New York: Basic, 2001.

Yoshino, Kenji. "Assimilationist Bias in Equal Protection: The Visibility Presumption and the Case of 'Don't Ask, Don't Tell.'" *Yale Law Journal* 108, no. 3 (December 1998): 485–571.

Yu, Henry. *Thinking Orientals: Migration, Contact, and Exoticism in Modern America.* New York: Oxford University Press, 2001.

CHANDAN REDDY is associate
professor of English at the University
of Washington.

Library of Congress
Cataloging-in-Publication Data

Reddy, Chandan, 1972–
Freedom with violence : race, sexuality, and
the US state / Chandan Reddy.
p. cm.—(Perverse modernities)
Includes bibliographical references and index.
ISBN 978-0-8223-5091-0 (cloth : alk. paper)
ISBN 978-0-8223-5105-4 (pbk. : alk. paper)
1. American literature—African American
authors—History and criticism.
2. African Americans—Intellectual life
—20th century.
3. United States—Race relations.
I. Title. II. Series: Perverse modernities.
PS153.N5R434   2011
305.0973—dc22   2011015676